AF265536

GYE NYAME
[Except for God]

WITHOUT GOD,
WE CANNOT
MAKE IT

Rev. Dr. John A.K. Bonful

GYE NYAME

[Except for God]

WITHOUT GOD,
WE CANNOT
MAKE IT

Rev. Dr. John A.K. Bonful

Gye Nyame (Except for God) Without God, We Cannot Make It
Copyright ©2009 by Rev. Dr. John A. K. Bonful
ISBN 978-0-9817603-7-7
Library of Congress Control Number: 2010940615

Published by:
Seed Word Communications
P.O. Box 16615
Tallahassee, FL 32317
Phone: +1.850.765.0386
www.seedword.com

Interior design, copyediting and research assistance: Alan Prescott
Cover design and photography: Alan Prescott
prescott_alan@comcast.net
alanjayprescott@gmail.com
prescottdesignshop.com
Phone: 949.412.4548

Photograph of Rev. Bonful by Mr. Frank Osei Poku of Calvary Redeeming
Methodist Church, Rockville, Maryland.
Photograph of Mrs. Bonful by K. N. Gestathi of Sears Store, P. G. Plaza,
Hyattsville, Maryland.

Unless otherwise indicated, Bible quotations are taken from the *New International Version (NIV)*, copyright ©1996 by AMG International Inc.

GYE NYAME
(EXCEPT FOR GOD)

**A Symbol of the Supremacy of God
with All His Attributes:**
omnipotence, omniscience, omnipresence, sovereignty, holiness,
majesty, justice, faithfulness, unconditional love, mercy, glory and peace

**In the African concept of God, the *Gye Nyame* symbol speaks of God
in His capacity as a Supreme Being**

*E*ven though the continent of Africa has been endowed with natural resources—gold, diamond, cocoa and timber, to name a few—there has been a persistent lack of economic and social progress of which it is capable and deserves to achieve.

After growing up in Ghana, West Africa, and serving as an ordained minister there for several years, The Rev. Dr. John Bonful has been serving congregations for two decades in the United States. Dedicated service and research in both countries have led him to conclude that part of the challenge many Africans—and people everywhere around the globe—face is that they are not fully aware that true freedom, peace, joy, wisdom and the power to succeed come from the Creator of the Universe and through His Son Jesus Christ.

This book will help you rediscover who you are and how you can continue to move closer to your God-given potential.

Dr. Joseph Amanfu, PMP, CCP, MBCS, CTM, CPC, ELI-MP, Ph.D.
President & CEO
Seed Word Communications, USA

TO THE
GLORY OF GOD,
and to Calvary Redeeming Methodist Church,
Rockville, Maryland, U.S.A.,
which is a part of the
living witness of the mighty work of
God in the name of Jesus Christ
through the ministry of the Holy Spirit.

Table of Contents

Foreword

The writing of this book was inspired by a vision that the author, Rev. Dr. John A.K. Bonful, strongly believes came from God; thus, he wrote this book from the heart. I've known John as a seasoned minister of God for several years; but most importantly, this book carries a simple but soul-stirring message very vital to our humanistic world today. There's more to this book than meets the eye: it has a very illuminating message about the necessity of reliance on the Almighty God, the Maker of the universe. He's done a great job presenting a very poignant message about God's love, peace and power.

He uses a powerful Ghanaian/African symbol, *Gye Nyame* (except for God), that speaks of the supremacy of God with all His attributes of omnipotence, omnipresence, omniscience, sovereignty, majesty, holiness, love, goodness, mercy, truth, righteousness, peace, etc., which we very much need in these times—for the transformation of Africa in particular and of the world in general.

It's important that the message this book brings is received in good spirit. The message covers a plethora of issues, but I'll highlight a few, with the hope of whetting your appetite for the whole book. It flows like a journey—one that takes you through some of the author's personal experiences and through God's will for our lives and the way forward.

First, he points out the fact that the concept of God is universal and that we're all created equal in His image. This point is very basic to our understanding of what He can do *for* us and *through* us. It's important that we understand this fact if we're to consider the essence of this book.

If we understand that God is there for us, that He has made us in His own image, and that He seeks what's best for us, then we'll acknowledge that we can't succeed in the world we live in without His role in our lives.

Another point worthy of mention—one that's been a bane to human beings throughout the centuries in man's relationship with God—is the issue of idolatry. Throughout the Bible we read of many people who had initially earned His approval but lost it because of idolatry. The list includes Saul and Solomon, and yet to date, many people haven't recognized that idolatry and worship of God are at war with each other.

This point is stressed in the book from the perspective that idolatry isn't only the worship of idols, but also the craving of material things. In today's materialistic world, many Christians find themselves craving things, most of which they rarely need. They turn their attention to material things so often that God—or the things of God—are pushed to the background. For example, many of us are willing to use our money to buy things we don't need, yet grumble when it comes to giving tithes and offerings for His work. The point being made isn't that we shouldn't desire things that make life easy for us; rather, we shouldn't let them consume our attention so much that the things of God are forgotten or become secondary.

Finally, a very practical solution is provided: reliance on the Almighty God, the Creator of heaven and earth. The point doesn't need much emphasis, because that's the essence of the book. Even the title tells it all—that we have to go back to Him, for we're nothing without Him. As human beings, we've tried all ways to be self-reliant, but all of our efforts haven't yielded the desired result. Despite our failures, some of us still haven't come to the realization that our lives are meaningless without our Maker.

John's book raises that poignant fact, and it's my prayer that by the time you finish reading it, you'll come to acknowledge your need for God more than ever in your life.

In conclusion, I want to thank Rev. Dr. Bonful for putting together this important book and for allowing me to be part of this great endeavor. God bless and guide you in your reading.

The Most Rev Dr. Robert Aboagye-Mensah
Past Presiding Bishop of the Conference
Methodist Church—Ghana, Accra, Ghana

*I*n the first place, I'm eternally grateful to the Almighty God for His grace through His Son, Jesus Christ, in enabling me by the power of the Holy Spirit to serve Him in His vineyard for the past 42 years. Indeed, no words are adequate to express my gratefulness to Him for His providence, particularly for the great vision He has gradually, under His guidance, led me to commit to writing for all to read.

Secondly, I would like to express heartfelt gratitude to my wife, Georgina, for being with me all these years, and for the spiritual, moral and financial support she's constantly offered me, especially when I quit my full-time secular job eight years ago to concentrate on doing the Lord's work.

Thirdly, I want to express my deep appreciation to the past presiding Bishop of the Conference of the Methodist Church—Ghana, the Most Rev. Dr. Robert Aboagye-Mensah, who, despite his busy schedule, managed to write the Foreword to *Gye Nyame*. His words set the tone for the book, for which I'm most grateful.

Also, my sincere thanks and appreciation go to Prof. Alex Kobina Armoo formerly of Baltimore International College, Baltimore, Md., U.S.A., who was the first to read the manuscript, worked on the initial design, and put the pieces together into a printable format. Without his help, this would have been a totally different book. May God bless you, Alex, for your efforts and in all your endeavors.

Furthermore, I'm wholeheartedly grateful to Dr. David McAllister-Wilson, President of the Wesley Theological Seminary, Prof. Albert

Wright, Chairman of the Africa Water Task Force and Caretaker of the Ghana Wesley Methodist Church, Va., Dr. George Ebo Bonney, Professor of Genetics at the School of Medicine of Howard University in Washington, D.C.; Rev. Dr. Emmanuel Lartey of Atlanta Theological Seminary; Rt. Rev. Ebenezer K. Dadson, former Senior Pastor of the Ghana United Methodist Church in the Bronx, N.Y., who spared their precious time out of their busy schedules to read through the manuscript and offered their valuable advice. I am equally thankful to Mr. Otoo Kofi and Jeffrey Marshall for helping me with my computer problems and for their excellent work in terms of corrections, comments and sound advice, which helped to enhance the contents and quality of the book.

The leadership and members of my local church, the Calvary Redeeming Methodist Church of Rockville, and also, the New Creation Gospel Church, formerly headed by Pastor Albert Amo-Mensah, deserve to be mentioned here for standing together with me all the way in prayer and with initial financial support.

To my senior brothers, Rev. Father Joseph K. Bonful and Dan; my sister, Agnes Harvey Ewusi; and my children, James, Emma, Esther, together with their spouses, I extend grateful thanks and appreciation for keeping me in their thoughts and prayers.

Finally, I want to express my heartfelt gratitude to Dr. Joseph Amanfu, President and CEO of Seed Word Communications, LLC, Tallahassee, Fla., for his encouragement, the Memorandum of Agreement established between us, and for his staff of experts, who designed, printed and helped get the second edition of *Gye Nyame* into the worldwide market, including all and sundry who worked behind the scenes in one way or another in support of this divine project. God richly bless you all.

Rev. Dr. John A. K. Bonful

The date was December 9, 2001. My wife and I were on a plane from Baltimore–Washington International Airport heading to Accra, Ghana. This was a very important flight, because we were on our way to attend the wedding ceremonies of our children. Our son, Jim, was getting married on December 22, 2001, while our daughter, Emma, was having her wedding on January 5, 2002. We were really feeling blessed, because the weddings of two children two weeks apart rarely come anyone's way.

I looked out the window at the dark sky—no stars, no clouds, just pitch darkness—and wondered what was out there. I soon realized, all over again, how awesome God is. He had created everything: the entire universe out of nothing. *How awesome! How wonderful! How marvelous! That's the God I serve!*

After a while, I looked into my hand luggage and pulled out a book; it was Bruce Wilkinson's *The Prayer of Jabez*. This work—about the story of the prayer of Jabez—had gained much public attention within Christian circles. As I started to read, my mind kept drifting back to Jabez's prayer. He had "cried out to the God of Israel, 'Oh, that you would bless me and enlarge my territory! Let your hand be with me, and keep me from harm so that I will be free from pain.' And God granted his request" (1 Chron. 4:10).

I was so touched by this prayer that I began thinking about it more and more. I could relate to what Jabez had gone through. When I looked back at my life while in Ghana and my present situation in the

U.S., I found myself understanding his prayer in a lot of ways and, therefore, adopted the prayer as my own: *Oh, that you would bless me and enlarge my territory! Let your hand be with me, and keep me from harm so that I will be free from pain.* I believed that the Lord, "Jesus Christ is the same yesterday and today and forever" (Heb. 13:8), that He Who never changes would grant my request.

For the past thirteen years, I've been ministering to the Calvary Redeeming Methodist Church, a congregation of about 150 members. The church was founded in obedience to a vision the Lord had given me on the night of Sunday, February 2, 1997. My prayer had always been that He would increase the membership of His Church so that I might undertake a full-time ministry. As I read the book, I prayed that He would bless me and increase my territory, the membership of my church. I continued with this prayer throughout my trip to Ghana and even after my return to the United States on Sunday, January 20, 2002. However, that wasn't all I was praying about; I was also praying for Africa, my beloved continent.

My Prayer for Africa

Writing to the Christians in Rome, Paul said, "Brothers, my heart's desire and prayer to God for the Israelites is that they may be saved" (Rom. 10:1). I had similar concerns for my fellow Africans. My thoughts and prayers, for quite some time, had concerned the lack of political, technological, economic and spiritual development in Africa, creating a condition of extreme hardship in many countries on the continent today — notably Rwanda, Ethiopia, Liberia, Sierra Leone, Nigeria, and Ghana. Hence, many have left their countries for places where they can make a living.

The result is a reduction in the labor force and personnel in almost every profession: engineering, medicine, nursing, teaching, skilled labor, etc. The brain-drain syndrome has compounded the already existing underdevelopment of Africa. With these disturbing thoughts on my mind sometimes, I couldn't help asking God the following questions: *Why is it so difficult for most Africans to make progress in life? Why are we at the bottom rung of the ladder in terms of development — politically, technologically and economically? You made all human beings equal in your image as declared in your Word (e.g., Gen. 1:26). Why is it so hard for the nations of the continent to achieve political maturity? Why is Africa, which is so endowed with natural resources, so poor? What is our problem? What do the advanced nations have that*

Africa is missing?

Every now and then my mind wandered to a story I was told several years ago. My roommate at the seminary, who was from the Philippines, had told me an amusingly ridiculous Filipino folk story. We had been discussing the creation account in Genesis when he said that folklore tells how God had created all human beings with clay, baking each batch in a big oven. After He had put in the last batch, He became so busy with other creative activities that He forgot about the oven. When He finally remembered to take the creatures out, they had turned black. Those black creatures, according to the story, were Africans or people of African descent. Can you believe this? What a ridiculous story!

Although the story isn't true, my friend wasn't telling it to make fun of me (a black African), but rather to highlight one of the misconceptions some people have of the black race. Like all types of folklore, the Filipino story has no biblical or theological basis. Even if—and that's a big *if*—there were any truth in it, the story only answers the question of color, but not the situation in which black people find themselves. After all, the Almighty God "…will neither slumber nor sleep" (Ps. 121:4) and "…will not forget…" (Isa. 49:15) His own handiwork, leaving it to burn in the oven.

Above all, I know that black people are as beautiful as any other group. At the end of His creation, God observed "…all that he had made, and it was very good…" (Gen. 1:31). Hence, I recounted the Filipino tale merely to emphasize that all human beings were made in His image and likeness and that no race is better or worse than another. We are merely different from one another, yet each one of us bears the same imprint of God on the soul.

I'm not as bothered about my color as I am about the living conditions or situations in which black people find themselves today. There are many theologians and Bible believers holding the view that Africans are the descendants of "Ham, the father of Canaan…," who "…saw his father's nakedness…" and was cursed. As it's written, "When Noah awoke from his wine and found out what his youngest son had done to him, he said, 'Cursed be Canaan! The lowest of slaves will he be to his brothers…May God extend the territory of Japheth… and may Canaan be his slave' " (9:22, 24–25, 27).

According to Warren Baker, "The curse pronounced by Noah was fulfilled when the Canaanites became 'woodcutters and water carriers' for the Israelites" (*The Hebrew–Greek Key Bible Study Bible: Commentary on*

Genesis 9:20–27).

Whatever might have given cause to the African situation, it became one of my chief concerns and, therefore, one of my constant prayers to God; I believe He has a lasting solution. However, I'm always comforted and strengthened by the great truth He revealed to Peter when he went to the house of Cornelius. He said, "I now realize how true it is that God does not show favoritism but accepts men from every nation who fear him and do what is right" (Acts 10:34–35). These verses have encouraged my belief that there are a lot of spiritually talented Africans God could use for His glory—and the blessing of the entire continent and the world at large—just as He had done long ago.

There are other instances in the Bible supporting the significance of Mother Africa and her people to God. For instance, the role of Egypt in the history of Israel is unquestionable, particularly in the lives of Abraham, Joseph, Moses and even Jesus. His parents and the infant Christ took refuge in Egypt when King Herod sought to destroy the child (Matt. 2:13–14). Other examples include the role of the African Simeon from Cyrene, called upon to bear the cross for Jesus on the way to His crucifixion. Several scholars claim that Simon (referred to as "black" in Acts 13:1)—one of the leaders of the Church of Antioch, who consecrated Paul and Barnabas for their missionary work—was Simeon of Cyrene.

There are many other historical records proving Africans hadn't always been on the receiving end. Significant men like Simon and the Ethiopian official were biblically indisputable as being among the first Africans baptized, linking them to the Church in Africa. It's not known for certain who established Christianity there; however, the records point to the city of Alexandria in Egypt as the location.

According to Noel King, it was John Mark (the writer of Mark's Gospel), who was the first to plant the Church in Africa before the turn of the first century (Nya Kwiawon Taryor, *Impact of the African Tradition on African Christianity*, 1984, p. 30). Christianity in Africa spread, and from the second century onwards, the Church in Africa was strongly established enough that it became part of the universal Church. Again, according to Taryor, the first theological seminary was founded in Alexandria in the second century, while the monastic movement owed its origins to Egypt through the devotion of a black African named St. Anthony, born in 250A.D. It's worthwhile mentioning further that three of the popes of the early Church hailed from Africa: Victor I (189–199),

Mechaiades (311–314) and Gelasius I (492–496).

It's significant to note also that some of the most prominent early Church fathers, like Tertullian (220), Origen (254), Cyprian (258) and Augustine (430), were Africans (pp. 171–173). Both Taryor and Roar G. Fotland maintain that those were the Church fathers who took pains to formulate Christian doctrines and practices. If these African Church founders indeed were part of the early Christian community—who trusted in God, the Owner of the entire universe with all its fullness and riches, and "righteousness exalts a nation"—then, *Why is Africa not as developed as other parts of the world? Why are Africans still lagging behind in many areas of life? What went wrong with the faith of our fathers?* I sought the Lord in my daily prayers for answers to these mind-boggling questions.

The Vision: God's Answer to My Prayer

Finally, about 4:00A.M. on Thursday, January 24, 2002—while meditating on the Book of Jeremiah, chapters 16 and 17—I felt the anointing of the Lord mightily upon me. Instantly the room was filled with His presence, and the Holy Spirit began ministering to me in the spirit. He illumined my mind, giving me a deeper insight (i.e., revelation) about the spiritual condition of Ghana, as well as Africa and the world at large. God revealed to me (i.e., He enlightened my mind, as it were, to understand) why there's so much fear, mistrust and a strong sense of insecurity in the world today; why there's no peace or stability; and why so many are poor, suffering and dying of diseases (e.g., HIV/AIDS, etc.), hunger and poverty, especially in Africa.

Since the Lord reveals in order to redeem, He taught me what must be done to effect a change in the miserable condition of humankind. I quickly grabbed pen and notebook and wrote down the message. According to Him, it was to be delivered first to my fellow Ghanaians, then to other Africans and then finally, to the world at large. Just as in the past, He graciously revealed His secrets to the Prophets to be delivered to His people in Israel.

So the "…immortal, invisible, the only God…" (1 Tim. 1:17)—Who "…is the same yesterday and today and forever" (Heb. 13:8)—continues to speak to His church and all people everywhere. He does so through His anointed servants in visions and dreams today, as Amos declared, "Surely the Sovereign LORD does nothing without revealing his plan to his servants the prophets. The lion has roared—who will not fear? The Sovereign LORD has spoken—who can but prophesy?"

(Amos 3:7–8). Therefore, what follows is a divine message worthy of the serious attention of all people under the sun—irrespective of race, color, gender or rank—who sincerely desire to be saved from their sins in order to "…flee from the coming wrath" (Matt. 3:7).

I must clarify that although the vision was received on a particular day, writing down the entire message took me almost two years (January 2002–December 2003). Before dawn each day, I would be awakened from sleep and the Lord would draw my attention to the message, adding to it or straightening up what needed to be corrected. Therefore, it's very important to note before going any further that this vision is consistent with Scripture.

Now, I invite you to read on with an attitude of humility and openness of heart and mind. Expect the Lord to speak to you personally, so that "…you will know the truth, and the truth will set you free" (John 8:32) from sin and whatever entangles you. Then you'll be able to serve and worship the Living God with joy and enthusiasm under the inspiration of the Holy Spirit.

Gye Nyame

Akan, a group of languages mutually understood by most speakers, is spoken throughout Ghana and parts of Côte d'Ivoire (formerly Ivory Coast). The Akan compound word *Gye Nyame* is the name of a Ghanaian symbol used in many contexts, particularly as a graphic element in many arts, crafts and body art. Its meaning derives from the Ghanaian notion *nyimpa nnye, Gye Nyam* ("human beings are bad, except for God," i.e., "only God is good"). We might also put it this way: "with the exception of God, no one else is good." It has the same meaning as the proverbial expression *Nyame nntѕe ɗe oɗaѕanyi* ("God is not like a human being").

The Ghanaian concept *Gye Nyame* is commensurate with what the Scriptures say about God. For example, Numbers 23:19 states that "God is not a man, that he should lie, nor a son of man, that he should change his mind. Does he speak and then not act? Does he promise and not fulfill?" Psalm 92:15 also says, " 'The LORD is upright; he is my Rock, and there is no wickedness in him.' "

According to Prof. Kwame Gyekye, Africans in general hold the religious concept that, "goodness is the prime characteristic of God" (*African Cultural Values*, 1996, p. 9). This notion is in line with Holy Scripture, which affirms that God is good and what He does is good

(Ps. 119:67–68). But concerning human beings it's written that, "…There is no one righteous, not even one" (Rom. 3:10); in other words, only God is good. Jesus echoed the same truth in His response to the rich, young ruler who came to Him with a burning question: "Good teacher, what must I do to inherit eternal life?" (Luke 18:18). Jesus answered him, " 'Why do you call me good?… No one is good — except God alone.' " (Luke 18:19). When the young ruler claimed to have obeyed the commandments from his youth, Jesus finally said to him, " 'You still lack one thing. Sell everything you have and give to the poor, and you will have treasure in heaven. Then come, follow me.' " (Luke 18:22).

But the man could neither sell his goods nor follow Jesus. Instead, "he became very sad, because he was a man of great wealth" (Luke 18:23). By failing to follow Jesus, the rich man portrayed his selfishness, greed and lack of concern for the poor in his community. Thus, the Ghanaian/African expression, *Gye Nyame* is biblically and theologically sound.

Humans have no control over the daily affairs and circumstances of their earthly existence

Another meaning of *Gye Nyame* emerges from the African recognition of the unpredictability of the unforeseen, changing scenes of life confronting us daily. Thus, in saying *Gye Nyame*, the Ghanaian/African is acknowledging the truth that humans have no control over the daily affairs and circumstances of their earthly existence — except God, as the following Scripture declares:

> *Unless the LORD builds the house, its builders labor in vain. Unless the LORD watches over the city, the watchmen stand guard in vain. In vain you rise early and stay up late, toiling for food to eat — for he grants sleep to those he loves* (Ps. 127:1–2; also Prov. 3:5–6)

James, the Apostle of the Lord, also underscores the same truth as he writes:

> *Now listen, you who say, "Today or tomorrow we will go to this or that city, spend a year there, carry on business and make money." Why, you do not even know what will happen tomorrow. What is your life? You are a mist that ap-*

pears for a little while and then vanishes. Instead, you ought to say, "If it is the Lord's will, we will live and do this or that." As it is, you boast and brag. All such boasting is evil. (James 4:13–16)

In this connection, James calls everyone's attention to the necessity of submitting our plans to God, and to depend on Him for wisdom, guidance and strength to accomplish our aims in life. *Gye Nyame* stresses the African notion that God is powerful —*Nyame ye tumfo*—but humans are frail and that without Him, no human being is able to achieve or realize his dream/goal in life. An Akan (Ghanaian/African) maxim puts it this way: *"Ikwatsir kokromatsir a, renntum mmbo pow,"* meaning, "Without the thumb, one cannot tie a knot." The African concept "to tie a knot" is to succeed in reaching a particular target or one's goal in life. Thus, when used in a full sentence, *Gye Nyame* could be expressed as follows: "Without God, all human efforts are fruitless." To put it in another way, "We (creatures) cannot make it without our Maker (God)." This truth is affirmed by the following story written by Anne Cetas of Radio Bible School:

> A group of scientists decided that they would no longer need God. They said, "We have enough knowledge to clone people and do many miraculous things." "Very well," God responded, "Let's have a man-making contest. We'll do it just like I did it with Adam." The scientists agreed, and one of them bent down and picked up a handful of dust. God looked at him and said, "No! You have to make your own dust." And so they gave up the contest.

The irrefutable truth is that this is God's world and He put us here to fulfill His purpose. We can't live in this world and ignore Him —the very source of our life and existence. Therefore, as stated in the opening pages of the book, in the African concept of God, the symbol *Gye Nyame* reflects the totality of God —the Supreme Being who holds all of creation in His hands and controls it as He wills. It's a word picture, revealing, so to speak, every aspect of His character, namely, His omnipotence, omniscience, omnipresence, sovereignty, holiness, majesty, justice, faithfulness, unconditional love, mercy, peace —you name it, etc.

One may ask, *How were our ancestors, in their traditional religion —with reference to* Gye Nyame —*able to arrive at such a tremendous truth about God on one side and human beings on the other?"* I'm convinced that our forefathers gained this insight through intuition as well as daily human experience, including observation of their environment and through natural theology (Ps. 19:1–4). Gyekye expressed his view on this when he wrote, "Traditional African religion, not being a revealed religion, can only be regarded as a natural religion arising out of the people's own experience and view of this world" (*Values*, p. 56).

Hence, in Africa in general and Ghana in particular—unlike other parts of the world—there are no atheists. The African believes in the existence of God as well as other deities or spirits. Thus, every aspect of his life (e.g., birth, work, marriage, death, etc.) is permeated with religion. "As a people," writes Kofi Appiah-Kubi, "the Akans make little or no distinction between religion and culture, which has religion at its base" (*Man Cures, God Heals*, p. 5).

Now, with this introductory background, I warmly invite you to read on; and may you be richly blessed, as the Lord gives you insight into the truth revealed in this book: *Gye Nyame (Except for God): Without God, We Cannot Make It.*

CHAPTER 1

I am the third son of Opanyin Kweku Afedzie and Madam Efua Munkuah who lived in Bibiani, an industrial mining town in the Western Region of Ghana on the west coast of Africa. Since my parents were illiterate, my date of birth wasn't recorded. However, my senior brother, who was then in middle school, put it at 1940 or 1941. The day was Tuesday, but he couldn't trace the actual date or even the month in which I was born. After further research, we agreed to establish it as Tuesday, June 3, 1940. I have two senior brothers, Joseph (the most senior among us) and Daniel. My only sister, Agnes, came after me.

My father was a blacksmith, farmer and herbalist/fetish priest. My mom traded in fish and *kenkey* (boiled, mashed cornmeal), which is a staple food for many Ghanaians at home and abroad. Since my parents were average, middle-class people, they couldn't put all three of us in school until my senior brother had successfully completed middle-school education and secured a job as an electrician. There and then, my father decided to send Dan and me to school in January 1949.

However, we proved more intelligent than our mates, so we were promoted to Primary Two before the end of the first term. While in Primary Two, I was promoted to Primary Three (or Class Three) in the second term, and thus was admitted to Primary 4 (or Standard One) by January 1950. When Dan and I learned to speak and understand some measure of the English language, we enrolled in the Methodist church choir, of which our senior brother, Joseph, and his classmate, Quainoo, were members. Since our parents weren't Christians, our senior brother was our mentor. We loved to go to church, not because we were converted, but I guess we just wanted to join the choir and participate in the singing of anthems and hymns. We considered it a privilege to sing in the choir.

The Sudden Death of My Dad

In December 1950 my mom went home to visit her family in Patuako (a small town of about 200 inhabitants) in the Central Region of Ghana, near Mankessim. Unfortunately, while she was away, tragedy hit us at home in Bibiani: on January 1, 1951, my dad passed away unexpectedly in his sleep late in the afternoon. I was just about 8 or 9 years of age. My dad's death was like a dream to me, because I didn't understand why a person should die when he wasn't sick. My dad was a strong man of medium height—about five-and-a-half feet—light-colored and stoutly built. Though tender in age, I knew that a person might die after a serious accident or a period of illness; but my dad hadn't been ill.

He went out in the morning about 9:00 on New Year's Day to say, *"Afenhia Pa"* ("Happy New Year") to some of his close friends and colleagues. When he returned home in the afternoon, I observed that he was a little intoxicated, judging from his walk and the smell of alcohol in his breath. I was the only one at home at the time, and he asked me whether someone had come looking for him. I said, "No, Dad." Quietly, he walked past me and went to bed. That was the last time I heard my dad's voice. I couldn't believe he was dead until I called his colleagues nearby and saw that he couldn't move or respond to those who called his name several times. There and then I knew that my dad was gone indeed. I was confused, disappointed and completely devastated.

The puzzle that began to trouble my mind was this: *Who then would be responsible for our education?* I asked myself this in a kind of soliloquy, because my mom was poor and wouldn't have been able to shoulder this burden alone. By this time, all three of us—Dan, Agnes and I—were in primary school, and there was hardly enough money to see us through at least our middle-school education.

At any rate, my mom returned to Bibiani for the burial and the funeral obsequies. She had now become a widow and single mother of four. Since my senior brother, Joseph, was working, he managed to financially support our mom, who had assumed the full responsibility of caring for her household with the small income from the sale of fish and *kenkey*.

No Money or Scholarship for Secondary Education

I took my studies seriously, and though I was successful in the common entrance examination and was eligible for admission to Prempeh College and Mfantseman Secondary Schools in 1955 and 1956, respectively, I wasn't admitted because I had no one to sponsor my education. The fees were too much for my poor mom or senior brother to bear.

It soon became more economical for my brother Dan and me to live with a family friend of our dad's for about three years. Later on, we had to work as steward boys for European mining officials, who lived at Bibiani European Bungalow/Quarters, situated in a section of the town separated from the African-populated community in Bibiani. It wasn't until my final year in middle school that I had to leave that job in order to have enough time to prepare for the Standard Seven final year examination in December 1956. By the help of God, I passed with flying colors and left Bibiani for Kumasi, the Garden City, where I gained admission to the Technical Institute in January 1957. The annual fee then was five pounds sterling, and my senior brother, Joseph, boldly accepted the responsibility of seeing me through technical education (January 1957–June 1960).

Joining the Choir of the Wesley Methodist Church

During the month of July 1958, I enrolled in the Kumasi Wesley Methodist Church choir through the help of the late Mr. J.K. Paintsil, who worked in the carpentry section of the Technical Institute. My brother Joseph and his wife were both members of the Wesley Society. I loved singing in the choir, and regularly attended choir practice three times a week, and Sunday morning and evening services.

At this time, Dan was already living with Joseph while attending Government Day School in Kumasi. We were both later joined by our sister, Agnes, and so all three of us were living under the roof of brother Joseph. His wife, Mary, with two children, took us in as her younger siblings. Thanks to God for granting our brother and his wife the grace to undertake such a task. I perceived that it was indeed a big sacrifice for any Ghanaian young couple in the prime of their lives to make, yet their Christian virtues prevailed, and all their endeavors weren't in vain. Dan graduated in December 1957 and was employed at the Kumasi Circuit Court, while Agie gained admission to the Nursing Training School at the Okomfo Anokye Hospital in Kumasi.

Working as a Technician

In June 1960, I graduated with a Grade 2 diploma in mechanical engineering craft practice and was employed in the mechanical engineering department of the then-Kwame Nkrumah University of Science and Technology. While there, I decided to do further studies through correspondence courses to qualify for admission to the university toward a degree in architecture. My job as a technician was to assist the engineering students in their practical training at the workshop, a good number of whom became my friends through this process.

It was interesting work, creating a sense of self-worth and a degree of job satisfaction, knowing that I was at the service of Ghana's future mechanical and civil engineers. Besides assisting the students, I was occasionally assigned to work on a project presented by some of the engineering professors, such as Dr. Albert Wright, then head of the civil engineering section of the engineering department. Incidentally, by God's providence as some readers might have observed, Prof. Wright—presently working on a contract with the United Nations—is now the caretaker of Ghana Wesley United Methodist Church in Arlington, Virginia, and one of the original readers of the manuscript of this book's first edition.

None of us knew or even dreamed that we would meet in the U.S. and to serve as co-workers with God in the soul-winning business for His kingdom. Isn't that amazing—and isn't He wonderful in His dealings with humankind? Truly, as William Cowper wrote:

> God moves in a mysterious way
> His wonders to perform;
> He plants His footsteps in the sea
> And rides upon the storm.
>
> Deep in unfathomable mines
> Of never-failing skill
> He treasures up His bright designs,
> And works His sovereign will.
> (*MHB*, 503, verses 1–2, William Cowper, 1731–1800)

Now, what follows was the sudden, unexpected incident that was to turn my life completely around.

Spiritual Attack and Near-Death Experience

One morning, I became seriously ill following a terrible dream I had had about a week before. In the dream, I found myself being attacked by an angry man. He hit me hard on the mouth, causing me to bleed profusely. Sensing that I was about to die, I called on the name of the Lord, saying, "Jesus, save me!" At the mention of His name, I awoke from this bad dream full of fear as to who was after me. A few days afterward, I felt so sick that I went to see my doctor at the university hospital. I was examined and given some medications, yet no amount of treatment was effective.

The most frightening experience I had during this illness was the fearful, recurring dreams: being chased by a wild, fearsome animal, such as a tiger, wolf or lion seeking to devour me. I would run as fast as I could and when I awoke, I would feel almost exhausted and unable to go to sleep again, because I was afraid I might have another terrible dream. That continued for several nights, aggravating my already sickly condition. I couldn't go to work and was on sick leave for about a month without any improvement.

The Miraculous Healing and Conversion

After a terrible dream one night, I got up from bed and, kneeling beside the center table in my bedroom, I cried to the Lord Jesus Christ for deliverance from what I perceived was untimely death at the hands of evil forces. I confessed every sin I had committed, and with tears dripping down my face, I offered my life to the Lord, promising to live for Him if He would have pity on me and save my life from these wild beasts.

I offered my life to the Lord if He would have pity on me and save my life from these wild beasts

I went to bed after the prayer and had a good night's sleep. When I got up the following morning, I was healed, but it was so fast that I couldn't tell whether it was real. So, I walked around my living room just to assure myself that it was a real healing experience for me. And it was indeed, to the glory of God. *Praise the Lord! Hallelujah!* Not only was I miraculously healed, but I was also converted.

From that time on, I realized with deep faith how much the Lord loves me unconditionally. With that insight, I felt I owed Him a debt I could never pay; therefore, I dedicated the rest of my life to Him. I joined the Youth Fellowship in addition to being a regular member of the church choir. I stopped attending ballroom dancing and going to movies. I turned it all over to the Lord in accordance with the vow I had made to Him previously in my prayer.

A Call to the Ministry

At a prayer meeting organized by the Youth Fellowship in the evening of Monday, February 7, 1966, I heard the Lord's voice clearly saying to me, "Now is the time to offer yourself." I shared my experience with P.K. Kyei, then vice president of the Youth Fellowship, who had conducted the prayer meeting that evening. After this incident, there were elections for positions of secretary and assistant secretary. I was appointed the assistant secretary of the Fellowship, and in the following year promoted to the seat of the secretary.

The urge to preach the Gospel was also so strong that I enlisted in the Evangelical Group under Brother Morrison. Soon I was accepted at the Leaders Meeting as a local preacher in the Kumasi Circuit. Through the guidance and encouragement of the youth minister, the Very Rev. James Emmanuel Yarquah, and Essuamah Thomson, then chaplain of the University of Science and Technology (all three deceased), I passed the Trinity Theological Seminary entrance examination in 1968 and received four years of theological training for the ministry.

My seven ministerial classmates and I were commissioned by the Methodist Conference in August 1972, and I was stationed at Effia-Kumah in the Sekondi Circuit. When the Sekondi District was later divided into two separate districts (dioceses), I remained at Effia-Kuma, which came under Takoradi Circuit.

The next important stage of my life was finding a suitable life partner. By God's grace, my prayer was answered when I had met Georgina Gaisie earlier, in September 1971, at our Youth Fellowship meeting one evening. She accepted my marriage proposal but first wanted to complete her two-year professional teachers' training course at Wesley College in Kumasi. She earned the honor of being the first female student elected college secretary in the history of Wesley College. She was both a good example and a great inspiration to her fellow students, particularly the younger ones; she really made me proud.

We got engaged in June of 1972 after the completion of my ministe-

rial training at Trinity Seminary. Following the good counsel of my superintendent minister, the late P.R. Anderson, we made our wedding vows in a simple but colorful ceremony on Saturday, December 29, 1973 at Wesley College Chapel, officiated by then-president of the Conference, Rev. Charles K. Yamoah, B.D. (of blessed memory). A few weeks after our honeymoon, Georgina had to return to college in January to finish her studies. She finally joined me in June 1974 after successful-
ly completing her course of study as a trained teacher.

By the grace of God, I was ordained by the Methodist Conference on Sunday, August 11, 1974 at the Sekondi Wesley Methodist Church and transferred to the Winneba Circuit. We've since had the privilege of serving the following stations: Ghana Technical Secondary School—Takoradi Circuit, as chaplain, 1976–1982, and Samreboi in the Asankrangwa Circuit 1982–1985. By God's grace, we've been blessed with four children: James, Emma, Esther and Samuel (deceased).

It's worthwhile reporting at this juncture that September 1977 saw a dramatic change in my ministry in the form of spiritual gifts: tongues and their interpretation, healing, prophecy and visions. These gifts were used mightily, not only for the benefit of the churches in Takoradi and Sekondi Circuits, but also other non-members of the church. (Examples of healing and fulfilled prophecies are mentioned starting on page 295 of this book.) The Methodist Conference of 1985 appointed me to head the Asankrangwa Circuit as superintendent minister, a position that was my privilege to hold for three years.

All along, I had been praying for an opportunity to further my theological studies abroad. In August 1988, my heart's desire was graciously granted with a full scholarship for further studies at the Wesley Theological Seminary in Washington, D.C. While there, I successfully completed my master's and doctor of ministry degree programs in May of 1990 and 1993, respectively. Between 1989 and 1996, I served the then-United Christian Church as an associate pastor with Rev. Robert B. Ansah as my senior. When prevailing circumstances made it impossible for me to continue with my service in that church, I peacefully resigned to wait on the Lord for His direction.

After 21 days of prayer and fasting in two separate periods, He graciously instructed me through a vision to gather up those who are scattered to come together, study His Word, pray and worship Him, so that they might be empowered as witnesses to outsiders to come to Christ. That vision gave birth to the non-denominational Calvary Redeeming Church. Our maiden service was held in my living room on Sunday, May 4, 1997, with seven adult members: Sister Georgina Bonful (my wife); Baffour Amoateng; Sisters Charlotte Amoateng, Ruby Marshall, Bertha Marshall, Comfort Afriyie, and Margaret Sefa; and three teenagers.

After the second Sunday worship at my residence, we moved into a classroom at the Richard Montgomery High School in Rockville, Md. In August 1998, Calvary came under the Conference of the Methodist Church, Ghana, assuming the current name, Calvary Redeeming Methodist Church. Due to the compassion and generosity of the rector, Linda Poindexter of Christ Episcopal Church, and her successor, John McDuffie—together with their vestry toward us—we were given a place in their sanctuary. We've been worshipping in the afternoon from 1:00–4:00 on Sundays for the past ten years. Indeed, we can't thank them enough for their generosity toward us all these years.

Today Calvary is blessed with over 150 members, consisting of a formidable choir, Women's Fellowship, Men's Fellowship, Youth Fellowship and Children's Ministry. We've acquired property at 5600 Muncaster Mill Road and are looking forward to putting up a sanctuary in which we can worship the Lord both in the morning and afternoon on Sundays. Truly, as King David declared, "The LORD has done this, and it is marvelous in our eyes" (Ps. 118:23).

Now, looking back on my life and the mysterious work the Lord has done on me as a whole, I'm lost for adequate words in praising Him for the manifold blessings bestowed on me: saving my life from premature death, giving me a New Life and enlisting me among the preachers of His glorious Gospel. With the writing of *Gye Nyame (Except for God): Without God, We Cannot Make It*, I strongly believe that my prayers have been answered and that He has enlarged my territory, because I know that the message of this book will minister to many people reading it— men and women, young and old alike. Though I may not see their faces or meet them personally, God in His own mysterious way has extended my ministry to them for His own glory. *Hallelujah!*

CHAPTER 2

God Created All Human Beings Equal

$\mathcal{T}$hrough the ministration of the Holy Spirit, God confirmed to me the truth that all human beings—whether white, black or brown, male or female—were all created equal in His image, as declared in the Holy Scriptures:

> *"From one man he made every nation of men, that they should inhabit the whole earth; and he determined the times set for them and the exact places where they should live. God did this so that men would seek him and perhaps reach out for him and find him, though he is not far from each one of us. 'For in him we live and move and have our being.' As some of your own poets have said, 'We are his offspring' "* (Acts 17:26–28; *also* Gen. 1:26, 2:7)

On the same biblical principle of equality of the human race, 15 men representing the 13 original states of America boldly wrote down the *Declaration of Independence* on July 4, 1776 in the city of Philadelphia:

> We hold these Truths to be self-evident, that all men are created equal, that they are endowed by their Creator with certain unalienable Rights, that among these are Life, Liberty, and the pursuit of Happiness (*Encyclopedia Americana—International Version*, Grolier, Inc., vol. 8, p. 591).

Therefore, we must realize that the physical differences we find among one another—either in our race, color, rank or sex, like the various colors of the rainbow—are altogether intended to reveal the beauty of our Creator's handiwork, the unity that exists among the Godhead—God the Father, God the Son, and God the Holy Spirit (the Trinity)—and among humankind and creation as a whole.

There Is Power in Unity

Again, as we carefully observe "the white and black keys on the keyboard of the organ/piano," we realize how much they "illustrate the beauty and unity of the human race," as declared by the late Dr. Kwegyir Aggrey, a great son of Africa born in Anomabu in the Central Region of Ghana. In their separate ways, each key (black or white) exists alone, producing a monotone whenever touched; however, when played together by a competent musician, these same keys produce sweet sounds of harmonious, melodious music capable of restoring peace in the mind and soul. It imparts healing to the sick, both spiritually and physically, and eventually sets the troubled heart at rest.

Similarly, when we live in our various places with one purpose under God, there's no limit to what we can achieve for the benefit of the entire human race. God recognized power in unity when He saw the people united together to build the Tower of Babel and said, "If as one people speaking the same language they have begun to do this, then nothing they plan to do will be impossible for them" (Gen. 11:6).

Nevertheless, the tower's builders failed because they were full of pride and determined to reach great heights without God, "...so that we may make a name for ourselves..." (Gen. 11:4)—and they failed miserably. For it is written, "Unless the LORD builds the house, its builders labor in vain. Unless the LORD watches over the city, the watchmen stand guard in vain." (Ps. 127:1).

Are There Godless Americans?

As I write, there are people in America who—to my utter surprise—speak and act without reference to God, disbelieving in His existence. For example, an article published by the *Washington Post* on Sunday, November 3, 2002, showed pictures of people carrying placards, some of which read: "Godless Americans March on Washington," "Their Religion, Our Money, No Way!!" "God Is a Fairy Tale," and

"Keep Your Gods out of Our Schools." According to the report, the group consisted of "atheists, agnostics and other secular humanists" numbering between 2,000 and 3,000, with Ellen Johnson as their president.

Here's part of what she said: "Ladies and gentlemen, I see a sleeping giant that is waking up and is ready to assert its political and cultural influence." She was reported to have announced, "the creation of a 'godless' political action committee, which will henceforth be responsible for making their views heard on any political platform in America."

Can you believe this? Who would have thought that America, of all nations, would have in its midst such a large number of declared "atheists." This is a country whose founding fathers believed in God and boldly witnessed the same to the world by declaring this faith on her currency: "In God We Trust." What's happened over the years to give rise to such a large number of atheists with the temerity to raise their puny fists in the face of God? Aren't they fearful of Him, Who has the power to reduce humans to dust and ashes in a second by snuffing His life-giving breath out of us (2 Kings 19:32–35; Luke 12:16–21)?

The call to remove Him—and for that matter, the Bible—from schools is detrimental to our children, community and entire nation. Objection to teaching religion—especially Christianity—in schools was first made by an atheist and her advocates in the mid-1960s. Since then, the Bible's been taken out of the hands and backpacks of schoolchildren and classrooms. Yet it's written: " 'The fear of the Lord—that is wisdom, and to shun evil is understanding' " (Job 28:28).

Taking God out of Schools Spells Danger

Now, if children are being educated to acquire merely academic knowledge without "the fear of God," what do we expect them to do with morality? It's obvious from what we're hearing that there are many homes in which the Bible isn't taught or read for family devotions. Since God is the source of all goodness and morality, what do we expect from innocent schoolchildren raised and trained in homes and schools, where God and His Word have no place? Instead of Bibles, what do we find in the hands and backpacks of these children nowadays? We find drugs and guns, the latter of which some kids have used to murder their friends, teachers and parents.

A typical example is the recent case of a 15-year-old boy who shot and killed a fellow student, a good football player of the same high school. When God is driven out of the classroom, the Devil sets up his kingdom and reigns in the hearts and minds of innocent children, influencing them to commit all kinds of evil deeds at home, in the schools, and on the streets, making every place unsafe for all.

Sharing his thoughts on America's schools—in comparison with those of Ghana—Kwabena Aaron Jeter of Ohio University said, "Living and teaching in Ghana the past four months has allowed me to compare many of the educational similarities and differences to those in America. Lack of funding, oversized classrooms, understaffed, and underpaid teachers and administrators are all issues that burden many of America's school systems.

"Unfortunately," Jeter continued, "over the years as a result of legislation because of the frequency of lawsuits [concerning the ways students are disciplined in schools], the word *discipline* has been nearly erased in many of America's schools. Gangs, metal detectors, probation officers, and pregnant students are just some of the many challenges teachers are faced with on a daily basis. The 1999 Columbine High School incident that occurred in Littleton, Colorado—where two students walked into school with semi-automatic rifles killing 12 students, one teacher, and then themselves—will probably forever illustrate just how far America's schools and families have morally decayed... That is not to say all of America's schools are suffering from these problems.

"But what I have noticed," he continues, "in my experience teaching and talking with many teachers is that despite the economic hardships that many people of Ghana endure every day, they would never resort to or accept the type of chaos that exists in many of America's schools" (*Wesley Grammar School Magazine*, "Abrempon," 2000, p. 36).

I strongly hold the opinion that America is the strongest nation in the world today because some of the founding fathers of the nation, if not all, believed in God and built their families, communities, and hopes on Him. For instance, "John Witherspoon, James Madison, and George Washington," according to Bill J. Leonard, "were practicing churchmen" (*Early American Christianity*, 1983, p. 13).

Being firm believers, they trusted in God as their Maker, Lord and Savior, Provider and Sustainer of their lives. They didn't consider it a shameful act or a sign of weakness to acknowledge Him and to practice their Christian faith publicly, as Leonard's pointed out. Why? The basic reason was that they knew they couldn't govern America and make it a strong nation without His strength and guidance. Therefore, they relied completely on Him in the nation's leadership. Hence, He was on their side, so they were able to withstand the severe trials of their time, such as the Revolutionary War, the Civil War and, more recently, the Cold War.

The September 11, 2001 Attacks

I'm convinced it was the same faith as the founding fathers' that motivated thousands of Americans to hold on to God after the September 11, 2001 terrorist attacks on the World Trade Center in New York and the Pentagon in Virginia. Causing the loss of thousands of lives and valuable property, that attack was intended to destroy what I've come to describe as "The Three Strongholds of America:" the economic, military and political power represented by the World Trade Center, the Pentagon and Washington, respectively.

The terrorists were aware that America's influence in the world depended on these most important sectors. Nevertheless, there's one other stronghold—and the most important of all—that eluded the attackers, and that is "Trust in God," upon which the founding fathers built this great nation, and which is still held by millions of American Christians today. That trust or faith causes many to pray to Him daily for protection, unity and peace for the country.

Thus, by His intervention, the plan to hit Washington was foiled by a hijacked plane's brave passengers, putting their lives on the line and crashing the plane before it could reach its target. May the souls of such loving, courageous, patriotic citizens rest in perfect peace!

Commenting on the September 11 incident, Bishop John Bryson Chane of the Episcopal Diocese of Washington had this to say:

> Those who carried out these attacks and killed so many innocent victims had deserted God and had, out of their own ignorance, fear and hatred, chosen to desert the God of compassion, unconditional love and peace to follow a God they had created in their own minds—a graven image, an idol and a misrepresentation of the true God, who is at the center of Judaism, Christianity and Islam. They deserted the God of life and created a god of death. (*Washington Window*, vol. 73, no. 11, p. 2)

Though the loss of precious lives and property created a deep wound in the souls of many families and homes, it couldn't break the United States of America. As I've already pointed out, what the terrorists didn't realize was that America's soul—as far as believers are concerned—takes refuge "…with Christ in God" (Col. 3:3) and is maintained by His power; therefore, no one can destroy her. " 'For in him we live and move and have our being' " as God's children (Acts 17:28). As some of us observed, the Sunday following the September 11 attacks saw many churches full of worshippers praying to God, through Christ, to sustain America and comfort the families of those who had lost loved ones in the attacks. Thus, despite the enormous damage to human lives and the economy, America still goes on, upheld by His mighty hand.

Furthermore, the goodwill of the American people—moved by the love of God, compassion and generous contributions from various companies, and the hard work of agencies such as the fire services, the Red Cross and many individuals—played a significant role in maintaining the morale of bereaved families. I believe that all this was a fulfillment of God's promise to meet the needs of all who trust in and call on Him in times of trouble. As it's written in the Psalms: " '…call upon me in the day of trouble; I will deliver you, and you will honor me.' " (Ps. 50:15). That's why "Those who trust in the LORD," says the Psalmist, "are like Mount Zion, which cannot be shaken but endures forever" (Ps. 125:1).

A Loud Wake-Up Call

What have we learned from these brutal, merciless attacks? I consider September 11 as a loud wake-up call to America, the most powerful nation in the world today. It teaches her citizens not to rely on their military, political or economic power, or boast of what and who they are or can achieve by their strength. Nor should the leaders forget to look to God, Who is the source of all power and wisdom for direction in their daily deliberations. He wants us all to understand that every nation is made up of imperfect, sinful people; hence, there are loopholes in every security system whose discovery the enemy can use to destroy lives and property. That's why Scripture admonishes us: "Trust in the LORD with all your heart and lean not on your own understanding; in all your ways acknowledge him, and he will make your paths straight. Do not be wise in your own eyes; fear the LORD and shun evil" (Prov. 3:5–7).

Unlike the builders of the Tower of Babel and the emerging atheists of our time, we American Christians—together with every true believer who loves God and his neighbor—mustn't depend on our own abilities in striving for justice, peace, dignity and success. Rather, we must depend on Him, Who is the "Rock of Ages," "The Unmoved Mover," the Maker and Giver of all good things—both visible and invisible. He is capable of supplying whatever strength, wisdom and power we need in reaching the zenith of our goals in this life and in that which is to come. We must keep the tradition of our fathers' faith through practical, daily living in close fellowship with Christ in order to "obtain grace to help in time of need." Writing to the Corinthians about the hardships he and his team encountered in their missionary work, Paul shared the following:

> *We do not want you to be uninformed, brothers, about the hardships we suffered in the province of Asia. We were under great pressure, far beyond our ability to endure, so that we despaired even of life. Indeed, in our hearts we felt the sentence of death. But this happened that we might not rely on ourselves but on God, who raises the dead. He has delivered us from such a deadly peril, and he will deliver us. On him we have set our hope that he will continue to deliver us, as you help us by your prayers. Then many will give thanks on our behalf for the gracious favor granted us in answer to the prayers of many* (2 Cor. 1:8–11).

St. Paul and his team learned to trust in God and not in themselves; He asked for support in prayers from his fellow Christians for a successful ministry. Likewise, Americans as a people seeking to stand for freedom, justice and peace—not only for themselves but also for others—can't achieve this lofty goal by themselves unless the Lord, the Source of life, freedom, justice and peace, is on their side. For " '…apart from me,' " says Jesus, " 'you can do nothing' " (John 15:5).

Realizing the need for God in good governance, George W. Bush, the 43rd president of the United States, looked to Him for direction. Bush recounted the following concerning predecessors who relied on God in their hours of need. "The first president to live in this house composed a prayer on his second evening here for all who would follow him. Our 16th president, Abraham Lincoln, knew that his burdens were too great for any man, so he carried them to God in prayer. Over the radio on D-Day in 1944, Franklin Roosevelt prayed for God's blessing on our mission to 'set free a suffering humanity' " (*On God and Country*, 2004, p. 68).

According to Thomas M. Freiling, Bush is a practicing Christian who "believes in the God of the Bible, and His Son Jesus Christ. He believes in the power of prayer, and that all men and women are created equal by God. He believes the Bible commands us to love our neighbor and have compassion. He believes that evil exists in the world, that freedom is our God-given right, and that as Americans, we have a duty to protect the rights of all people to be free… He uses the Bible and prayer to find comfort and help, not to condemn or discriminate. Most importantly," he continues, "his religious beliefs are what drive his 'compassionate conservative' policies on issues like AIDS and his faith-based initiatives to help the poor and needy" (p. 12).

Thus, there's evidence that this great nation of ours didn't rise to greatness overnight, but by means of God's power, wisdom and guidance, which the predecessors and successors diligently and resiliently sought through daily prayer in Christ, personal integrity, human dignity and hard work. The founding fathers have left a lasting legacy for the living to follow. Being a Christian, Bush has also learned to lean upon God and not solely on the strength of his homeland. The following expresses his faith in the power, wisdom and guidance of God through prayer:

> "Prayer teaches humility. We find that the plan of the Creator is sometimes very different from our own. Yet we learn to depend on His loving will, bowing to purposes we don't always understand. Prayer can lead to a grateful heart, turning our minds to all the gifts of life and to the great works of God. Prayer can also contribute to the life of our nation. America is a strong nation, in part because we know the limits of human strength. All strength must be guided by wisdom and justice and humility. We pray that God will grant us that wisdom, that sense of justice and humility in our current challenges, and in the years ahead" (pp. 71–72).

It's gratifying to note here that as a firm believer in Christ, he was determined to follow the path of his predecessors, who laid America's foundation on solid ground through their faith. Like those before him, Bush has learned that to succeed as a leader, he must always wait on the Lord in prayer—through which he strongly believes he'll find strength, comfort and peace from His Word. As the prophet Isaiah declared:

> *He gives strength to the weary and increases the power of the weak. Even youths grow tired and weary, and young men stumble and fall; but those who hope in the LORD will renew their strength. They will soar on wings like eagles; they will run and not grow weary, they will walk and not be faint.* (Isa. 40:29–31).

Therefore, it's wise to put Him first in all our plans, looking to Him Who alone is the source of our life, strength, wisdom and power for achieving our purpose in life. My dear friend, are you working with Him today or going along without Him? He is interested in all the good things we want to do in making life meaningful and profitable. Knowing our human frailty, He is more than willing to help us reach our target; as He declared to Jeremiah: " 'I am the LORD, the God of all mankind. Is anything too hard for me?' " (Jer. 32:27). This message came in answer to the prophet's prayer, when he couldn't understand why he had been asked to buy land in Jerusalem from his uncle, land that God had declared would soon be destroyed.

Nevertheless, His promise to Jeremiah surely materialized when the Babylonian army came to destroy Jerusalem and take the Jews captive: he was spared and given a captain who took good care of him. Besides, the copies of the plot's deed of purchase were kept in a clay jar, which lasted for 70 years. It was protected by God's power until the return of the Jews from captivity (Jer. 32:6–16). Just as He proved faithful to the prophet because he trusted in Him, so will He be faithful to any person or nation trusting in Him. But unless we give Him a chance in our lives as individuals and as a people—regardless of who we are and where we live under the sun—we can't experience His presence among us, let alone His love and faithfulness.

Every Nation Has Some Knowledge about God

The Holy Spirit further made me understand that since God made every human being in His own image, everyone of us has the ability to recognize His existence (Rom. 1:20). He has planted within each person's soul the spark of the divine seed (Gen. 1:26); therefore, no one is ignorant of Him. However, due to the broken human condition (i.e., our sinful nature through the fall of humanity), by our own efforts we cannot know, love and serve Him or do His will (Ps. 53:2–3; Rom. 3:23).

Unfortunately, there are people who deny God's existence, because of pride, rebellion and selfishness. They don't want anybody—not even God—to tell them what to do or not do. They want to have their own ways of life and be the captains of their own ships. To such people, His Word declares:

...what may be known about God is plain to them, because God has made it

> *plain to them. For since the creation of the world God's invisible qualities—his eternal power and divine nature—have been clearly seen, being understood from what has been made, so that men are without excuse* (Rom. 1:19–20).

The different names by which He is called by different tribes and people throughout the world underscore the truth that the majority of humans, if not all, believe in His existence. For example, before the Gospel reached the shores of the west coast of Africa through European missionaries, ancestors of Ghana believed in the existence of God.

In his book *African Cultural Values*, Gyekye echoed this truth: "The African world into which European Christian missionaries entered in the late seventeenth century was a religious world in which the idea of God as the Supreme Being was already known and held by the people. Their idea of God is proved by the various names and appellations they attribute to God according to their various religious experiences." For instance, the Akans call God *Boadze/Boadee* (Creator); *Enyiansombea* (All-seeing); *Totrobonsu* (the Giver of sun and rain); *Nyankopon* (the best of all friends); *Twerduammpon* (Dependable One—the unmovable tree capable of supporting all who lean upon Him); *Nyame* (Fante/Twi); *Nyomo* (Ga); *Mawu* (Ewe); *Allah* (Hausa/Arabic), *Olu* (Yoruba), and *Chineke* (Ibo).

Ghanaian Artistic Symbols

Besides the various names, our ancestors used symbols and artistic patterns to speak of God or present a theological message (*please see below*). I've learned through this vision that of all the names assigned to various African symbols, the most important one requiring our deepest thought is *Gye Nyame*.

| Gye Onyame | Nsoromma | Mmusuyidee | Dwennimmen | Fihankra |

THE INTERPRETATION OF THE MOTIF:

| God | Son (of Sky) | Sacrifice | Ram | Household |

GOD'S SON BECAME A SACRIFICIAL LAMB FOR THE HOUSEHOLD

That proverbial expression means that without God's help, we humans can't do anything. For instance, we can't tie a knot without the thumb. Similarly, we cannot tidy up or put our broken lives back together, or succeed in achieving our God-given goals (according to His standard) without His power and wisdom. He is " '…the Alpha and the Omega…who is, and who was, and who is to come…' " (Rev. 1:8). Just as He spoke with John on the island of Patmos, so the Lord gave me insight to know from this vision that due to Adam and Eve's fall, all human beings, as their descendants, are imputed with sin (Gen. 3:6–24; Rom. 3:23, 5:12–14).

Therefore, every aspect of our lives is affected by sin, and it's only Him, our Maker (like the potter), Who can put us back together again. That's to say, He is the only One Who can recreate us or restore us in His image. Only He Whose prime characteristic is goodness can make us whole again, as good and upright as He wants us to be in fulfilling His good and eternal purpose for every human being. Apart from our Maker, nothing can transform humanity in achieving its divine purpose or realizing its God-given destiny.

Each Symbol Bears a Sign of a Cross

Did you notice a cross in each of the symbols above? Take a careful look from the first to the last and you'll discern a cross in each of them. Isn't that wonderful? Just as the five symbols together convey the message "God's Son became a sacrificial lamb for the household," each individual symbol bearing a cross conveys the Good News of the message of Christ's death at Calvary in the salvation of humankind. Thus, the cross is His Father's solution to the human problem of sin and its consequences: death (Rom. 6:23).

We offer thanks to Him for giving our ancestors the creative ability to design these powerful symbols and their divine messages. Though they didn't realize the full impact of these symbols, I strongly believe they were divinely led to create them for us and posterity.

It was to understand, treasure and derive the full benefits from these symbolic messages that God graciously gave me this vision. Otherwise, we would still be ignorant of the blessings He has in store for us. "In the past God overlooked such ignorance," says Paul, "but now he commands all people everywhere to repent" (Acts 17:30). We now live in the age of technology, where every piece of information needed is only a phone call or mouse click away; so we have no excuse to claim ignorance. "For since the creation of the world God's invisible qualities—his eternal power and divine nature—have been clearly seen, being understood from what has been made, so that men are without excuse" (Rom. 1:20).

That's why He instructed me to put in writing the vision's message, so that all people everywhere—particularly my fellow Africans—may get to know the truth. Knowing this truth, we should take hold of His power in Christ in overcoming the world: faith in His love revealed in His Son's earthly life, ministry, and crucifixion (John 3:14–16). We'll discuss the cross later in more detail as we proceed; however, let's return to our discussion on the various names of God, this time as discovered by the Hebrews.

The Hebrews (i.e., the Israelites) also have different names for the Almighty as a result of the various encounters they had with Him in their early history. For instance, Hagar called God *Beer lahai Roi,* meaning "...'You are the God who sees me'..." (Gen. 16:13–14). This happened when He graciously sent His angel to rescue Hagar and her child from imminent death. She thought no one cared for her, but He did. Gideon called Him *El-Shalom,* which means "...The LORD is Peace..." (Judg. 6:24).

In the booklet *God Is,* written by the World Church of God, there's further explanation of various names ascribed to Him by the Hebrews/Jews found in Holy Scripture, as follows:

> *Yahweh* or *Jehovah* designates God in a covenant relationship with those He created. *Yahweh* means "the Eternal, the Immutable One, the Everlasting God" (Gen. 21:33); *Yahweh-Tsidkenu* ("Yahweh, our righteousness") (Jer. 23:6); *El* ("the Almighty, the Omnipotent"); *Elohim* ("in all His strength, the God who possesses all") (Gen. 14:18–22); *El Shaddai* ("the God Almighty is the all-bountiful Giver of grace; He supplies all the needs of his people") (Gen. 17:1) (Thomas Nelson, Inc., *God Is,* 1992, pp. 12–13).

These names, to mention only a few, indicate that throughout human history, from one generation to another, God has graciously revealed Himself in diverse ways to humanity in our different situations and cultures. Therefore, the phrase *Gye Nyame* is loaded with meaning. More importantly, *Without God, We Cannot Make It* expresses the fact that our lives, as His creations, are so rooted in Him that unless He is with us every step along our earthly paths, our efforts are fruitless. In other words, no successful venture by any person, group of people or nation is possible without His power. For without His "breath"—His life-giving Spirit in us (Gen. 2:7)—we are independently no more than dust and ashes. *Gye Nyame*, indeed.

History's amply demonstrated that one nation after another rose high and failed to make its mark, because it abandoned the Maker whose Kingdom rules over the universe. Therefore, no individual, group of people or nation can succeed without Him. This is the message that the Almighty, wants me to communicate not only to Ghanaians, but also to all Africans and the world at large.

CHAPTER 3

Hindrances to Africa's Success and Prosperity

*I*t was further revealed that the majority of African countries, including Ghana, are lagging in development because our nation-builders—ancestors, founding fathers, traditional chiefs, political leaders, priests, people in authority and Africa's citizens—didn't put God first in our plans. Our Ghanaian ancestors believed in the existence of *Nyame* (God) and called Him by different names, but they neither really knew Him in biblical terms nor sought Him with the view of worshipping Him "…in spirit and in truth" (John 4:24).

Kwame Gyekye wrote the following: "A European traveler to West Africa around the end of the seventeenth century observed that the Africans believed in a supreme God, that they had 'an idea of the true God, and ascribe to Him the attributes of Almighty and Omnipresent; they believe He created the universe, but they do not pray to Him or offer sacrifices to Him.' " (*African Cultural Values*, pp. 3–4).

When the Bible speaks of "knowing God," it refers to having a close relationship with Him. For instance, in Genesis 4:1, it is written, "Adam lay with [knew] his wife Eve, and she became pregnant and gave birth to Cain…" That's to say, he entered into "intimate relationship" through sexual intercourse with his wife and they bore a child, which is a gift from God—not from any other god, goddess or ancestors, as heathens are wont to believe. Thus, to know Him is to have a close and personal relationship with Him, in a sense comparable to the relationship between husband and wife.

Another example could be cited from the prophet Hosea's message, expressing God's lamentation over His people: "...my people are destroyed from lack of knowledge..." (Hosea 4:6). That means Israel's rejection of God's instruction through His prophets had made them ignorant of knowing how to live in a covenant relationship with Him; they were no longer following His way of righteousness through commandments. Their rebellious attitude had separated them from Him, and they were no longer under His arm of protection. As a result, they were destroyed by their enemies (Deut. 28:25).

Similarly, the failure of our ancestors to know and worship the true God (*Nyame*) made it impossible for them to build the land of Africa on a foundation firm enough to withstand the storms and turmoil of life. Consequently, the continent crumpled under various attacks from European traders, who scrambled for its riches, a process upon which I'll now expand.

The Partition of Africa

This is what Europeans did in partitioning Africa, as R.R. Palmer and J. Colton wrote:

"The Berlin conference of 1885 had laid down, for expansion in Africa, certain rules of the game—a European power with holding on the coast had prior rights in the back country; occupation by administrators or troops; and each power must give proper notice to the others as to what territories it considered its own. A wild scramble for 'real occupation' followed. In fifteen years the entire continent was parceled out" (*A Modern History of the World*, p. 623). How was the land distributed?"

The writers continue: "First, somewhere in the wilderness, would appear a handful of white men, bringing their inevitable treaties—sometimes printed forms. To get what they wanted, the Europeans commonly had to ascribe powers to the chief which by the customs of the tribe he did not possess—powers to convey sovereignty, sell land, or grant mining concessions" (p. 623). The only African nation that stood against the whites was Ethiopia: "Some 80,000 Ethiopians, however, slaughtered and routed 20,000 Italians in pitched battle at Adowa in 1896. It was the first time that native Africans successfully defended themselves against the whites, and it discouraged invasion of Ethiopia by the Italians (or other Europeans) for forty years" (p. 626).

The rest of the African continent was easily seized by the Europeans. Let's take the following example: between 1882 and 1884, H.M. Stanley, who returned to the Congo from Europe, "concluded treaties with over 500 chiefs, who in return for a few trinkets or a few yards of cloth put their crude marks on the mysterious papers and accepted the blue-and-gold flag of the Association, known as 'the International Congo Association, founded at Brussels in 1878, with a few financiers,' including Leopold II, king of Belgium" (p. 621).

The next question to ask is, *What happened to the natives after their lands had been taken away from them?* Palmer and Colton answer as follows: "Labor was the overwhelming problem… The result was that Europeans all over Africa resorted to forced labor. Or the new government, once installed, might allocate so much land to Europeans as private property (another foreign conception) that the local tribe could no longer subsist on the lands that remained to it. Or the whole tribe might be moved to a reservation, like Indians in the United States" (p. 624). Thus, Africans were not only dispossessed of their native lands, but also displaced and demoralized by the European settlers. Read again, the following report:

> In any case, while the women tilled the fields or tended the stock at home, the men would move off to take jobs under the whites for infinitesimal pay. The men then lived in "compounds," away from family and tribal kindred; they became demoralized; and the labor they gave, unintelligent and unwilling, would scarcely have been tolerated in any more civilized community. In these circumstances everything was done to uproot the Africans, and little was done to benefit them. The old tribal or village society collapsed, and nothing replaced it (p. 624).

Europeans' mistreatment of Africans must help readers of this book and other sympathizers understand why we're lagging behind in many areas of development—spiritually, economically, politically and technologically. What can we do to improve the situation? We don't have to continue living the rest of our lives in this stifling quagmire of degradation. As in the story of the four leprous men sitting outside the gate of Samaria, we have to ask ourselves the question: "…'Why stay here until we die?' " (2 Kings 7:3).

> ## We don't have to continue living the rest of our lives in this stifling quagmire of degradation

As the story continues, they gathered up courage, arose at dawn and went in faith to the camp of the Arameans, who had besieged the city of Samaria for weeks. When they reached the camp, the soldiers had quit their post, "for the Lord had caused the Arameans to hear the sound of chariots and horses and a great army, so that they said to one another, 'Look, the king of Israel has hired the Hittite and Egyptian kings to attack us!' So they got up and fled in the dusk and abandoned their tents and their horses and donkeys. They left the camp as it was and ran for their lives." (2 Kings 7:6–7).

We know from the rest of this story that not only did the Good Lord rescue and feed four lepers, but also, through their witness, the entire city of Samaria and its surrounding towns were saved from Aramaen domination with food in abundance. In his comment, Haddon Robbinson put it this way:

> You and I have discovered that salvation is found in Jesus Christ. It is a breakdown of basic integrity to keep that truth to ourselves. If we have found the cure for a guilty conscience, If we have found the food of life, we are obligated to share it with others. Evangelism is one hungry beggar telling another beggar where to find bread (*Daily Bread*, February 23, 2005).

Therefore, despite our present predicament, let those of us who believe in Christ rise up with faith and boldly approach Our Father's throne with a plea for deliverance. He Who delivered Samaria from war and hunger through the faith of four pathetic outcasts is still a miracle-worker in the business of deliverance. He will certainly deliver us, too.

Bribery and Corruption

In many cultures of the world—black or white—it's customary for individuals to express their gratitude to benefactors by presenting them with gifts in cash or in kind for services rendered. However, if the gift *precedes* the act of kindness, it's tantamount to bribery: the person concerned is naturally influenced by the weight of the gift in acting contrary to his will or conscience. This happens in various circumstances of life.

For example, if three people—Amponsah, Badu and Takyi—have applied for the same position as a salesman, it's up to the management to choose the best of the three applicants. During the interview, Amponsah proves to be the best, yet Takyi's hired, because prior to the interview he had offered a substantial gift through a friend to the chief executive. So Takyi starts work, fails to measure up to expectations, sales suffer and the company sustains a drop in profits. Under normal circumstances, he should be fired, but the chief executive can't do it because of the bribe. If the situation isn't remedied, the result may be closure of the business, simply because of incompetence coupled with selfishness and greed.

This has happened to countless business sectors throughout the African continent and thus hindered her progress as a people. A notable example was cited by Palmer and Colton in the following report:

> All Africa inland from the coasts was considered to be, like America in the time of Columbus, a *"terra nullius,"* without government and claimed by nobody, wide open to the first civilized persons who might arrive. Stanley, returning to the Congo in 1882, in a year or two concluded treaties with over 500 chiefs, who in return for a few trinkets or a few yards of cloth put their crude marks on the mysterious papers and accepted the blue-and-gold flag of the Association (*Modern History*, p. 621).

It's for this reason that the Scriptures offer strict warning to judges, kings and others in authority against receiving gifts, as follows:

> *"Do not deny justice to your poor people in their lawsuits. Have nothing to do with a false charge and do not put an innocent or honest person to death, for I will not acquit the guilty. Do not accept a bribe, for a bribe blinds those who see and twists the words of the righteous"* (Exod. 23:6–8). *Follow justice and justice alone, so that you may live and possess the land the LORD your God is giving you* (Deut. 16:20).

Though we're aware that the majority of countries in Africa are politically independent, for many reasons—e.g., bribery, corruption, mismanagement and nepotism—they're still tied to the apron strings of their colonial masters or governments. As stated in the above Scriptures, we won't possess the land unless we follow justice, because "Righteousness exalts a nation, but sin is a disgrace to any people" (Prov. 14:34). Read as a typical example the following excerpt in *The Washington Times* headed "UGANDA SHAKEN BY FUND SCANDAL: Millions Stolen in Health Grants:"

> Uganda, which continues to win praise from President Bush and others as a model of success battling AIDS, is reeling from the disclosure that top officials, their relatives and colleagues siphoned off

tens of millions of dollars in grants from the Geneva-based Global Fund. Money went to charities that did not exist, into the personal bank accounts of government employees and even to fund a nation-wide campaign to scrap term limits so that President Yoweri Musev-eni could run for a third term in office.

The most prominent official named was Jim Muhwezi, who had served as health minister until his recent ouster. Also named were two other senior ministry officials, Alex Kamugisha and Mike Mukula, with further investigation recommended. Commenting on the scandal, Jus-tice James Ogoola, the top judge of the Uganda High Court, said, "This was assistance for people who were dying, who had absolutely no hope. This is exactly what the Global fund was created for. The money came and people were diving in for the kill" (reported by Willis Witter, Fri-day, June 16, 2006).

It's obvious that the high officials involved in the scandal were con-cerned about their own welfare and prosperity. Why did they divert public funds for their own benefits instead of the sick? They were con-sumed by selfishness, lacking the slightest sympathy or compassion for the sick and those dying of AIDS among them.

It's been noted that the root cause of our hearts' corruption is the ab-sence of faith in God through Christ. He is the only way to a new life of righteousness and peace, as well as political, social and economic stabil-ity. But as discussed in previous passages, our reliance on the powers of other gods and ancestral spirits, and the elite's practice of occultism, have plunged Africa into darkness and poverty.

What can we do to emerge from this dismal prospect, to follow the light of God, which leads to peace and prosperity? Since "...all have sinned and fall short of the glory of God" (Rom. 3:23), none of us is ex-empt; we're all part of the problem. We ought to repent and turn to Him for the answers to our problems, remembering always Christ's spoken, unalterable Truth: "...'I am the way and the truth and the life. No one comes to the Father except through me...Apart from me, you can do nothing'" (John 14:6, 15:5). "'Come to me, all you who are weary and burdened, and I will give you rest'" (Matt. 11:28).

In order to understand our past, cleanse our misunderstanding and seek the Living God with all our heart, soul and mind as one people, we need to explore further our ancestors' religious backgrounds, discussed as follows.

What God Did Our Ancestors Worship?

I pose a necessary, legitimate question: *If our ancestors didn't worship God, the Creator of the universe, then what kind of god* did *they worship and call upon in times of need?* The undeniable, honest answer is that they worshipped other gods and goddesses, as some still do today. After calling upon these gods in times of trouble, was anybody saved from sin, misfortune, poverty, disease, or death? The answer is clearly *NO!*

Just as the people of Israel fell prey to their enemies in forsaking the true God (*Yahweh*), so have we become victims to Europe's capitalist nations, selfish political leaders in Africa, and the demonic forces unleashed by our archenemy, the Devil, who "…comes only to steal and kill and destroy…" (John 10:10).

In this connection, the Lord reminded me of my African traditional studies under the tutelage of Reverends Joseph DeGraft Johnson (deceased) and Dr. J.K. Agbetie, both of Trinity College, Legon, in Accra, Ghana (1968–1972), now known as Trinity Theological Seminary.

Furthermore, both my master's and doctoral studies—completed at Wesley Theological Seminary in Washington, D.C., under Professors Josiah Young, Recinos, James Shopshire and James Logan (1988–1993), to mention only a few—gave me access to books on African theology. I pass on to readers a detailed, broadened understanding of our ancestors' religious worldview (cosmology) in the next chapter.

CHAPTER 4

*O*ur ancestors viewed the world as consisting of a hierarchy of spirit-beings with the Supreme Being (the Akan *Nyame*) at the apex, below whom are the ancestors, followed by other gods, then lesser gods (such as dwarves). At the bottom of this hierarchy is Satan, the Devil (*Sasambonsam*).

In addition, there's a myth about the transcendence of God. The story has it that long ago, *Nyame* was so close to human beings that one could easily reach out to Him in the sky. However, one day an old woman accidentally hit *Nyame*'s dwelling place with a pestle while pounding *fufu* (mashed plantain/yam/cassava). She apologized and begged Him to move up a little further, which He agreeably did. After many repetitions, *Nyame* went up so high that no human being could ever see or hit Him anymore, forever. As funny and unrealistic as this story may seem, it explains, at least for the African, the transcendence of God—the reason that no one can see or reach Him.

"In traditional African religion," says Kwame Gyekye, "God is the Supreme Being but not the object of direct worship. Worship is directed to trees, rocks, rivers, and mountains… It is believed that objects of nature are inhabited by spiritual beings or deities who are thought to exist in the universe as intermediaries between God and humans but who cannot be seen by the human eye" (*Values*, pp. 6–7).

Whatever reason might have prevented our forefathers from worshipping the true deity, the Lord made me understand that it was a choice they made themselves without coercion. Just as our first parents,

Adam and Eve, made a conscious decision in obeying the voice of the serpent (Satan) instead of God's, so our ancestors, influenced by their environment, chose to worship other gods and spirits. People poured libation and sacrificed to them and dead ancestors, hoping to receive both spiritual and material support. In his book, *Towards African Theology*, John S. Pobee, wrote:

> The idea of mediator between God and man is not foreign to [the African]. The West African nature gods are said to be children of God, sent by Him as His representatives in human form; they can be seen, whether in the natural phenomena or in the symbol placed in their shrine (e.g., rock, tree or river) and so it is easier for man to approach them with offerings and prayer than the invisible high God (p. 48).

Indeed, what he says in the above passage is true, and I have a personal testimony to substantiate it.

A few days after graduating from Trinity Theological Seminary in Accra, I went home to visit my mother and family, all of whom had gathered in welcome. After a few words, the elder of the family (Nana Kojo Kum, not his real name) poured a cup of soda, readying for libation as a thanks-offering to the gods and ancestors. Respectfully restraining him, I explained that the Lord had made known to me that what he was about to do is tantamount to idol worship.

Despite my great respect for Nana Kum as the elder of the family or clan, like Peter I had decided to " '…obey God rather than men!' " (Acts 5:29). Instead, I offered a prayer thanking Him Who had saved me from sin and imminent death in preparing me for His ministry. Those present then amicably joined me in saying the Lord's Prayer.

Just as I was about to leave for Kumasi the following morning, Nana Kum asked me for a bottle of schnapps as a fee for juju/voodoo, which he said would give me protection and power for a successful ministry. Once again, I politely refused his well-intentioned offer, firmly assuring him that the Almighty God, Who had called me into His Son's ministry, would never leave or forsake me. He will ever be my Guide, Strength, Wisdom, Salvation and All-in-All. Realizing now that I was fully dependent on God for everything, Nana Kum shook my hand and wished me success.

Indeed, I knew he meant well in wanting to help me succeed in life, but his source of power for success — juju/voodoo — conflicted sharply with my faith. While on vacation a year later, I went back home and shared the Gospel with my people—including Nana Kum. This proscription makes it the duty of those privileged to know God through Christ to reach out with the Good News to our people so He may draw them from the power of darkness into the marvelous light of His Kingdom.

The Elite and Occultism

In addition to God's revelation that some of our ancestors or people in authority consulted diviners, medicine men or spirits of the dead, he made it known to me that some of the elite in our African societies and most countries of the world delve in occultism. According to *Webster's Dictionary*, the *elite* refers to "a socially superior group; a powerful minority group—inside government" or the ruling class of the community, including others in institutions, corporations, the army, the police, the church, etc.

Then, what is *occultism*? It's "belief or study of the action or influence of supernatural powers" (*Webster's New Collegiate Dictionary*, p. 794). Owing to their high positions in government or society and the respect accorded them, the elite indulge in these practices secretly. Hence, no member dares divulge what takes place behind closed doors. Norman Mackenzie writes that for most of them, the purpose of joining the group is mainly for "self-development," which is not wrong in itself. However, since members seek power, influence or success from spirits, angels or deities other than God in violating His Word, they incur His anger. As it's written:

> *Ahab son of Omri did more evil in the eyes of the LORD than any of those before him. He not only considered it trivial to commit the sins of Jeroboam son of Nebat, but he also married Jezebel daughter of Ethbaal king of the Sidonians, and began to serve Baal and worship him. He set up an altar for Baal in the temple of Baal that he built in Samaria. Ahab also made an Asherah pole and did more to provoke the LORD, the God of Israel, to anger than did all the kings of Israel before him* (1 Kings 16:30–33).

We suffer His displeasure by rejecting the One Who made us in His image in favor of fallen angels, other deities or spirit-beings who are creatures other than God. In spite of such supernatural beings' help in attaining certain positions of authority, in the end there's disappointment and shame. That's the main reason this book was written: to constantly remind everyone that "Unless the LORD builds the house, its builders labor in vain. Unless the LORD watches over the city, the watchmen stand guard in vain" (Ps. 127:1).

The pity is that sometimes we may not even be aware of our sinful behavior's magnitude until it's revealed to us. Let me share with you my own testimony here. Though I hadn't personally poured libation prior to my studies at Wesley Seminary and previously withstood my family elder's tradition, I had allowed myself nonetheless to be influenced by the opinions of other writers on African theology, compromising to some extent my own. Thus, in the presentation of my thesis, I wrote in favor of libation, describing it as an acceptable African way of prayer, as follows:

> Libation is an appeal made to *Nyame*, the Source of all things, before turning to any other in the hierarchy of being. After God, a portion of the wine is poured to *Asaase Yaa* (Mother Earth) and also to the ancestors, and finally to the other deities or gods. Libation is therefore a traditional way of praying (John A.K. Bonful, *Applying Both Hands to the Plough: Preaching and Healing Ministries of the Church*, 1993, p. 33).

A few weeks after graduation, while I was still in Washington, I had a dream in which I saw myself sitting on a bench together with idol worshippers before a diviner's shrine in Ghana. When I woke up, I was confused. For clarification, I asked the Lord during my early morning meditation for the meaning of the dream. He said to me, "Since you have written in favor of libation and are willing to teach others to do the same, aren't you just like one of those heathens, who worship other gods?"

That was an eye-opener. I realized that it's always necessary for believers to stick uncompromisingly to the Truth revealed in God's Word instead of following a tradition, or the opinions of theologians, or respectable people in authority. Traditional rites and opinions, however sincere, *have not saved* and *never will save* anybody. The only exception is when such an opinion or tradition doesn't conflict with Scripture. I thank God for giving me a dream to reveal a mistake, quickly withdrawing me from it before I could impart it to anybody else. We should always be skeptical when prophets or spirits approach, testing the authenticity of their message against what we know to be true. If it isn't of God or in line with Scripture, we'll fall or be deceived (Mat. 7:15–20; 1

Cor. 10:12; 1 John 4:1).

Another example follows. The leader of an elite group had been selling books on occultism to new members. After some time, the Lord sent me to convey the following message to him: "If you had been selling Bibles to members, you would have helped lead some to heaven, but since you've been selling books on occultism, you've sent more people to hell than you can imagine." Naturally, these words upset the boss, but I assured him that the Lord loves him and doesn't want him and others to be condemned and destroyed in hellfire; that was why He sent me to him. Besides, as His messenger I loved him, too; hence, I didn't hesitate to bring him a message of warning and salvation—saving grace possible through faith in Jesus Christ alone, and no one else.

He calmed down and after a little more conversation prayed with me. You may be surprised to know that he was a preacher for a local church in Ghana, yet God knew he hadn't surrendered his life to Christ. Years later, the elite group's big boss died, and only God knows where he'll spend eternity—with Him in heaven or with Satan in hell.

A third example was the case of a seasoned minister, who ha4d gained fame in the healing ministry. After several years in various places, complaints reached his bishop and church authorities that he had been indulging in occultism and that his powers of healing weren't God-given. Investigations produced other witnesses, proving him guilty of violating the Church's doctrinal principles of ministry; the minister was prematurely retired.

At this juncture of our discussion, I think Isaiah's question to his fellow Jews after they had delved in idolatrous practices is relevant: "When men tell you to consult mediums and spiritists, who whisper and mutter, should not a people inquire of their God? Why consult the dead on behalf of the living?" (Isa. 8:19).

My brothers and sisters, there are two questions in the above passage that require answers:

1. *Shouldn't a people inquire of their God?* The answer is an emphatic *Yes!* The Good God graciously invites all the people of this world to seek Him out, saying, " 'Call upon me in the day of trouble; I will deliver you, and you will honor me.' " (Ps. 50:15). Again He says, " 'Turn to me and be saved, all you ends of the earth; for I am God, and there is no other' " (Isa. 45:22). In other words, there's no other god or power that can deliver human beings from the original problem of sin, insecurity and chaos, except God (*Gye Nyame*), Je-

hovah, the "...I am who I am..." (Exod. 3:14), the Unchangeable One.

2. The second question is, *Why consult the dead on behalf of the living?* The reason is that people often want quick answers to their problems and to follow the path of least resistance in obtaining their hearts' desires. But it's demonic, and those who follow such ways soon fall into the snare of the Devil, as we've noted in previous passages.

King Saul Consults the Dead

God no longer spoke to Saul, first king of Israel, through a prophet, dream or *Urim* (instruments of divination), because of his disobedience to the Lord's Word, which He had previously sent to him through Samuel. Samuel, who had played the double roles of priest and prophet of Israel up until that time, had died. Besides, the king was embittered against David and wanted to kill him, because the latter had killed Goliath, thereby winning more praise from the women than the former. The women danced as they sang: "...'Saul has slain his thousands, and David his tens of thousands' " (1 Sam. 18:7).

In envious anger, he thought, " 'They have credited David with tens of thousands...but me with only thousands. What more can he get but the kingdom?' And from that time on Saul kept a jealous eye on David" (18:8–9). Aware that he would be the next monarch instead of his son, Jonathan, Saul was filled with a murderous jealousy, and their once cordial relationship turned to hatred.

Worse still, the Philistines were pressing in furiously against Saul for battle, and David, his strong and faithful captain, was now fearfully hiding from his master. In his frustration, the king disguised himself to seek help from a witch (medium) at Endor, where he consulted Samuel's spirit for advice on the impending battle. "Samuel said to Saul, 'Why have you disturbed me by bringing me up?' 'I am in great distress,' Saul said. 'The Philistines are fighting against me, and God has turned away from me...' " (28:15).

> *Why do you consult me, now that the LORD has turned away from you and become your enemy? The LORD has done what he predicted through me. The LORD has torn the kingdom out of your hands and given it to one of your neighbors — to David. Because you did not obey the LORD or carry out his fierce wrath against the Amalekites, the LORD has done this to you today. The LORD will hand over both Israel and you to the Philistines, and tomorrow you*

and your sons will be with me…" (28:16–19).

Though Saul consulted Samuel through the medium's divination, the prophet's spirit couldn't offer him the power to overcome the invading Philistine army. God had neither commanded human beings to seek help from the dead nor empowered their spirits to help the living. We need to be reminded here that earlier in his reign, when Saul was in His good standing, he courageously carried out a religious reformation. He had purged Israel of all wizards, mediums and acts of witchcraft and divination (28:3) in accordance with God's commandment: "A man or woman who is a medium or spiritist among you must be put to death. You are to stone them; their blood will be on their own heads" (Lev. 20:27).

Through Scripture, Saul was aware that God wanted His people to depend totally upon Him at all times for fulfillment of their needs, and not to turn to any other god, goddess or spirit of the dead for help. He says, " 'and call upon me in the day of trouble; I will deliver you, and you will honor me.' " (Ps. 50:15). We have another comforting promise: "Cast all your anxiety on him because he cares for you." (1 Pet. 5:7) These and many other wonderful, faithful promises of the Almighty tell us that we mustn't turn to any other god or ancestors. They can't save or help us in any way; we must trust in Him alone. Yet King Saul violated the very principles of God that could have preserved his life and his people.

Samuel's stern message to Saul teaches us several important lessons deterring us from calling on the dead or diviners:

1. ***Calling on the Dead Is a Disturbance of Their Peaceful Rest:*** For example, we read, " 'Yes,' says the Spirit, 'they will rest from their labor, for their deeds will follow them.' " (Rev. 14:13). Hence, the last sentence pronounced by a priest over the dead at a burial service is this: "May the soul of the faithful departed rest in perfect peace." "Rest in Perfect Peace," are the four most important last words all relatives and loved ones leave with their dead, often abbreviated on tombstones as "R.I.P." To awaken them from their peaceful rest in spirit is a great harassment to their quiet souls (1 Sam. 28:8). For God's sake, don't disturb the dead as they rest in peace!

2. ***Calling on Dead Ancestors Is an Act of Disrespect:*** Our ancestors have earned honor, even in death. Children or adults who honor their parents and elders dare not make noise in a house or room where a parent or elder is sleeping. If one parent is sleeping, the other will warn us against disturbance. Disregarding such parental caution isn't just a sign of disrespect, but also arrogance deserving due punishment. The Bible commands us to honor our fathers and mothers, including both the dead and the living, so that we'll have long and fruitful lives (Exod. 20:12).

3. ***Calling on the Spirits of the Dead Is Provocative to their Souls:*** By so doing, we're demanding from them what God alone can provide. Jesus tells the story of a rich, greedy, selfish man who died and found himself tormented in hellfire. Yet poor Lazarus went to rest in Abraham's bosom in heaven because he had trusted in the Lord. In agony, the formerly rich man, not wanting his five equally unbelieving brothers to suffer in hell upon their deaths, begged Abraham to send someone from the dead to warn them on earth. He responded: "…They have Moses and the Prophets; let them listen to them" (Luke 16:29). But the man still insisted that a witness from the dead would prove more credible to his brothers than Moses and the Prophets. Abraham finally said: "If they do not listen to Moses and the Prophets, they will not be convinced even if someone rises from the dead" (16:31).

Abraham's response stresses the fact that the dead cannot help the living, that we shouldn't call or depend on them for any help or guidance, apart from the Living God through Jesus Christ.

The Psalmist wrote:

> *Do not put your trust in princes, in mortal men, who cannot save. When their spirit departs, they return to the ground; on that very day their plans come to nothing. Blessed is he whose help is the God of Jacob, whose hope is in the LORD his God, the Maker of heaven and earth, the sea, and everything in them — the LORD, who remains faithful forever* (Ps. 146:3–6).

One Advantage of the African Christian

Perhaps the only advantage the concept of libation offers to the African Christian is that it reconciles with the belief in life after death. For instance, Moses and Elijah showed up at the transfiguration of Jesus and spoke with Him (Matt. 17:3–6; Luke 9:28–35). Luke tells us there was communication between Abraham's spirit in heaven and the rich man's in hell (Luke 16:19–31). Additionally, in Jesus' resurrection, He revealed Himself to Mary Magdalene in speaking with her outside the tomb (John 20:11–17). Such evidence confirms the fact that "the dead are still alive," but not to be worshipped or consulted. God is our Provider, Refuge and Strength forever, and *not the dead.*

With this in mind, the African Christian finds tenable the Scriptural doctrine of the Resurrection of Christ, His Second Coming, the hope of everlasting life for righteous believers and hell for the wicked. Nevertheless, one thing is certain: we're biblically forbidden from calling on the dead, because they absolutely *can't* help the living. That's why both Peter and Paul invite us, as taught by Christ Himself, to come to our Heavenly Father with all our concerns. He will care for us, give us peace and meet our needs according to His glorious riches in Jesus (Matt. 11:28; 1 Pet. 5:7; Phil. 4:6–7, 19).

We're biblically forbidden from calling on the dead, because they absolutely can't help the living

Gyekye puts it this way: "In Africa…the belief that the ancestors are always around to provide help of various kinds has led to excessive and incessant attention to the ancestors. We must surely remember and praise our forebears for their achievements. But we must not expect them to bestow favors on their descendants." He emphasizes the point that "the post-colonial problems of Africa clearly show that the ancestors cannot be helpful. The greatest reverence we, the descendants of the ancestors, can give to them is to let them rest in peace" (*Values*, p.167).

Finally, the most important reason we shouldn't call on the dead is the fact that it's forbidden by God in Scripture:

> *Let no one be found among you who sacrifices his son or daughter in the fire, who practices divination or sorcery, interprets omens, engages in witchcraft, or casts spells, or who is a medium or spiritist or who consults the dead. Anyone who does these things is detestable to the LORD, and because of these detestable practices the LORD your God will drive out those nations before you. You must be blameless before the LORD your God* (Deut. 18:10–13).

That means we must trust in God alone and no other, as did King David, who always looked to Him as his Maker, Savior, Refuge, Strength and Provider. He was never found wanting, because God had promised everyone who sincerely trusts in Him: " 'Never will I leave you; never will I forsake you' " (Heb. 13:5). Thus in the following passage, David praises Him, describing how much He means to him: "Praise be to the LORD my Rock, who trains my hands for war, my fingers for battle. He is my loving God and my fortress, my stronghold and my deliverer, my shield, in whom I take refuge, who subdues peoples under me" (Ps. 144:1–2).

Like David, we must cast our care upon God, trust Him and depend on Him to lead us in victory over our enemies. Furthermore, we ought to look to Him to supply all our spiritual and material needs "…according to his glorious riches in Christ Jesus" (Phil. 4:19). Each of us can then boldly say with David, "Surely goodness and love will follow me all the days of my life, and I will dwell in the house of the LORD forever" (Ps. 23:6).

In a public address on a special occasion in September 2002, Capt. Effah Nkrabea Dartey, Ghana's Deputy Minister of the Interior in the NPP Government, called on Ghanaians to stop pouring libation to other gods and ancestors during State functions and other occasions, saying it didn't yield benefits to the nation or its citizens in any way. Instead of heeding the minister's wise counsel, some traditional leaders and their supporters criticized him in the media.

When the Israelites abandoned the God Who made them and rejected their Savior, they incurred his wrath. "They made him jealous with their foreign gods and angered him with their detestable idols. They sacrificed to demons, which are not God—gods they had not known, gods that recently appeared, gods your fathers did not fear. You deserted the Rock, who fathered you; you forgot the God who gave you birth" (Deut. 32:16–18).

Privileged as we are to be living in the last days of the Spirit's dispensation and the Gospel's spread—with all the advantages of computerized communication—it's vital that we not worship idols or ancestors as did our ignorant forefathers.

I'm certain that if they had had the knowledge of the Holy Scriptures as we do today, they probably would have been better Christians than some of us currently are. For this reason, it's not my intention to criticize or pass judgment on our forebears. What we all need to do in our generation is to follow Paul's sound counsel: "Therefore, my dear friends, flee from idolatry" (1 Cor. 10:14).

We Came into This World with Nothing

Perhaps it'll do us some good to be reminded that whoever we are — black or white, male or female — we neither created ourselves nor entered this world with anything in our hands. We were all made by God for His purpose. Therefore, apart from Him and His purpose for our lives as individuals, we have nothing — and there's nothing any of us can do. In all our ways, the Bible exhorts us to "...approach the throne of grace with confidence, so that we may receive mercy and find grace to help us in our time of need" (Heb. 4:16). Whoever we are and whatever we have — materially and spiritually — it all belongs to God, "...who richly provides us with everything for our enjoyment" (1 Tim. 6:17).

Especially for leaders of nations, business enterprises or religious organizations, we're all accountable to no ancestors or gods but our people and ultimately our Creator. Therefore, our help comes from Him alone. "For there is one God and one mediator between God and men, the man Christ Jesus, who gave himself as a ransom for all men — the testimony given in its proper time" (2:5–6). Through His one sacrifice, all who accept the Savior receive forgiveness of sins and become children of God (John 1:12).

These verses are in line with Krakye Denteh's interpretation of the theological message presented by the Adinkra patterns on page 19: "God's Son Became a Sacrificial Lamb for the Household." Besides, Jesus rose from the dead, according to the Scriptures, giving eternal life to all confessing faith in Him. By the same theological interpretation, the Ghanaian artist has the Adinkra symbol representing His resurrection.

For this reason, we don't have to maintain the traditions of our ancestors, attempting to pacify gods and spirit-beings with animal blood and liquor. We sacrificed to them in the false belief that the gods were owners of the land. But according to the Bible, "The earth is the LORD's, and everything in it, the world, and all who live in it" (Ps. 24:1; also Lev. 25:23; Isa. 8:8). Even though He graciously gave our ancestors the wisdom to make inspiring symbols — including the signs of the cross and the resurrection of Christ, with their profound theological meanings — they didn't fully grasp the real implications of the Good News for the transformation of their lives.

The New Covenant Replaced the Sacrificial System of Old Covenant

The Jewish sacrificial system faced the same problem of tradition, and so the Jews had to learn to accept "a new and living way" (Heb. 10:20), which God had provided through His Son, described as " '…the Lamb of God, who takes away the sin of the world' " (John 1:29). The following underscores the importance of the sacrifice of Christ:

> *"Day after day every priest stands and performs his religious duties; again and again he offers the same sacrifices, which can never take away sins. But when this priest had offered for all time one sacrifice for sins, he sat down at the right hand of God…because by one sacrifice he has made perfect forever those who are being made holy." The Holy Spirit also testifies to us about this. First He says, " 'This is the covenant I will make with them after that time,' says the Lord. 'I will put my laws in their hearts, and I will write them on their minds.' Then he adds: 'Their sins and lawless acts I will remember no more.' And where these have been forgiven, there is no longer any sacrifice for sin"* (Heb. 10:11–12, 14, 16–18).

The above certifies the assurance of believers in God's promise of eternal life through Christ's sacrificial death on the cross. "Heaven and earth will pass away, but my words will never pass away" (Mark 13:31). Therefore, the letter to the Hebrews strongly encourages believers: "Let us hold unswervingly to the hope we profess, for he who promised is faithful" (Heb. 10:23). Our faith must thus rest in the Lord and His Word, and not in ancestors or traditions.

CHAPTER 5

Libation in the Old Testament

*T*here are two particular instances in the Old Testament when libation was poured to God. The first example is seen as a memorial to a certain place or a patriarch's special encounter with Him. He appeared to Jacob on his return journey from Paddan Aram and blessed him:

> *And God said to him, "I am God Almighty; be fruitful and increase in number. A nation and a community of nations will come from you, and kings will come from your body. The land I gave to Abraham and Isaac I also give to you, and I will give this land to your descendants after you"* (Gen. 35:11–12).

After He had spoken with him, He departed. To mark this occasion as significant in Jacob's life, he set up a stone pillar where God had appeared to him and "…he poured out a drink offering on it; he also poured oil on it" (35:14). This example of libation is significant for the following reasons:

- It's his token of thanks-offering to the L0iving God for blessings received, and not to any other god or dead ancestor, such as Abraham or Isaac.
- It's a memorial to future generations of God's revelation to him at that particular place and time in his life.
- It's a testimonial of God's loving kindness toward the patriarch whenever his life's story is read.
- It marks the ancestors' footsteps, that is, their relationship with Him, drawing the attention of children to fear, love and worship

the God of their fathers.

- It's sometimes considered as a form of prayer, as the following example shows:

> *Then Samuel said, "Assemble all Israel at Mizpah and I will intercede with the LORD for you." When they had assembled at Mizpah, they drew water and poured it out before the LORD. On that day they fasted and there they confessed, "We have sinned against the LORD." And Samuel was leader of Israel at Mizpah* (1 Sam. 7:5–6).

- It shows both present and future generations how much their fathers trusted in God and depended upon Him alone for salvation and victory over their enemies.
- It teaches them to trust in the God of their fathers, and to learn to obey and serve Him as they had done.

Careful observation of both libation examples above enables us to realize that unlike the Ghanaian/African type of libation, the oil or water was poured not to other gods, spirits or ancestors, but to the One Who alone is the Source and Sustainer of our lives. Therefore, only He is worthy of worship by human beings (Exod. 20:1–6). In addition, He calls on us to direct our prayers to Him alone (Jer. 33:3). Interestingly, there are several places in the Old Testament where a patriarch might have built an altar and called on His name (i.e., worshipped) at that particular spot, without necessarily offering Him any drink or libation (Gen. 12:8, 35:7; Josh. 4:1–9).

Commenting on Isaiah's message concerning Israelites' indulgence in "…offering sacrifices in gardens and burning incense on altars of brick," and "…sit[ting] among the graves and spend[ing] their nights keeping secret vigil" (Isa. 65:3–4), Nicky Gumbel said, "This refers to the false cults, probably involving Canaanite fertility rites and sexual immorality. Often, people think that it does not matter what you believe so long as you are sincere. But here we learn that the worship of such gods is offensive to God. 'To sit among the graves,' means to consult the dead. This is expressly forbidden in the Bible (Lev. 19:31; Deut. 18:10–12), and any attempt to contact the dead through mediums or séances is not an option for Christians" (*The Heart of Revival*, p. 169).

Whenever the people of God had followed the pagan practice of sacrificing or calling on other gods or spirits of the dead, they were sharply rebuked and punished by Him through the prophets (Exod. 32:25–8; 1

Kings 18:39–40; Isa. 63:3–4, 6).

Their occasional disobedience caused God to withdraw His protection and provision, making them helpless and hopeless at the hands of their enemies; in trouble afterward, they repented and cried to Him for deliverance. This was the type of religious roller coaster in which they found themselves during the period of the Judges (Judg. 1:1–21; 1 Sam. 28:15; 1 Kings 21:20–28; 1 Cor. 8:4–8; 1 John 5:21).

These events taught them the truth, warning future generations against disobedience of His Word:

> *See, the storm of the LORD will burst out in wrath, a whirlwind swirling down on the heads of the wicked. The anger of the LORD will not turn back until he fully accomplishes the purposes of his heart. In days to come you will understand it clearly"* (Jer. 23:19–20).

This is as well as an exhortation to rise above similar situations that otherwise may lead to destruction.

The New Testament Teaching on Idolatry

In their letters, the Apostles earnestly taught believers to avoid idol worship. For instance, writing to the Corinthians, Paul offered Christians a strong caution to flee idolatry, referring to the punishment their fathers suffered as a result of their disobedience (1 Cor. 8:4–8, 10:1–12, 14–22; also 1 John 5:21). In his letter to the Ephesians, he issues the following alarm: "…'Wake up, O sleeper, rise from the dead, and Christ will shine on you.' Be very careful, then, how you live—not as unwise but as wise, making the most of every opportunity, because the days are evil" (Eph. 5:14–16).

CHAPTER 6

Traditional Chiefs Entrusted with Authority

*T*he Bible counsels all people, especially believers, to submit to those in authority, because they are put there by God:

> *Everyone must submit himself to the governing authorities, for there is no authority except that which God has established. The authorities that exist have been established by God. Consequently, he who rebels against the authority is rebelling against what God has instituted, and those who do so will bring judgment on themselves. For rulers hold no terror for those who do right, but for those who do wrong. Do you want to be free from fear of the one in authority? Then do what is right and he will commend you. For he is God's servant to do you good. But if you do wrong, be afraid, for he does not bear the sword for nothing. He is God's servant, an agent of wrath to bring punishment on the wrongdoer* (Rom. 13:1–4).

That means those entrusted with authority represent God and are expected to exercise their authority in accordance with His will, whether for the good of citizens or employees of a particular business. Anyone in a leadership position is accountable to Him, as well as to the people through whom He elevated him or her. The Bible has several examples of men and women—Joseph, Moses, Miriam, Joshua, Gideon, Deborah, Esther, Peter, and Paul—who had weaknesses just as we do. Yet they discharged their tasks successfully by depending on God rather than their own abilities or wisdom.

For instance, when Joseph was brought from an Egyptian prison and presented to the king to interpret his dream, Pharaoh said, " '...I have heard it said of you that when you hear a dream you can interpret it.' 'I cannot do it,' Joseph replied to Pharaoh, 'but God will give Pharaoh the answer he desires.' " (Gen. 41:15–16). After interpreting the dream, he asked the king to "appoint commissioners over the land" to be in charge of the reservation of food for Egypt. Pharaoh then asked his officials: " '…Can we find anyone like this man, one in whom is the spirit of God?' " Then he turned to Joseph and declared in the presence of all his officials: " 'Since God has made all this known to you, there is no one so discerning and wise as you…I hereby put you in charge of the whole land of Egypt' " (41:34, 38–39, 41).

As people in authority, what lessons do we learn from Joseph? First, he believed in God, and so His Spirit dwelt in him (39:2–5, 37–8). Second, he feared Him and obeyed His commandments (39:6–10). Third, He didn't claim special abilities in interpreting dreams on his own. He gave all the glory to God, drawing Pharaoh's attention to Him, Who has the power to " '…[reveal] to Pharaoh what he is about to do…God will give Pharaoh the answer he desires' " (Genesis 41:25, 16).

Ghana, like many African countries, is blessed with a rich heritage of chieftaincy (a tradition of chiefs and queens), including elders, who are placed in authority by God (through the people) to govern. It follows, therefore, that these authorities mustn't exercise their power for their own personal interests, but for the well-being of all people. According to tradition, before a king/chief/queen takes office, he or she is given a traditional sword or scepter as a symbol of royal authority. Now, standing before the assembly of kingmakers, elders and the entire populace, the new king or queen swears an oath of allegiance, avowing the faithful exercise of authority at all times for the progress of everyone.

In order for Ghanaians to maintain their cultural values and simultaneously advance as a distinct African people, ancestors and predecessors bequeathed to their succeeding kings, chiefs and queens vast acres of land to be developed or cultivated for everyone's benefit. In addition to land and treasures of gold and silver, Ghana's traditional chiefs were entrusted with a rich religious heritage, among which are symbols or patterns that present a theological message for the people.

Precious religious endowments from God, they're intended to reveal His character through various names, as discussed in Chapter 2. Similarly, it's believed that the various names our ancestors used for Him arose out of their experiences and ideas about Him. It was to preserve their religious tradition that they represented these names and ideas in artistic patterns and symbols in a piece of wood, clay or cloth for use by their successors and posterity.

Unfortunately, this rich religious inheritance of Akan–Adinkra patterns—each of which conveys a unique theological message—was kept a secret treasure in the king's palace. Some of them were used to make beautiful designs in costly *kente*—the name of the specially woven cloth worn on certain occasions in Africa, particularly in Ghana—and various other textiles (such as tie-dye) or wooden carvings and stools or on the walls and gates of houses.

Nowadays, a good number of carpenters and potters also use them in producing attractive handiworks, purchased by both black and white people for decoration in their homes, offices and hotels. Though such uses aren't bad in themselves, they don't serve their original divine purpose: drawing our mind toward God so that we might know Him and walk in His ways. Regrettably, that didn't happen. The chiefs, political leaders, other authority figures and Ghanaians in general didn't put God first in our lives.

That's why after 53 years of independence as a sovereign nation, Ghana, like other African countries—such as Uganda, Congo, Nigeria, Côte d'Ivoire, Liberia, and Sierra Leone, to mention only a few—is still lagging behind in terms of spiritual, moral and economic advancement. It's important for every reader of this message to note here that Ghana has been cited. God pointed her out to me as an example, knowing I'm Ghanaian and can speak about her better than I can any other nation. Nevertheless, what applies to that country applies to others and their people, because " '...God does not show favoritism but accepts men from every nation who fear him and do what is right' " (Acts 10:34–35).

Just as the ancient builders of the Tower of Babel failed miserably because they chose to pursue their aim without first seeking God's power, wisdom and guidance, so will come to ruin the plans of every human organization unless it turns to Him. For instance, the United Nations, heads of states, religious and political leaders, elders of tribes, parents, teachers and students may all set forth laudable goals; yet without God, the result won't be to His glory or in service to His purpose for the community. When the leaders of Israel, for instance, had neglected the Holy Scriptures, they fell into a similar situation. God then laid the blame squarely on the leaders' shoulders, saying: "Those who guide this people mislead them, and those who are guided are led astray" (Isa. 9:16).

Isaiah's statement isn't different from Jesus': " 'Woe to you, teachers of the law and Pharisees, you hypocrites! You travel over land and sea to win a single convert, and when he becomes one, you make him twice as much a son of hell as you are' " (Matt. 23:15). It follows that due to lack of the true knowledge of God, both teachers and students are in danger of destruction (Hosea 4:6). It behooves us, therefore, to let Christ's admonition be our guiding light and principle, in order that we might seek His wisdom and guidance in all our ways. Otherwise, those of us in leadership positions, together with those under us, will eventually be sadly disappointed.

> **Whatever, whoever we may be— we're merely flesh and blood by nature and, therefore, liable to sin**

How can we avoid this failure? I'm convinced that the inevitable answer to such a situation is found in the Word of God: "Unless the LORD builds the house, its builders labor in vain. Unless the LORD watches over the city, the watchmen stand guard in vain" (Ps. 127:1). As nations consisting of people from different cultures—whether white or black, however rich or poor, strong or weak, whatever we are, and whoever we may be—we're merely flesh and blood by nature and, therefore, liable to sin.

It's not within our own strength and wisdom to order our ways. The horrible events of September 11, as well as the sniper shootings of Ocober 2002, should humble all human beings, wherever we are, to seek God and to learn of His ways through His only Son, Jesus Christ, who is the Savior of the world (Isa. 45:22; John 3:16–17). As He said, " '…apart from me you can do nothing.' " (John 15:5). This stresses the need for us to look up to Him, Who is "…the power of God and the wisdom of God" (1 Cor. 1:24), as well as " '…the light of the world…' " (John 8:12). With our limited human resources, we can do very little to protect ourselves from danger and enemies.

But with Christ as our Guide, we'll receive necessary direction in every aspect of this life, finding moreover true success, happiness, peace and security. Otherwise, we're prey to our enemies who, like lions, hide in the dark looking for people to devour. The following was part of a report from staff writer Manju Subramanya in the *Wheaton Gazette*, under the headline "In the Grip of Terror," and subtitled "Indiscriminate Murder Shocks, Unsettles County:"

> Montgomery County has seen its share of bizarre and horrific crimes, but nothing has prepared the County for the random, seemingly motiveless shootings that have gripped the region with fear, locking down our schools and changing the way we conduct our daily business. Even veteran police and prosecutors who remember the Samuel Sheinbein dismemberment case, the Golf family murders in Potomac or Bradford Bishop's disappearance after he killed his family are flummoxed by the events of this past week, which have left six people dead and two badly wounded. [*Note:* the number of the dead had risen to ten by the following Tuesday, October 22, with the killing ofConrad Johnson, a bus driver].

What could we do as a church? Though no particular bishop or church leader was called upon to join hands with law-enforcement agencies in the search for the perpetrators, we couldn't sit unconcerned about this horrible situation. Bishops, pastors and various leaders of religious organizations called their members to prayer vigils, among the greatest weapons of the Church. So on Sunday, October 13, 2002, members of my church, the Calvary Redeeming Methodist Church in Rockville, met solely for prayers toward a solution and for the bereaved families. It was our conviction that if we lifted up our voices with one accord and prayed unto God in Jesus' Name, He would hear and come to our rescue, as He has said, "…'Call upon me in the day of trouble; I will deliver you, and you will honor me.' " (Ps. 50:15). He has also assured us, " '…Not by might nor by power, but by my Spirit…' " (Zech. 4:6).

The Only Hiding Place

If one man with his teenaged companion as a gunman could terrorize such a security-conscious region as the Washington, D.C., Metropolitan Area, then we must realize there's no safe place or haven anywhere, except in God. In "The Hiding Place," David Roper's words are very relevant here: In this world's misery, there is only one sure hiding place: God Himself. "…He is a shield for all who take refuge in Him" (Ps. 18:30).

> To "trust in" comes from a Hebrew word that means "to take refuge in" or "to hide in" or "to hide with." It suggests a secret place of concealment, a "hidey hole," as we used to say in Texas.
>
> When we're exhausted by our efforts, when we're bewildered by our

problems, when we're wounded by our friends, when we're surrounded by our foes, we can hide ourselves in God. There is no safety in this world. If we were to find safety here, we would never know the joy of God's love and protection. We would miss the happiness for which we were made.

The only safe place is God Himself. When storm clouds gather and calamities loom, we must run into His presence in prayer and remain there (Psalm 57:1).

George MacDonald said, "That man is perfect in faith who can come to God in the utter dearth of his feelings and desires, without a glow or an aspiration, with the weight of low thoughts, failures, neglects, and wandering forgetfulness, and say to Him, 'Thou art my refuge.' "

> How safe and blessed we are!
> O the sweet unfailing refuge
> Of the everlasting arms;
> In their loving clasp enfolded,
> Nothing worries or alarms.
> —Hennessay
> *Our Daily Bread*, March 10, 2004

CHAPTER 7

*G*od is so faithful and true to His promises that those who believe in and call on Him surely experience that faithfulness aplenty. As many believers intensified their prayers on the killing spree gripping the nation over the previous 10 days, the snipers—John Muhammad (41) and John Lee Malvo (17)—were arrested by the police at about 3:30A.M. on Thursday, October 24, 2002, while sleeping in their blue Chevy Caprice at a rest stop in Frederick County. Our church had held a prayer vigil on October 13 and the snipers were caught eleven days later.

Together with many others who had knelt in humility, God had answered our prayer for deliverance, using human agents to apprehend the perpetrators. Indeed, the news of the arrest drew a big sigh of relief from thousands of people living in fear of such unexpected, unprecedented, random death in Washington, D.C., Virginia and Maryland.

We give praise and glory to God for coming to our rescue through the combined efforts of the prayer-warriors of the church, law-enforcement agencies and the cooperation of the public as a whole. As Alfred, Lord Tennyson said, "More things are wrought by prayer than this world dreams of." Surely, without His timely intervention, the snipers wouldn't have been caught so soon, and the killings would have continued for a much longer time than they did. "But thanks be to God! He gives us the victory through our Lord Jesus Christ" (1 Cor. 15:57). Indeed, He hears the prayers of His servants when they sincerely cry unto Him in troubled times, as promised in His Word (Ps. 50:15).

Commenting on the case in the *Gazette*'s Regional News after the arrest, Parris N. Glendening, then-governor of Maryland, said, "The death penalty should be used to punish those responsible for 10 sniper-related killings in Maryland, Virginia and Washington, D.C." (Wednesday, October 30, 2002, p. A-22). Held in police custody, the suspects were later tried separately and found guilty of murder by a jury in Virginia. Mohammed was sentenced to death for masterminding the crimes, while Malvo, the teenager, had his sentence commuted to life in prison for carrying out the shootings. After seven years in police custody, Mohammed was finally put to death by lethal injection in November of 2009.

Catholic Schools Prayed for Peace

The news of the snipers' arrest thrilled members of churches, organizations, institutions and schools to such a degree that special services were held in various places to thank God for answered prayers. Karl Hille, staff writer for *The Montgomery Journal*, reported on the front page concerning a service held by Catholic schools in the county as follows:

> **Services Held in Appreciation of Police, Sniper Task Force**
> Catholic schools across the Archdiocese of Washington on Thursday held prayer services for peace and to show their appreciation for Montgomery County Police and other members of the sniper task force. At Mary of Nazareth School in Darnestown, more than 300 students gathered to honor the police officers of District 1, as well as their teachers and the parents who volunteered to patrol their wooded campus. Patricia Weitzel-Oneill, superintendent of the archdiocese schools, had planned to offer prayers on Thursday morning, and many classrooms composed letters to Montgomery County Police Chief Charles Moose and their local police stations (col. 1).

No words are adequate to express our heartfelt thanks to God for using the teamwork of all the law-enforcement agencies and many volunteers to arrest and bring the two snipers to justice. Again, it ought to be noted that had the Lord not intervened in response to prayers, all human efforts would have been in vain, and the snipers could still have been killing innocent people. Glory be to His name and may His wonderful deeds be praised by His people from generation to generation.

The point emphatically repeated in this book is the truth that human ability, authority or military/scientific/political power can neither rule nor order our lives according to God's will or expectation unless it seeks divine wisdom and guidance. Why? Because it's God Who created us: " '…in him we live and move and have our being'…" (Acts 17:28). This is similar to the prophet Isaiah's cry of woe (Isa. 31:1) to those not seeking help from the Lord, preferring to make an alliance with Egypt (29:15). He stressed, "…the Egyptians are men and not God; their horses are flesh and not spirit…" (31:3). Just as a child can't survive without its parents/nurse/caregiver, as humans we can't make it without God—our Maker, Strength, Provider and Sustainer. The Psalmist affirms this truth:

> *I lift up my eyes to you, to you whose throne is in heaven. As the eyes of slaves look to the hand of their master, as the eyes of a maid look to the hand of her mistress, so our eyes look to the LORD our God, till he shows us his mercy* (Ps. 123:1–2).

Surely, my friend, it's never been possible in generations down the centuries to do without the Almighty. Besides, He has neither changed in the nature, character, or principles by which He operates or governs the universe, nor is He the respecter of people. Therefore, every head of state, president, prime minister, king, and queen—including all people under the sun who breathe "…the breath of life…" (Gen. 2:7)—had better take a cue from this book's revealed vision for their own good, their family's, and that of all people.

God Reveals in Order to Redeem

Those who acknowledge their need of God, sincerely trusting and calling on Him in their hour of trouble, receive deliverance. But those who rely on themselves or any other god or military/scientific powers for success/victory often end up in utter disappointment, frustration, destruction or suicide. The reason is that as humans, we neither created ourselves nor dropped down from the sky into this world, nor can we protect or redeem ourselves from danger and sin with their deadly consequences.

The security guard hired to protect you, me or the President, easily becomes tired and sleepy, and soon falls asleep when we do, but the Almighty God "…will neither slumber nor sleep" (Ps. 121:4). He watches over you, me and all His creation day and night throughout the year (2 Chron. 16:9). He alone keeps us secure under the shadow of His mighty wings. We can confidently say with the Psalmist:

> *God is our refuge and strength, an ever-present help in trouble. Therefore we will not fear, though the earth give way and the mountains fall into the heart of the sea…The LORD Almighty is with us; the God of Jacob is our fortress* (Ps. 46:1–2, 7).

Gina's Story: A Miraculous Deliverance from Death

Toward the middle of the month of May 2009, my wife, Gina (short for Georgina), noticed a change in her urine and that her legs and thighs had become swollen. She consulted her primary-care physician and received the recommended treatment, but without improvement in her condition. Referred to a specialist at Sibley Hospital in Washington, she was admitted on May 27. When her condition was examined again, she was diagnosed with nephrotic syndrome (derived from nephrosis: "non-inflammatory degeneration of the kidneys chiefly affecting the renal tubules").

After a team of specialists had examined Gina a few days following admission, they said in their concluding remarks to one another, as they were almost out of her room, "Everything has shut down—the kidneys aren't functioning and could no longer respond to treatment." Lying quietly in her bed, she overheard their comment, suddenly recalled Lazarus' hopeless situation in John 11 and said to herself, *As for my God, He specializes in hopeless cases, and thereby proves His mighty power over cases that are impossible with men.* In thus speaking to herself, she believed that though her condition was hopeless and beyond the abilities of the specialists, Jesus Christ, the Greatest Physician, would intervene with His miraculous touch to arouse and heal her weakened body.

Skeptical of their diagnosis, one of the doctors, a specialist in nephrotic disease, decided to tackle Gina's condition using steroids, which also have negative side effects. When the church was informed about this, some of the members joined me in prayer and fasting, interceding on behalf of my wife's recovery.

With faith in God, Gina started taking the steroid treatment on Sunday, July 2, 2009. Her condition had raised such an alarm in the Bonful family that our daughter, Adoma, who was in London with her husband, flew to the U.S. to be with her mom at the hospital. Within a week after the start of treatment, the doctor came with the good news that her kidneys had bounced back by 20% of their working capacity. Then her condition kept improving day by day, with the kidneys' capacity improving to 60% within a couple of weeks. We kept praying for a miraculous healing. In short, by divine intervention, her kidney function had miraculously risen to the normal condition of 100%. Surely, what had broken down was then completely restored.

On hearing this report from her doctor, my wife exclaimed, "Praise the Lord!" Standing by her bedside and beaming with a broad smile and sparkling eyes, her doctor acknowledged the words and said, "Yes, indeed! This is all God's doing. It's a miracle! We give God the glory. I don't take any credit for myself." Yes, it's true that we agreed with the doctor, but we also assured him that he had a human role to play in the healing process by being an obedient vessel, whom God could use to fulfill His purpose for Gina in such critical times.

On Monday, August 3, 2009, she was discharged from the hospital. Thanks to God for answered prayers and to the nephrotic specialist, as well as all the nurses assigned to her case. Isn't the Almighty awesome and wonderful, yet merciful, gracious and faithful to all who sincerely call on Him? He has promised believers, " '…call upon me in the day of trouble; I will deliver you, and you will honor me' " (Ps. 50:15).

Of course, after Gina had come home, we attended church the following Sunday, giving thanks to God and everyone who had helped us in prayer and other ways. In her honor, a special party was organized in the Church Hall, where she had the privilege of delivering a glorious testimony and expressing personal gratitude to God for making her a living example of what prevailing prayer can do for those who trust in Him.

Cases of Suicide Involving Celebrities

It's surprising that a disproportionate number of suicides have been been committed by celebrities and the rich of this world rather than the poor. Why? In exploring the cause, the reason is not hard to find: many rich people pin their entire livelihood—their love, family life, happiness, hope, peace, and destiny—on their wealth. It becomes their all-in-all, that is, their god. Francis Bacon, Sr., said, "Money is a good servant, but a bad master." Whenever the rich discover that material wealth alone doesn't satisfy, they inevitably have no other solid object or safe haven to run to for security. Eventually, they become not only disillusioned, but miserable and depressed, hateful of themselves, their family and society at large.

Finally, they feel completely out-of-joint and rejected, with life becoming empty and meaningless. They hit rock bottom. Then, of course, life is no longer worth living. Some end it slowly through alcohol or drugs and, finally, overdose and die. But the aggressive end their lives at once to curtail their shame, loneliness, and misery.

A typical example was the case of Billy Jojoe, one of the greatest musicians the twentieth century had ever known. He had his music, popularity, money, a luxurious mansion, many friends and everything that could make a man happy by worldly standards. Yet all these things couldn't prevent Jojoe from fear when diagnosed with a serious medical condition: stress leading to high blood pressure. His condition had been partly triggered by the divorce of his wife, who had fallen in love with a close friend, who was there regularly to comfort her because of the loneliness brought on by her husband's many trips away from home.

The situation worsened still when their 14-year-old daughter, who had fallen into bad company, wouldn't go to school or come home. In his hopelessness and inability to hold on any longer, Jojoe decided to end his troubles altogether rather than face them and, eventually, committed suicide by drug overdose. This was an unexpected, unnecessary and tragic end of a man who wasn't just rich by worldly standards, but also very popular because of his extraordinary musical talent. Then why couldn't he stand up to his trials?

The answer is that God did not design human beings so that we could obtain from material things the helping hand or saving grace that He alone can provide during the turbulence of our earthly lives. As Jesus declared, "…'A man's life does not consist in the abundance of his possessions' " (Luke 12:15). Jojoe had everything but Jesus Christ, the Savior. Despite many friends and riches, they didn't have the power to help him overcome or cope with his problems, or deliver him from death by his own hand. But I can bet with confidence that he would still have been alive had he known Jesus as his Lord and Savior, the One to Whom to turn in times of trouble—particularly when facing helplessness (Ps. 46, 50:14–15; Matt. 11:28–30).

The sad end of Jojoe—and other precious lives shortened by tragic accidents, natural disasters and others' wickedness—should cause all of us to ponder now and again the brevity of life. As we do so, we'll realize life is too short to be treated carelessly. After meditating on the span of our fleeting, earthly life, Moses prayed to God: "Teach us to number our days aright, that we may gain a heart of wisdom" (Ps. 90:12).

My dear brothers and sisters, the truth is that human beings weren't made to derive their inward satisfaction from material things. God made us in a unique way—"in His own image"—so that humans will live in loving relationship with Him through faith in Christ. And with their neighbors, they'll find—through the indwelling Holy Spirit—lasting love, peace, joy, patience, gentleness, faith, self-control, contentment and fulfillment (Gal. 5:22). Anything other than His Way revealed in the Scriptures—and affirmed by Christ's life, death, and resurrection (Matt. 22:3–40; Mark 10:42–45; John 14:6, 15:13–14; Luke 23–24)—leads humans astray.

We're faced with disappointment, frustration, emptiness, and misery, too often culminating in self-destruction. But if we walk with God in obedience to His will (1 Pet. 4:2), He will sustain us by His mighty hand and loving care in the midst of the storms of our lives (Isa. 43:1–2; John 16:33). This is also affirmed by both Peter and Paul: "…put no confidence in the flesh" (Phil. 3:3); for "…'God opposes the proud but gives grace to the humble.' Humble yourselves, therefore, under God's mighty hand, that he may lift you up in due time. Cast all your anxiety on him because he cares for you" (1 Pet. 5:5–7).

> **If we walk with God in obedience to His will, He will sustain us by His mighty hand and loving care**

Dear reader, I encourage you to believe the Scriptures in saying that the Lord has power to walk you through every "Red Sea" (Exod. 14:15–31; Job 1:42; Isa. 43:1–2) that you have to cross in the wilderness of your life. He is able to speak His Word of Power to make a way in the sea or calm down the raging storms of your life. Like the Israelites and the Disciples, you'll exclaim with wonder, "…'Who is this? Even the wind and the waves obey Him!'" (Mark 4:41).

Just remember that as human beings, we can't do without God. Our lives—together with our goals and fulfillment as one package designed according to divine plan—depend on our relationship with Him, Who made us in His image, and by grace redeemed us through His Son. Without Him in our lives, we're never content, because nothing can fill the place He has created in the human heart for Himself. Yes, that's quite true; without Him within us fulfilling the purpose of our lives, there's always chaos and discontentment. Nothing really satisfies the soul, the real personality especially designed to relate to Him.

Rev. Dr. Michael Youssef, introducing his latest book *Divine Discontent: Pursuing the Peace Your Soul Longs For*," said:

> Are you convinced that if things were different, you would be happier and more at peace? Are you finding less fulfillment in the things that consume most of your time and energy? Is there a steady background hum in your life—the dull hum of dissatisfaction? This deep-seated discontentment is not limited to those who are struggling with life's hurts and tragedies. In fact, a sense of dissatisfaction with life is often more pronounced among people who—from all outward appearances—seem to have it made. One's level of success does nothing to minimize the symptoms of discontent. And Christians are not immune. Large numbers of believers are angry with God, disappointed in their church, or troubled by the requirements that Scripture makes on their lives. Their faith seems to be powerless to quiet the hum of discontent. The nagging inner voice insists, *There has to be more. Something is still missing.*

He continues:

> While most people pursue earthly solutions to quiet their restlessness, God's Word makes it clear that our lack of peace and satisfaction in life is a spiritual issue. As we study the Scriptures, we see that the loss of contentment can push us in one of two directions. The search can either lead us down paths cluttered with false promises of fulfillment, or it can bring us to a place of turning, where the journey takes on a redemptive quality. Our search for contentment can ultimately lead us to the heart of God, which is the only place where we will find rest, a place of belonging, and ultimate contentment.

In conclusion, Youssef writes:

> God wants to refresh your soul—to replace anxiety with peace, to give you rest in place of weariness, to provide a place of belonging that will quiet your restlessness. In other words, God wants you to find contentment in His love and grace ("Leading the Way," January/February 2004, p. 1).

Paul's Testimony of Coping with Trials

It's encouraging to discover from the Apostle Paul's vivid testimony following that you're not alone in life's challenges, distresses and disappointments.

He and his companions experienced a lot of suffering while spreading the Good News among the Jews and Gentiles of the Roman Empire. In 2 Corinthians 6, for instance, he enumerated their outward trials, their inward traits and characters, and their spiritual resources (verses 4–6). Let's try to imagine the circumstances in which all these things interacted—beatings, patience, imprisonment, kindness, distress, and love. Although they were broken physically, depleted emotionally and tested spiritually, the authenticity of their faith in Christ enabled them to stand fast, their feet deeply rooted in Him and the source of their strength.

Paul and his friends were "sorrowful, yet always rejoicing; poor, yet making many rich; having nothing, and yet possessing everything" (verse 10). That is exactly the message of this book: that we live by the power of God, and not by anything else. With boldness and clarity, Jesus says, " '...apart from me you can do nothing.' " (John 15:5). The Good News is that "...'What is impossible with men is possible with God" (Luke 18:27).

CHAPTER 8

*L*et us take another specific example from the political history of Ghana.

The Rise and Fall of Kwame Nkrumah

In the early days of his regime, Dr. Kwame Nkrumah acknowledged that he couldn't make it without God. He sought His wisdom, strength and direction for political leadership. When he considered it necessary, he would occasionally retire to a quiet, secluded place, reading and meditating on the Holy Scriptures with prayer and fasting. The local newspapers (e.g., the *Sunday Mirror*, *Evening News*, etc.) would publish his picture, showing him dressed in a white suit, sitting alone and somber on a rock or log in silent meditation.

Most certainly, that was the figure of a man who acknowledged his need of the Omnipotent and humbly but fervently sought divine counsel and protection, relying on Him for the fulfillment of his political aspirations for Ghana in particular and Africa in general.

Eventually, Nkrumah succeeded, bravely achieving for the country his long-desired goal: political freedom from British rule on March 6, 1957, thus making Ghana the leading nation south of the Sahara to gain independence. With God, he made strides in politics and was highly respected both at home and abroad, becoming Africa's pioneer in the struggle for the total liberation of the continent.

During the first few years, Ghana lived in peace, freedom and justice, becoming a shining example in showing the way for all other leaders in the goal of political emancipation in their countries. With God, Nkrumah succeeded—his views and foresight were highly respected at home and abroad. I would venture that he put the African personality in an enviable position in the world's political marketplace. He proved to everyone, especially to the Western world, that Africa, too, had a precious contribution to make toward world peace.

In pursuance of his goal, Nkrumah initiated the formation of the Organization of African Unity (OAU), with Ghana, Guinea and Mali as the nucleus. To further his political aspirations, he organized a series of international meetings and rallies, sharing his unique knowledge of political science and organizational spirit with African leaders to encourage them in their struggles for freedom. Among his many powerful and inspirational utterances, there was one that greatly spurred on many of his political peers: "The independence of Ghana is meaningless unless it is linked with the total liberation of Africa;" the audience often responded with resounding applause.

He was, indeed, one of God's greatest gifts to Africa; he was able to achieve a lot for the continent. For example, he succeeded in putting Africa on the international scene and positively projected the African personality by appearing at international meetings (e.g., at the United Nations) in a gorgeous, rich *kente* cloth. With his foresight, wisdom and valuable contributions at the UN and other international gatherings, he lifted high the image of Africans in the eyes of the world.

Then, at the zenith of his political career, Nkrumah attributed his achievements to his own ingenuity, ascribing to himself certain divine names, such as *Osagyefo* (Mighty Savior). "Nkrumah never dies" was often recited on the national radio by the Ghana Young Pioneer's Movement of that day. As if these were not enough, he went further still and, without the fear of God, twisted a text from Jesus' Sermon on the Mount (Matt. 5–7): "Seek first the political kingdom, and all other things will be given to you as well." The actual text as Christ put it reads: "But seek first his kingdom and his righteousness, and all these things will be given to you as well" (6:33).

When the Christian Council of Ghana sent a delegation to Nkrumah, respectfully counseling him not to ascribe divine qualities to himself or twist God's Word to suit his political aspirations, he paid no heed. His rejection of their counsel, as I see it, meant equally his rejection of God and His divine counsel. The Council spoke with the leader as His mouthpiece; and for Nkrumah to have ignored them wasn't only a proof of his repudiation of God, but also of the only power that could deliver him from imminent destruction. It became obvious that he had found another god in whom to place his trust. He chose to rely on a newly found god (*Kankan Nyame*) to achieve his goal. Nonetheless, to his utter shock and woeful disappointment, he was suddenly and unexpectedly overthrown from his "political kingdom" by a military coup d'état on February 24, 1966.

Since then, Ghana, the Shining Star in the West Coast of Africa, which was to lead the way for the total liberation of Africa, has ceased to be a beacon for its neighbors. Her leaders didn't put God first in the administration of the country for the good of all, and particularly for His glory. Today, after many decades as a sovereign nation, instead of advancing, the nation had retrogressed so far that by the year 2000, it was classified among the world's poorest—economically known as "Highly Indebted Poor Countries" (HIPC).

According to the Bible, other national leaders in ancient times suffered a similar fate when they forsook God as Nkrumah would later do. It's an unfortunate human trait that people don't often learn from history's tragedies. The Old Testament stories of King Nebuchadnezzar of Babylon and his successor, Belshazzar, in the Book of Daniel are notable examples. Their stories were recorded in the following:

> *God gave…Nebuchadnezzar sovereignty and greatness and glory and splendor. Because of the high position he gave him, all the peoples and nations and men of every language…feared him. Those the king wanted to put to death, he put to death; those he wanted to spare, he spared…But when his heart became arrogant and hardened with pride, he was deposed from his royal throne and stripped of his glory. He was driven away from people and given the mind of an animal; he lived with the wild donkeys and ate grass like cattle; and his body was drenched with the dew of heaven, until he acknowledged that the Most High God is sovereign over the kingdoms of men and sets over them anyone he wishes* (Dan. 5:18–21).

Anyone who's read Nebuchadnezzar's story might reasonably think his successor would take a cue from it, but he didn't; rather he did worse things than his father had done, as the following account shows:

> *Belshazzar, the son of Nebuchadnezzar, succeeded him as King of Babylon. On one special occasion, in the cool of the night, Belshazzar sat on his throne surrounded by his wives and concubines and all the nobles of his kingdom. "Instead, you have set yourself up against the Lord of heaven. You had the goblets*

from his temple brought to you, and you and your nobles, your wives and your concubines drank wine from them. You praised the gods of silver and gold, of bronze, iron, wood and stone, which cannot see or hear or understand. But you did not honor the God who holds in his hand your life and all your ways" (5:23).

As a result, God sent a hand with the following inscription:

"MENE, MENE, TEKEL, PARSIN
"This is what these words mean:
"Mene: God has numbered the days of your reign and brought it to an end.
"Tekel: You have been weighed on the scales and found wanting.
"Peres: Your kingdom is divided and given to the Medes and Persians"
        (5:25-28).

That very night, after Daniel had explained to Belshazzar the meaning of the inscription on the wall, the king was slain and his kingdom was taken over by Darius the Mede.

> **Those of us in authority must forgo pride and arrogance in the exercise of our powers**

These and several other similar stories that abound in the Bible are to warn all of us, especially those in authority, to forgo pride and arrogance in the exercise of our powers. We should take this seriously lest we incur the displeasure of the Almighty God, Who is the Ultimate Ruler and Judge of this world, King of Kings, and Lord of Lords, before Whom "…'All men are like grass, and all their glory is like the flowers of the field…' Surely the nations are like a drop in a bucket; they are regarded as dust on the scales…" (Isa. 40:6, 15).

That was why after he and the elders of the people had provided sufficient money and materials for the building of the Temple, David saw the need to sound the following warning to his son, Solomon, who had succeeded him as king of Israel:

Unless the LORD builds the house, its builders labor in vain. Unless the LORD watches over the city, the watchmen stand guard in vain. In vain you rise early and stay up late, toiling for food to eat — for he grants sleep to those he loves (Ps. 127:1–2).

We must bear in mind that what David said to Solomon many years ago is still relevant and applicable to all in authority today, black or white, and disregarding this warning is to their own detriment and the destruction of those they govern.

The following story may serve as another good example. Uzziah was just 16 when he became king of Judah, but despite his youth, it's recorded, "He did what was right in the eyes of the LORD, just as his father Amaziah had done. He sought God during the days of Zechariah, who instructed him in the fear of God. As long as he sought the LORD, God gave him success" (2 Chron. 26:4–5).

Uzziah's fame spread abroad and his army grew increasingly stronger: 307,500 soldiers commanded by 2,600 officers, helping him to defeat all enemies in neighboring countries. Then, like Nkrumah in his heyday, we sadly read, "But after Uzziah became powerful, his pride led to his downfall…" (26:16).

That was most unfortunate, wasn't it? Commenting on his downfall, Albert Lee said, "It is tragic to witness someone starting out well in life and then finishing poorly… Uzziah had failed to remember the One who had given him success and who had given godly counsel. He sinned against the Lord when he burned incense in the temple, and God struck him with leprosy (26:16–19)." He remained a leper 'until the day he died' (26:21).

"To finish well," says Lee, "we need to avoid having a heart that is 'lifted up.' Let's remind ourselves often of the warning in Proverbs 16:18: 'Pride goes before destruction, a haughty spirit before a fall.' And let's keep seeking the Lord, obeying Him, and thanking Him for all He has done" (*Our Daily Bread*, RBC Ministries, Sunday, February 8, 2004).

Disobedience to God Has Disastrous Consequences

I cap this portion with yet another example worthy of notice. Since "…there is no authority except that which God has established…" (Rom. 13:1), it follows that those in authority should exercise it according to His will. Like Solomon, Ahab—who became King of Israel after the death of his father Omri—reigned for 22 years. During this time, we are told:

> *Ahab son of Omri did more evil in the eyes of the LORD than any of those before him. He not only considered it trivial to commit the sins of Jeroboam son of Nebat, but he also married Jezebel daughter of Ethbaal king of the Sido-*

nians, and began to serve Baal and worship him. He set up an altar for Baal in the temple of Baal that he built in Samaria. Ahab also made an Asherah pole and did more to provoke the LORD, the God of Israel, to anger than did all the kings of Israel before him (1 Kings 16:30–33).

What was the effect of his idolatrous reign upon himself, his family and the nation?

- There was no rain in the land for three-and-a-half years, resulting in severe famine and death. For example, Elijah's encounter with Ahab's 450 prophets of Baal (the god of the Canaanites) ended in their slaughter in the Kishon Valley (18:40).
- God spoke to Ahab through Elijah: " 'I am going to bring disaster on you. I will consume your descendants and cut off from Ahab every last male in Israel — slave or free' " (21:21). He was eventually killed in his war against Ramoth Gilead (22:35–37).
- His wife, Jezebel, was thrown down from a window "…and some of her blood spattered the wall and the horses as they trampled her underfoot." (2 Kings 9:33).
- Ahab's 70 sons in Samaria were slaughtered, their heads sent in baskets to Jezreel Valley by the command of Jehu (10:7).
- Jehu went to Samaria and proclaimed a solemn "…'assembly in honor of Baal' " When the temple was crowded with worshippers, "…it was full from one end to the other." Jehu offered a sacrifice and then commanded the guards to kill all the worshippers. "They demolished the sacred stone of Baal and tore down the temple of Baal…So Jehu destroyed Baal worship in Israel" (10:20–21, 25, 27–28).

All this evil came upon Ahab and his household — and the nation as a whole — because he had forsaken God and His commandments in following other gods. Once again, this is a caution to all holding positions of leadership: "It is a dreadful thing to fall into the hands of the living God…for our 'God is a consuming fire' " (Heb. 10:31; 12:29).

As reiterated throughout this book, the poor state of affairs in Africa, Europe, Asia, etc. — spiritually, emotionally and economically — boils down to the fact that we've abandoned God, His commandments and the provision He has made through Christ for the solution of our earthly problems.

Hence, the need for everyone to take God's Word seriously can't be overemphasized here; it's worth our lifetime commitment. He offers abundant blessings to those worshipping Him and obeying His commandments in their daily affairs. His blessings make us rich so that we can be channels of blessing to our descendants and others. He laments not being able to give us His blessings as a result of our disobedience through the prophet Isaiah:

"If only you had paid attention to my commands, your peace would have been like a river, your righteousness like the waves of the sea. Your descendants would have been like the sand, your children like its numberless grains; their name would never be cut off nor destroyed from before me" (Isa. 48:18–19).

Knowing that disobedience to His Word means disastrous results for individual people and nations, Jesus did not turn away from the Holy Scriptures. He said, " 'I know that his command leads to eternal life. So whatever I say is just what the Father has told me to say' " (John 12:50). He has set for us a perfect example and wants us to follow it: anything done outside His Father's will is sin and means deadly consequences for us.

It was for this reason that Christ wept over the city of Jerusalem when the Jewish leaders of His day rejected Him (Luke 19:41). He had foreseen the result of their rejection—massive destruction of the city and the death of its people, including children, at the hands of Roman soldiers—which was to come on them 40 years after His death at Calvary. With deep sorrow and compassion, He lamented for the people:

"O Jerusalem, Jerusalem, you who kill the prophets and stone those sent to you, how often I have longed to gather your children together, as a hen gathers her chicks under her wings, but you were not willing. Look, your house is left to you desolate. For I tell you, you will not see me again until you say, 'Blessed is he who comes in the name of the Lord' " (Matt. 23:37–39).

The Jews' rejection of Jesus meant their abandonment of God's Word: "For it is by grace you have been saved, through faith—and this is not from yourselves, it is the gift of God" (Eph. 2:8). By rejecting Christ, " '...the light of the world...' " (John 8:12), they chose to live in

"...darkness instead of light because their deeds were evil" (3:19).

Furthermore, by rejecting Jesus, who is "the light of men" and " '...the truth and the life...' " (1:4, 14:6), they chose death instead. What was the consequence of forsaking the Messiah, Lord and Savior of their lives? The city of Jerusalem was completely destroyed by the Romans in 70A.D., as He had foreseen and accurately predicted.

There are important lessons for us to learn from Christ's statements:

- As a nation and as individuals, there's a limited time within which we're to receive salvation while we live here on earth. Jesus put it this way: "As long as it is day, we must do the work of him who sent me. Night is coming, when no one can work" (9:4).

- We must be willing to accept salvation through faith in Him at the time it's graciously offered to us through Gospel preachers, or we'll miss that opportunity forever and become eternally doomed . As the saying goes, "Opportunity once lost is never regained." Thus, Isaiah cried out to the wayward people of Judah, "Seek the LORD while he may be found; call on him while he is near" (Isa. 55:6).

- We have no control over our lives or tomorrows; therefore, whatever needs to be done must be done *now* (John 9:4), because tomorrow may be too late. "...'In the time of my favor I heard you, and in the day of salvation I helped you.' I tell you, now is the time of God's favor, now is the day of salvation" (2 Cor. 6:2).

- It's inevitable and irrevocable that those who forsake God are cursed and doomed to destruction as a result of their rebellion against Him. The only choice left to them is to fall victim to the Devil, who "...comes only to steal and kill and destroy..." (John 10:10). There's only one clear decision, no neutral ground: you're either for Christ or Satan. The choice is in your hands, but you know my counsel by now.

- Had leaders of Jerusalem accepted Jesus and His teachings about the Kingdom of God, the city would have been spared destruction. As it's written: "For whoever finds me finds life and receives favor from the LORD. But whoever fails to find me harms himself; all who hate me love death." (Prov. 8:35–36).

This is a strong warning for those rejecting the Lord. As a pastor of His flock, I am passionately counseling you to turn toward wisdom, because there's neither a hiding place for our sins nor can we pay the cost; it's too high. Besides, "Salvation is found in no one else," said Peter to the Sanhedrin (the Jewish Supreme Court), "for there is no other name under heaven given to men by which we must be saved" (Acts 4:12). That verse underlines the truth that there's neither a human being on earth nor an angel in heaven worthy enough to plead for our salvation before the presence of Almighty God, except His Son. As John wrote:

> *I wept and wept because no one was found who was worthy to open the scroll or look inside. Then one of the elders said to me, "Do not weep! See, the Lion of the tribe of Judah, the Root of David, has triumphed. He is able to open the scroll and its seven seals."…He came and took the scroll from the right hand of him who sat on the throne. And when he had taken it, the four living creatures and the twenty-four elders fell down before the Lamb…And they sang a new song: "You are worthy to take the scroll and to open its seals, because you were slain, and with your blood you purchased men for God from every tribe and language and people and nation. You have made them to be a kingdom and priests to serve our God, and they will reign on the earth"* (Rev. 5:4–5, 7–10).

Therefore, salvation and abundant blessings exist for those who fear God and humbly receive His Son as Savior and Lord of their lives. Calamity and the destruction of precious lives await those refusing the gift of eternal life through "the Savior of the world" (John 3:36, 4:42; Rev. 20:11–14).

CHAPTER 9

*T*he Holy Spirit further gave me insight into the fact that idolatry may not always necessarily involve concrete objects like the gold, silver, trees, rivers, stones or clay worshipped in the religions of other cultures. There's also what the Book of Ezekiel describes as "idolatry of the heart" (Ezek. 14:1–8).

By the time my wife joined me in the U.S. in September of 1989, I had enrolled in the Master of Theological Studies Program at Wesley Theological Seminary. We had only a few material possessions; even the furniture in our room belonged to the seminary, because we had none of our own. After completing the Doctor of Ministry Program in 1993, we had to find our own apartment in Washington, obtain work permits and then get Green Cards, so that we could work to support ourselves and our children in Ghana.

It had never crossed my mind that we could be materialistic. After all, I was working only part-time in a grocery store and as an associate pastor in a small Ghanaian church (formerly the United Church of Ghana) in the Washington Metropolitan Area. Nevertheless, feelings of discontent began to occupy my heart, and before long, we were craving nice things in a secret resentment for not having them. Then, quite recently, as my wife and I were meditating on Ezekiel, the Holy Spirit suddenly opened our eyes with a "disturbing" insight: *Materialism isn't necessarily* having *things; it can also be* craving *them.*

There we sat side by side quietly on our bed with our Bibles in our laps, convicted of materialism! The Lord had exposed our discontentment for what it really was, an idol in our heart. My friends, I'm afraid that many of you reading this story may be equally guilty of this obscure sin: "the idolatry of the heart."

That hour, as we each repented and humbly asked the Almighty to mercifully forgive us and cleanse our hearts of this subtle sin, He graciously regained our hearts as His rightful throne. Right there on our bed, we were filled with a deep sense of contentment and peace based not on things we had or wish we had, but on Him alone. Our faith was so much strengthened by His Word: "Delight yourself in the LORD and he will give you the desires of your heart" (Ps. 37:4).

In the days of Judah's prophet, Ezekiel, the Lord exposed the idolatry in the hearts of His people, who had come to seek His counsel as follows:

> *"Son of man, these men have set up idols in their hearts and put wicked stumbling blocks before their faces. Should I let them inquire of me at all? Therefore speak to them and tell them, 'This is what the Sovereign LORD says: "When any Israelite sets up idols in his heart and puts a wicked stumbling block before his face and then goes to a prophet, I the LORD will answer him myself in keeping with his great idolatry."' I will do this to recapture the hearts of the people of Israel, who have all deserted me for their idols. Therefore say to the house of Israel, 'This is what the Sovereign LORD says: "Repent! Turn from your idols and renounce all your detestable practices!"'"* (Ezek. 14:3–6).

It's easy to be deceived into thinking you haven't set up an idol in your heart. I humbly appeal to you to allow the Holy Spirit to search it and lead you to a decisive conviction in the light of His Word, which is

> *...living and active. Sharper than any double-edged sword, it penetrates even to dividing soul and spirit, joints and marrow; it judges the thoughts and attitudes of the heart. Nothing in all creation is hidden from God's sight. Everything is uncovered and laid bare before the eyes of him to whom we must give account* (Heb. 4:12–13).

Idolatry remains a problem for Christians, as well as all other worshippers of God. The danger is that it's not always open or plain to the human mind. In our so-called civilized age, idols are usually more subtle and difficult to recognize, because they set up their home in the hidden places of our heart.

Commenting on "Idols of the Heart," David Roper of Radio Bible

Class (RBC) Ministries had this to say:

> If we want to know our idols, we need to consider our predominant
> thoughts, for what we think about most of the time may be an idol.
> Our last thought before we sleep, our first thought when we awake.
> Our reveries throughout the day are spent on the items and issues we
> treasure and trust.
>
> Any possession or person we put our hope in to bring us fulfillment,
> any goal or aspiration that becomes more important to us than
> God—these are the "gods" that attract all our allegiance and subtly
> control our lives.

He emphasized in concluding, "only God can satisfy the deepest
needs of our heart and make us truly alive." That's why we would be
wise to heed the loving counsel of the apostle Paul: "Therefore, my dear
friends, flee from idolatry." (1 Cor. 10:14). Should you find yourself
convicted by the Spirit as I was, you'll do well rather to repent in humility and be freed from the subtle sin of the heart easily besetting all of
us, even when it escapes our notice. Then we can truly yearn for God
to recapture our souls and minds as we altogether turn to our Savior, "in
Spirit and truth," with a penitent heart, singing prayerfully the following hymn:

> Return, O holy Dove! Return,
> Sweet messenger of rest!
> I hate the sins that made Thee mourn,
> And drove you from my breast.
>
> The dearest idol I have known,
> Whate'er that idol be,
> Help me to tear it from Thy throne
> And worship only Thee.
> (*Methodist Hymn Book [MHB]* 461, verses 4–5, by William Cowper,
> 1731–1800)

Like St. Augustine, Cowper echoes in this solemn hymn—which is
one of my personal favorites—the truth that God has made human beings for Himself. And for that reason, no earthly thing can save us or
satisfy the heart's deep longing other than Him. As I meditated on this
much further, the Holy Spirit made me realize, once again, the futility
and foolishness of striving in our own human effort or ingenuity to solve

our individual or national problems, or to find success, happiness, peace and comfort through other sources of power, such as magic or voodoo. Thus, we seem to Him as though we've lost our senses and can no longer think or reason correctly. Indeed, we look like silly children before Him.

The Folly of Idolatry

Now, the logical question to ask here is this: *If nothing, apart from God, is able to satisfy the deepest need of the human heart, why then do we bother ourselves to seek refuge, success, riches, strength, hope, comfort, etc., in other sources rather than Him alone?* The Bible declares, "Trust in the LORD with all your heart and lean not on your own understanding; in all your ways acknowledge him, and he will make your paths straight. Do not be wise in your own eyes; fear the LORD and shun evil" (Prov. 3:5–7). As it's written: "The fear of the LORD is the beginning of wisdom…" (Ps. 111:10).

So when we lean on our human intellect instead of trusting Him, our so-called wisdom turns to ignorance (1 Cor. 1:20–21). In order to point humans to the true way of life, He revealed to His chosen people, Israel, through the prophet Isaiah, the futility of idolatry in the following extended but exquisitely poetic passage:

All who make idols are nothing, and the things they treasure are worthless. Those who would speak up for them are blind; they are ignorant, to their own shame. Who shapes a god and casts an idol, which can profit him nothing? He and his kind will be put to shame; craftsmen are nothing but men. Let them all come together and take their stand; they will be brought down to terror and infamy. The blacksmith takes a tool and works with it in the coals; he shapes an idol with hammers, he forges it with the might of his arm. He gets hungry and loses his strength; he drinks no water and grows faint. The carpenter measures with a line and makes an outline with a marker; he roughs it out with chisels and marks it with compasses. He shapes it in the form of man, of man in all his glory, that it may dwell in a shrine. He cut down cedars, or perhaps took a cypress or oak. He let it grow among the trees of the forest, or planted a pine, and the rain made it grow. It is man's fuel for burning; some of it he takes and warms himself, he kindles a fire and bakes bread. But he also fashions a god and worships it; he makes an idol and bows down to it. Half of the wood he burns in the fire; over it he prepares his meal, he roasts his meat and eats his fill. He also warms himself and says, "Ah! I am warm; I see the fire." From the rest he makes a god, his idol; he bows down to it and worships. He prays to it and says, "Save me; you are my god." They know nothing, they understand nothing; their eyes are plastered over so they cannot see, and their minds closed so they cannot understand. No one stops to think, no one has the knowledge or understanding to say, "Half of it I used for fuel; I even baked bread over its coals, I roasted meat and I ate. Shall I make a detestable thing from what is left? Shall I bow down to a block of wood?" He feeds on ashes, a deluded heart misleads him; he cannot save himself, or say, "Is not this thing in my right hand a lie?" (Isaiah 44:9–19; *also* Jeremiah 10:1–15).

Let's now turn to the next chapter wherein I discuss some areas of Ghanaian religious and social life, in which tradition makes void the Word of God.

CHAPTER 10

Areas of Ghanaian Life in Conflict with Scriptures

*T*here are several aspects of Ghanaian religious and social traditions that conflict with the Word of God. Following are a few examples:

Marriage

The typical Ghanaian traditional marriage consists of two stages: the engagement (known in Akan as *esiwaah*) and the actual marriage ceremony (*aware*). On each of these occasions, the elder of the family pours libation to the gods and the spirits of ancestors, invoking their blessing and support for the engagement or marriage. The elder prays to grant the newly married couple many children (twins, triplets, etc.), riches and material prosperity.

Again, the question is: "…Why consult the dead on behalf of the living?" (Isa. 8:19) Is it possible for the dead ancestors of our clans or for other gods—who have never, ever before created human beings—to provide couples with children and material wealth? Of course not!

- "Sons are a heritage from the LORD, children a reward from him" (Ps. 127:3).
- " 'The silver is mine and the gold is mine,' declares the LORD Almighty" (Hag. 2:8).
- "…remember the LORD your God, for it is he who gives you the ability to produce wealth…" (Deut. 8:18).
- "No one from the east or the west or from the desert can exalt a man. But it is God who judges: He brings one down, he exalts another…The earth is the LORD's, and everything in it, the world,

and all who live in it" (Ps. 75:6–7, 24:1).

Thus, the Scriptures teach us that neither gods nor ancestors have power or any other means to provide any married couple with children or riches. It's high time we stopped calling on gods and spirits of the dead for help. Instead, we ought to look to God, our *Creator*, Who alone is able to meet every need of ours—spiritually, emotionally and materially, "...according to his glorious riches in Christ Jesus" (Phil. 4:19).

We must remember that the many marriages in which traditional rituals have been performed without the renewing power of God's Spirit don't have the benefit of His blessings. We need to know without a doubt that "Unless the LORD builds the house, its builders labor in vain..." (Ps. 127:1). According to the Scriptures, we realize that "Every good and perfect gift is from above, coming down from the Father of the heavenly lights, who does not change like shifting shadows" (James 1:17).

Many couples can testify that such traditional rituals tend to render them childless. For instance, a couple came to me for counseling and prayers because they had been married for over two years and were still childless. In their attempts to have a baby, the husband had taken his wife to a fetish priest in Praso in the interior of the Western Region, where she was made to stand naked in the River Pra so that the god of the river could impregnate her. Two years after consulting the fetishist, there was still no sign of a child. He then began blaming her for their childlessness.

However, medical examinations conducted later on both of them showed that the husband's infertility was responsible (i.e., his sperm was too weak to fertilize his wife's egg). After receiving the medical report, his wife no longer found the situation tenable and eventually divorced him on account of his dishonesty and fetishistic tendencies. She later married another man with whom she had two children. Truly, children are blessings from God, the Creator of heaven and earth, and not from any other god or ancestor.

My dear reader, I humbly remind you that no god, spirit or ancestor has ever created a child anywhere in this universe. Therefore, it's a deception on the part of diviners or fetish priests and priestesses to offer to married couples with infertility problems vain promises that their gods and spirits can bless them with children. It's a big lie; don't listen to them. We know that with the help of modern medical science, physicians can sometimes enable a childless mother to conceive and bear children through artificial insemination, but they can't *by themselves* create sperm and eggs to produce them. The power to do so is God's prerogative and glory, which He will not give to any man or idols (Isa. 42:8).

The Traditional Role of a Wife in the Home

Many African married men lay heavy burdens on their wives, unaware of any wrongdoing. For instance, in some African homes where there are no children or servants, it's the wife's duty to clean the house, including the bathroom. In addition, she does the laundry, shops for groceries, cooks the meals, sets the table and cleans the cooking utensils and dishes—while the husband does nothing. Thus, tradition compels the woman's larger role as both wife and servant in the house.

I've been told that my father-in-law, the late S.O. Gaisie—perhaps the first Ghanaian District Commissioner in the country—became furious when he saw a man coming from his farm with empty hands, while his pregnant wife, loaded down with a basketful of cassava, was also carrying a baby on her back. Gaisie quickly had the man arrested and charged with negligence of marital responsibilites. Such treatment of his wife was a typical example of the subjugation of women by many husbands; it's un-Christian and unfair to human dignity. We must aim at banishing all forms of ill treatment of our female counterparts in Africa in order to maintain healthy and enjoyable marital relationships with our wives in fostering greater respect for females in general.

Campaign in Africa to Eradicate Male Violence against Women

Taking a strong view of the effort to affirm the dignity of African women in the home and community, Ban Ki-moon, UN Secretary General, "called on the support of African leaders to give new impetus to his campaign to end the violence suffered by women on the continent. He called them 'unsung heroines' of development in the region. We know African women are often a linchpin keeping families, communities, and nations together," declared Ban at the African launch of his

"UNiTE to End Violence against Women." According to Okey Ndiribe of Addis Ababa, Ethiopia, the Secretary General launched his campaign in 2008, calling "for all countries to put in place strong laws, action plans, preventive measures, data collection, and systematic efforts to address sexual violence by 2015." (*The New Ghanaian*, January 2010, vol. 10., p. 24)

At this juncture, it's relevant to call to mind a conceptual insight of Dr. Kwegyir Aggrey, another great son of Africa, regarding the value of women in society. He said, "Educate a man, and you educate an individual; but educate a woman, and you educate a nation." Surely, no one could have said it better than Aggrey did. In fact, he sees eye-to-eye with Ban's campaign on behalf of this important issue, with regard to African women in particular and women in general. If what Aggrey said is true—and the truth that women are the foundation of nation building is undeniable—then how can we continue to mistreat them and blindly disregard their precious role in the community?

Furthermore, Nancy Leigh Demoss, addressing a group of women participating in the *Revive Our Hearts* radio series on the theme "Becoming a Woman of Discretion," quoted John Adams, the second president of the United States. "From all that I have read, of history, and of Government, and of human life and manners, I have drawn this conclusion: that the manners of women were the most infallible parameter to ascertain the degree of morality and virtue of a nation." In uncovering any country's moral standards, we begin by examining closely the life of its women.

Thus, Adams had made observations congruent with those of such diverse leaders as South Korea's Ban and Africa's Aggrey. God endowed women with considerable influence, the ignorance of which negatively impacts the moral standards of our homes, churches, communities and nations at large. Therefore, it's imperative that men, particularly of African descent, respect and encourage women as much as possible in fulfilling their role for the good of all societies.

The King of Ashanti Sets an Example for Change

It's encouraging to note further that within Ghanaian society, there are a number of people in authority determined to bring about necessary changes in our tradition. One such person in a key position is the current king of the Ashantis, Nana Otumfuo Osei Tutu II. The following article was published about him by Stella Nkrumah Ababio:

A King with a Difference:
Transformation in the Asante Kinship

The Asantehene, Otumfuo Osei Tutu II, has forever transformed the tradition governing the role and place of the king's wife. He has caused a mini-revolution. Recently, very boldly and proudly, he exhibited his wife at an official gathering in Holland. Not only was the beautiful lady seated by her husband but also the king, her husband, was not embarrassed to include her in his address to the gathering.

I am confident that a lot of folks there will agree that the present Asantehene has taken Ghana by storm. In many respects, he has shown us what a dynamic leader can do with any institution. Today, we do not picture palanquins solely when thinking of the Asantehene. One rather sees the thousands of Ghanaian children benefiting from educational scholarships; brilliant conflict-resolution skills among chiefs; the tourists bringing in foreign exchange as they travel from far and near, to visit the king; and his campaign against HIV/AIDS, to mention a few of his laudable initiatives.

Therefore, when the dailies surreptitiously announced the new marriage of the Asantehene, I wondered how he was going to manage this aspect of his life. Additionally, a few colleagues and I spent close to 45 minutes discussing the merits and demerits of a tradition that tacitly discourages kings from appearing in public with their wives.

A popular Ghanaian maxim intimates that behind every successful man is a woman. But these women, for a large part, have been faceless, formless, invisible, neutral and voiceless, especially in Ghanaian royal corridors.

In the past, the wifely advice, strategies and concepts offered to the king have been offered in private. But today, the modern king has dared to rock the boat... In his address, he publicly acknowledged her presence by saying *"Me ne me ho kafo"* (my wife and I) in a lot of the statements he made, thereby communicating that his thoughts and statements represented those of his wife as well.

"This public gesture," says Stella, "though small, is symbolically ripe with meaning. By this gesture, the Asantehene, as the lead man of Ashantis, has rewritten the code of ethics of Ashanti kings. He has made history. I want to believe that this gesture will not only occur when the king is outside Ghana.

We the women of Ghana would love to see the king honor and acclaim his wife publicly and officially in Kumasi and, indeed, in Ghana as often as is practical. He has definitely made a statement for the ongoing gender debate and we believe all other kings, chiefs and men will take a cue from this exemplary 21st-century leader.

The Asantehene has made women proud. He has recognized the rightful position of women and shown by example that culture need not be static but should evolve with the times. He has also demonstrated that "Culture was made for man and not man for culture." Nana, we look forward to more of such groundbreaking reforms in Akan kingship (*Daily Graphic*, Tuesday, August 27, 2002, p. 7).

To read such news about the Asantehene is very intriguing, since the Ashantis are the most traditional among all Akans. For instance, in order to keep the Asante chieftaincy tradition in the Washington Metropolitan Area and New York, they installed their kings and queens, who dress in their national costumes and sit in high positions on special occasions such as funerals and marriage ceremonies. That's why the example set by Nana Otumfuo Osei Tutu II is so highly regarded, especially by women desirous of progress in the transformation of traditional life.

In rural areas, a married woman's position is even more compromised than it is in the cities. For instance, in many rural towns, the usual practice is that whenever a husband and wife visit their farm, she struggles home with a basketful of foodstuffs while he carries a piece of wood on his shoulder and a cutlass in his hand. This is despite the clear fact that the man is genetically the stronger of the two and is supposed to bear a much heavier burden than the woman. Because many men are blind to this reality due to tradition, things must change now in order to give women the relief, respect and dignity they rightly deserve.

Every husband ought to remember that God created his wife to be his better half and not his servant. Being responsible for his wife, a husband has the duty to love and cherish her. Thus, it's understood that the woman was made for the man to love and treat tenderly and gently, not to be mistreated as though she were inferior to him. As the Bible points out, the husband thereby proves that he loves himself, for the wife is mystically a part of his body. "After all," Paul says, "no one ever hated his own body, but he feeds and cares for it, just as Christ does the church" (Eph. 5:29).

Since marriage is a sacred institution God created for the mutual enjoyment of husband and wife, we can't derive its full benefits without relying on Him. Despite realizing that marriage thrives on love and "Whoever does not love does not know God, because God is love" (1 John 4:8), human beings are nonetheless still basically selfish. Hence, no couple can enjoy their union to the fullest without committing themselves to Christ as their Savior and Lord, allowing Him to govern their lives. For " '...apart from me,' " says Jesus, " 'you can do nothing' "

(John 15:5).

We therefore always need to feed fat on God—the source of all life and love—in order to feel love in ourselves and share it in wedlock toward enabling its steady maturity. We can only give and share what we've received from Him. Calling on other gods and ancestors will *never* bring us the much-needed virtue of *love*, the *bedrock* of every happy and successful marriage. Many marriages are deficient in love, and some have ended in divorce because of too much adherence to tradition, an unforgiving spirit and bitterness harbored by one against the other. They're denying themselves the authentic, loving relationship that should characterize every true marriage. They ultimately lose not only the Holy Word of God—which nourishes their souls and lighten their paths in life—but also His blessing on their marriage.

However, this isn't to suggest that customary marriage is somehow inferior to Christian marriage. The most important point I want to make is that marriage is a sacred institution intended to forge a lasting relationship between a husband and his wife. Without God, who instituted marriage, men and women in their own strengths can't make it, regardless of whether they're in a Christian or customary marriage. And whether we admit or dismiss it, this is an undeniable, proven fact. It's out of His concern in redeeming our marriages and rekindling the love among all members of the family as a whole that this truth's been revealed. We must all examine closely our marital relationships in making necessary amends, until our good is better, and our better best.

Same-Sex Marriage

There are remarkable numbers of men and women who've been so disappointed with traditional Christian or customary marriage (i.e., between a man and a woman as ordained by God) that they've chosen to enter into what's now known as "same-sex marriage," a term that until recently was deemed so shameful to be mentioned in public that it was hidden in the closet.

Today, it's garnered attention in certain quarters, including the media, TV shows and the movies. Well, such a lifestyle doesn't solve a marital problem; instead it's multiplied and made untenable. In the first place, it violates God's principle of marriage between men and women. Second, it perverts human sexuality. In His infinite wisdom and love for humanity, He designed both male and female bodies to complement and fulfill each other spiritually, emotionally and physically (Gen. 1:27, 2:18,

20–24; Matt. 19:4–6, 8–9; 1 Cor. 7:1–5).

Furthermore, same-sex marriage doesn't fulfill God's purpose of procreation in marriage (Gen. 1:28; Ps. 127:3–5). If every man married a male of his choice, and every woman a female, there would be no children to eventually replace the present generation of people when we're gone. Therefore, gay and lesbian lifestyles seek to annihilate the roots of the family system, community and nation as a whole. It's detrimental to human existence, nothing but a figment of our sinful hearts and evil imaginations. I stems from a rebellious attitude toward God, our Creator, and the Savior of humankind.

It may be admitted that some marital problems (e.g., barrenness, incompatibility and impotence) can render a marriage unsuccessful. However, the solution doesn't lie in human hands, but in God's. He is our Maker and Provider of all our needs—spiritually, emotionally and physically. He created marriage for companionship and the mutual enjoyment of husband and wife. It's He "...who richly provides us with everything for our enjoyment" (1 Tim. 6:17), including sex in the context of marriage. Hence, without His providential care of creation, we can have nothing.

That's why Paul, in his Christ-like, fatherly manner, counsels every one of us in these words: "Do not be anxious about anything, but in everything, by prayer and petition, with thanksgiving, present your requests to God. And the peace of God, which transcends all understanding, will guard your hearts and your minds in Christ Jesus" (Phil. 4:6–7).

Therefore, if you've chosen a gay or lesbian lifestyle, it's not too late for you to turn to Jesus, the Friend of sinners, Who " '...came to seek and to save what was lost' " (Luke 19:10). He has the power to turn your life around. There are others like you whose lives have changed since coming to Him. They're in support groups, working at their jobs and enjoying normal lives. Christian counselors are abundant and ready to help you. I encourage you to consult any of them for counseling and necessary assistance.

Naming Ceremony

As its name implies, this ceremony's conducted to enable a married couple to make known publicly to family members and friends their gift of a new baby. Since many parents name their children after their great-great-grandparents, an elderly member of the family is often asked to pour libation and call upon the spirits of ancestors to enter the child to shield it from harm. But since children are gifts from God, why don't we pray to Him alone for their safety, well-being and the fulfillment of their purpose on earth? The Bible urges us as parents to "…bring them up in the training and instruction of the Lord" (Eph. 6:4).

Neither gods nor ancestors can create or bless our children, let alone equip them with the virtues enabling them to achieve their goals in life. Besides, pouring libation to spirits at the naming ceremony of a child will open up avenues for evil forces to invest their diabolical plans in the child's life. As Christians, therefore, I suggest the following pattern.

> In most African cultures, naming ceremonies take place in the parents' home or church hall. To begin, a close relative or friend is chosen as the master of ceremonies (MC). After an opening hymn or chorus, a priest or a Christian elder of the family offers prayer, thanking God for the gift of a new baby in the family and for all the invited guests assembled in the house. In Africa, a child is a gift not only to the biological parents but also to the extended family and community as a whole. Hence, prayers are offered, touching upon the needs of all concerned.
>
> This is followed by the introduction of all the invited guests and a statement of the purpose of their meeting on that particular occasion. Then, two glasses — one filled with water and the other with wine — are placed on a table. The father writes the name of the child on a piece of paper and hands it to the officiating minister/elder family member appointed to perform the ceremony. The priest/godfather/ elder holds the child gently in his arms and announces to the people the name of the child, explaining the reasons for that particular choice. Usually, a child is named after a grandfather/grandmother, whose life' had a good impact on the entire family. It's believed that a child named after such a great person will naturally cultivate similar characteristics and lead a similarly virtuous life.
>
> After making the name known, the celebrant dips his fourth finger into the glass of water and touches the tongue of the child, saying to him/her, "*So-and-So, se ese nsu a, nna nsu a,*" meaning "So-and-So, if you say this is water, then it's truly water." This act is repeated three times. After this, he dips the same finger into the wine and touches the tongue of the child as before, saying, "*So-and-So, se ese nsa a, nna nsa a,*" meaning "So-and-So, if you say this is liquor, then it's truly liquor." This is in conformity with Scripture, admonishing us as follows: "Let your 'Yes' be yes, and your 'No,' no, or you will be condemned" (James 5:12).

Therefore, the significance of this ritual is to inculcate in the child the spirit of honesty and truthfulness, so that as he or she grows up, these traits will develop toward creating a reliable and dependable citizen in the family and community.

At this juncture, final prayers are offered for the baby and parents, asking for God's blessings and protection for them and all the guests. Then the father presents his gift (usually money) to the child, followed by the rest of the guests, generously offering their individual gifts of cash or in-kind to the baby. These are all gratefully received by the MC on behalf of the parents in respect of the child. It should be noted here that in African culture, a child is born into a community and not as a single individual belonging to a married couple living in isolation.

Finally, the ceremony comes to an end with food and refreshment for the guests' enjoyment. There's no actual closing time for this—sometimes the festivities continue until midnight, because as some leave, others also come in to welcome the new baby with their presents.

Let's turn our attention to what we do for twins.

Ritual For Twins

Again, it's good to be reminded that all children—whether twins, triplets, quadruplets, or septuplets—are gifts from God, to Whom we must be thankful. However, due to false traditional beliefs, Ghanaians and many other Africans maintain that twins are special gifts from the gods of the land or clan. Hence, a slightly different ritual is performed for the twins during the naming ceremony. A fetish priest/priestess prepares two amulets or wristbands (*abam*) to be worn on each of the twin children's wrists. It's believed that the spirit in the *abam* protects and identifies them as children of the gods, thus maintaining the relationship among them all. It's also believed that the gods speak through the spirit to parents concerning what they should do or not do for the twins and the gods.

It's very important to note here that since these gods truly have no power to create human beings, they have none of the divine virtues of love, mercy or compassion for them, whether adult or child. Inability to meet the high demands that fetish priests or priestesses impose upon parents usually results in serious illness for the children and sometimes death.

These demands can be compared to those of Baal, the god of the Cannanites (1 Kings 18:25; Jer. 19:5), or "…Ashtoreth the goddess of the Sidonians, Chemosh the god of the Moabites, and Molech the god of the Ammonites…" (1 Kings 11:33), all of whom demanded the sacrifice of Israel's children by fire to pacify them, as stated in the previous passage. Therefore, the Israelites were seriously warned against such idolatrous and wicked acts of worship, because it provoked God to anger and brought disastrous consequences upon Israel whenever they indulged in them (Lev. 20:1–5).

That's why, in the Gospel of John, Jesus, Who " '…came to seek and to save what was lost' " (Luke 19:10), seriously cautions all Christians about the ways of the Devil, saying, "The thief comes only to steal and kill and destroy; I have come that they may have life, and have it to the full" (John 10:10).

There are Christian parents who refused *abam* rituals for their twins, simply dedicating them to the Lord, the Giver and Sustainer of all human beings. Their children are still living to His glory. Whatever He created—the world and all its fullness, including human beings—was intended to bring Him glory, i.e., "everyone who is called by my name, whom I created for my glory, whom I formed and made" (Isa. 43:7).

Of course, since Christians are not exempt from sickness and death, twins may fall sick and die; but we should not attribute their death to the refusal to perform the *abam* rituals.

Funeral Ceremony

During funerals, the MC usually calls upon an elderly man from the bereaved family, who's then accompanied by two or three other members. They stand in the middle or corner of the hall, and the ritualist lifts up a cup of drink toward heaven, ostensibly showing it to God for His approval. He then pours two or three drops of liquor to the ground for *Asaase Yaa* (Mother Earth), and begins to call on the names of the gods and the ancestors of the various clans, inviting them to receive a drink. He follows this with an appeal to them to provide protection and prosperity for the community, especially for the bereaved family, and the country as a whole.

Sometimes there's suspicion that the family member's death was caused by an enemy through witchcraft, voodoo or a curse. In such cases, the spirits are called upon to retaliate, paying evil for evil. Again, this is contrary to the will of God as revealed in the Holy Scriptures. Retaliation brings neither peace nor victory, but rather further destruction of precious lives. Hence, He commands us to "love your enemies and pray for those who persecute you" (Matt. 5:44). The Bible declares, "Do not take revenge, my friends, but leave room for God's wrath, for it is written: 'It is mine to avenge; I will repay,' says the Lord. On the contrary: 'If your enemy is hungry, feed him; if he is thirsty, give him something to drink. In doing this, you will heap burning coals on his head.' Do not be overcome by evil, but overcome evil with good" (Rom. 12:19–21).

Therefore, during funeral ceremonies, elders of the people should speak words of comfort and encouragement to the bereaved family instead of invoking the powers of gods and ancestors for retaliation, which doesn't do anyone any good—not even the bereaved family or the children within the community. The truth of the matter is that our adherence to tradition has left a bad example for posterity to follow. The time to change for the better is now.

Installation of a Traditional King or Chief

It's a very special day in the life of the people in any Ghanaian city or community when a new chief/king/queen takes office or swears the oath of allegiance to the head of state, paramount chief, elders and people as a whole. One of the most significant functions on the occasion's agenda is libation. As the elder pours libation, he prays to the ancestors and the spirits of the land to give the new chief/king/queen the necessary strength, foresight, wisdom and courage to deal justly with all people without discrimination, fear or favor.

> Neither gods nor ancestral spirits can help a people achieve their goals on earth honorably except God

The question, again, is: *Who in heaven or beneath it is able to provide the king and his elders with the virtues of wisdom, honesty and courage leading a nation to success and prosperity except for God?* In calling upon lesser gods and the spirits of our ancestors for help, we're violating His commandments (Exod. 20:1–6). The pity is that neither gods nor ancestral spirits are able to help a nation or people achieve their goals on earth honorably except Him.

By resorting to other gods and spirits of the dead for help, we leave God completely out of our plans. Because He is an Almighty, Holy and jealous God, He has declared, " 'I am the LORD; that is my name! I will not give my glory to another or my praise to idols" (Isa. 42:8). When we pour libation to gods and ancestors on the day of a chief's installment, praying to them to meet our needs, we're only provoking Him to anger, as declared by the prophet Zechariah:

> *...it is the LORD who makes the storm clouds. He gives showers of rain to men, and plants of the field to everyone. The idols speak deceit, diviners see visions that lie; they tell dreams that are false, they give comfort in vain. Therefore the people wander like sheep oppressed for lack of a shepherd. "My anger burns against the shepherds, and I will punish the leaders; for the LORD Almighty will care for his flock..."* (Zech. 10:1–3).

God's anger still burns against our chiefs, kings and religious leaders who compromise their faith, because they're the ones entrusted with the authority to lead people in the right direction, seeking Him and following His righteous ways. But unfortunately, many of our leaders follow their own selfish ways, mislead the people and abuse the trust vested in them. We have to remind ourselves as leaders that He Who entrusts us with authority, unique gifts and the talents to fulfill our different roles for His divine purpose also knows our weaknesses as human beings:

> *For he knows how we are formed, he remembers that we are dust. As for man, his days are like grass, he flourishes like a flower of the field; the wind blows over it and it is gone, and its place remembers it no more. But from everlasting to everlasting the LORD's love is with those who fear him, and his righteousness with their children's children* (Ps. 103:14–17).

Therefore, as kings, heads of nations, leaders of tribes and communities, and Christian leaders, we should acknowledge not only our trespasses as human beings, but particularly our inability to do without God, Who is the source of our life, and the very power that sustains all living things. Hence, without Him, we're hopeless and helpless; indeed, we're headed for failure, disgrace and complete disaster.

It's like building our castle in the sand instead of upon the solid Rock. Such a house, however big and beautiful, is bound to collapse and fragment in the face of life's storms, because its foundation is nothing but sinking sand (Matt. 7:24–27). "For no one can lay any foundation other than the one already laid, which is Jesus Christ," therefore, "Unless the LORD builds the house, its builders labor in vain..." (1 Cor. 3:11; Ps. 127:1).

As humans, that means we're not made independent of God but rather dependent on Him in all we do, so that He might direct our paths to success. He never fails or disappoints those placing their trust in Him. Hence, Paul declared, "I can do all things through Christ which strengtheneth me" (*KJV*, Phil. 4:13). We know that he encountered spiritual and physical suffering in his ministry among the Gentiles (2 Cor. 6:4–10, 12:7–10), yet by the grace of God, he "fought the good fight and finished the race" set before him. If that's the case, then all of us entrusted with positions of authority should follow his good example by choosing Christ as our Lord and Savior.

We must remit ourselves entirely into His able hands so He might transform, empower and lead us to "do all things" in fulfilling His pleasure and receiving the blessings promised to His obedient children. On this note, He drew my attention immediately to what is written in the Book of Proverbs by King Solomon:

> *Choose my instruction instead of silver, knowledge rather than choice gold, for wisdom is more precious than rubies, and nothing you desire can compare with her. "I, wisdom, dwell together with prudence; I possess knowledge and discretion. To fear the LORD is to hate evil; I hate pride and arrogance, evil behavior and perverse speech. Counsel and sound judgment are mine; I have understanding and power. By me kings reign and rulers make laws that are just; by me princes govern, and all nobles who rule on earth. I love those who love me, and those who seek me find me. With me are riches and honor, enduring wealth and prosperity…I walk in the way of righteousness, along the paths of justice, bestowing wealth on those who love me and making their treasuries full"* (Prov. 8:10–18, 20–21).

The wisest of all the kings who ever reigned and are yet to reign on earth, Solomon indicates through these wise words that he learned this lesson from personal experience with God during his tenure as king of Israel. Unless we live our lives in submission to His guidance, all wisdom, purpose, wealth and earthly pleasure are "…'Utterly meaningless! Everything is meaningless' " (Eccl. 1:2).

Such was Solomon's miserable existence. In spite of his many wives, concubines and riches uncountable, he found life empty and meaningless, because he turned from God to worship the gods of his foreign wives. In the process, his love for Yahweh grew cold; his heart was no longer whole toward Him Who crowned him king of Israel. His experience reminds us that joy, happiness, comfort and the peace of mind and soul we crave can't emerge from the abundance of our earthly possessions, but instead come from God alone.

He blessed us with the gift of procreation and gave us dominion over the earth and everything in it, including birds of the air, and the fish in the sea (Gen. 1:27, 28–30). In choosing to worship idols or material possessions, it follows that our nations' leaders and others holding authority will bring unimaginable hardships on themselves, the community and the people they represent. But with God, we all become channels of blessing and "righteousness, which exalts a nation."

CHAPTER 11

Leaders Who Fear Losing Their Positions

*L*et's ask ourselves this question: *Why do some people in authority refuse to accept Jesus as Savior and Lord of their lives?* The truth of the matter is that "most of the people in power today," as Burke Hedges describes them, "are scared to death. Their overriding concern is the fear of loss, that is, loss of their own power! Everywhere they turn, they see the handwriting on the wall and they don't like the message. So what do they do? They shoot the messenger" (*Who Stole The American Dream*, p. 107).

For instance, when Jesus raised Lazarus from death, news of the miracle quickly spread throughout the city of Jerusalem and its surroundings. But when the leaders of the Jews found out, they hurriedly convened and took counsel to kill Jesus. John, the beloved disciple, reports on their plans as follows:

> *Then the chief priests and the Pharisees called a meeting of the Sanhedrin. "What are we accomplishing?" they asked. "Here is this man performing many miraculous signs. If we let him go on like this, everyone will believe in him, and then the Romans will come and take away both our place and our nation." Then one of them, named Caiaphas, who was high priest that year, spoke up, "You know nothing at all! You do not realize that it is better for you that one man die for the people than that the whole nation perish."* (John 11:47–50).

Although the ancient leaders of Jerusalem rejected Jesus, secretly plotted to kill Him, and did kill Him indeed, there are today several countries whose leaders and citizens refuse His entry into their lives out of pride, jealousy and selfishness. They have neither fear of God nor regard for their neighbors. They neither follow Christ nor even want to hear His name mentioned. But the Bible declares that " '...there is no other name under heaven given to men by which we must be saved' " (Acts 4:12) — except the name *Jesus*.

The angel of God spoke to Joseph about this *Name*: " '...you are to give him the name Jesus, because he will save his people from their sins' " (Matt. 1:21). He is the Almighty's answer to the human condition of sin, death and eternal damnation.

We should remember that the rejection of Christ by the Jewish leaders eventually led to the destruction of Jerusalem and precious lives. We also need to be reminded that as descendants of Adam and Eve, all people naturally inherited a tendency toward sin; it's in their blood. Therefore, just as they were cursed and suffered in the aftermath of their sin, so is all humanity under a curse and its fatal consequences.

As human beings we must thus realize that we can't save ourselves (Gen. 3:16–19), because we didn't bring ourselves into this world — God did. (1:26–27, 2:7, 18–24). It's abundantly clear that we need Him to rescue us from the mess in which we find ourselves — now as much as then, and tomorrow. The prophet Jeremiah wrote:

> *This is what the LORD says: "Cursed is the one who trusts in man, who depends on flesh for his strength and whose heart turns away from the LORD. He will be like a bush in the wastelands; he will not see prosperity when it comes. He will dwell in the parched places of the desert, in a salt land where no one lives. But blessed is the man who trusts in the LORD, whose confidence is in him. He will be like a tree planted by the water that sends out its roots by the stream. It does not fear when heat comes; its leaves are always green. It has no worries in a year of drought and never fails to bear fruit"* (Jer. 17:5–8b).

His emphatic message is that God is the source of who we are and all that we possess here, now and in the future — we either choose to be with Him in heaven or Satan in hell. He represents human beings' sole power for success and prosperity. His Son sounded the same caution: " '...apart from me, you can do nothing' " (John 15:5), and Paul adds his powerful voice to the chorus, warning, "For we brought nothing into the world, and we can take nothing out of it." Whatever we have is a gift from God, "...who richly provides us with everything for our enjoyment" (1 Tim. 6:7, 17).

Life without God Is Meaningless

As I've earlier indicated, King Solomon eventually discovered the unassailable truth in this most fundamental statement. "A man can do nothing better than to eat and drink and find satisfaction in his work. This too, I see, is from the hand of God, for without him, who can eat or find enjoyment?" (Eccl. 2:24–25). Excepting His presence in our hearts, there's no lasting satisfaction or unqualified enjoyment in any aspect of our lives, no purpose or meaning. *If so, what are we here for?* Are we like Judah's hedonists who said, "Let us eat and drink…for tomorrow we die!" (Isa. 22:13), seeing no hope or value in life due to the impending doom in their rebellion against God?

It behooves us not to rely on ourselves or our possessions, because even when wealth or riches abound, we've been cautioned against casting our life-and-death aspirations on them. As Jesus pointed out to the rich fool in His parable, our lives as individual human beings do " '…not consist in the abundance of [our] possessions' " (Luke 12:15). Instead, our lives are in the hands of God, our Maker and Sustainer.

On behalf of the greater good and fulfillment of our lives and purposes on earth, in His divine wisdom, He did not create us to live in isolation from Him. To the contrary, life in its highest fulfillment of God's purpose was designed to flourish in loving relationship with Him through daily obedience to Him, and in loving fellowship with one another as prescribed in His Word (Matt. 22:36–40). Anything inferior to the divine plan is not only meaningless but also sinful in His sight, with disastrous consequences.

In the following text, the Lord specifically addresses those nations and individuals boasting of their possessions and making their riches, knowledge, wisdom, technology, military power, talent, magic or voodoo as idols to be worshipped, and in which they place their trust, hope and confidence:

> …*"Let not the wise man boast of his wisdom or the strong man boast of his strength or the rich man boast of his riches, but let him who boasts boast about this: that he understands and knows me, that I am the LORD, who exercises kindness, justice and righteousness on earth, for in these I delight"*… (Jer. 9:23–24).

To illustrate this message: Israel's King Solomon, the wisest and richest man who ever lived on this planet, had the privilege of marrying 700 beautiful women from all parts of the globe, as well as his own country.

In addition, he kept 300 concubines, enjoying every pleasure his heart desired. As any other man would have thought, he regarded these material and carnal pleasures as delivering happiness and fulfillment, but he was to be miserably disappointed. He wrote:

> *Yet when I surveyed all that my hands had done and what I had toiled to achieve, everything was meaningless, a chasing after the wind; nothing was gained under the sun...So I hated life, because the work that is done under the sun was grievous to me. All of it is meaningless, a chasing after the wind* (Eccl. 2:11, 17).

What a sorrowful expression of bitterness from the man who thought he had it all together! Now, if Solomon—who'll remain forever unsurpassed in terms of wisdom, riches and worldly pleasures—failed to find fulfillment from such material blessings, then none of us, can ever find satisfaction without God, our most earnest efforts to the contrary. *Why?*

According to biblical records, among the many wives Solomon had married were foreign women—Egyptians, Moabites, Ammonites, Sidonians and Hittites—hailing from nations whose people the Lord had specifically warned the Israelites not to marry. He knew they would surely turn the hearts of His people to their own gods (Exod. 34:15–16), but despite this clear message, Solomon didn't honor His command.

Consequently, Solomon's foreign wives eventually turned his heart toward their gods:

> *He followed Ashtoreth the goddess of the Sidonians, and Molech the detestable god of the Ammonites. So Solomon did evil in the eyes of the LORD...The LORD became angry with Solomon because his heart had turned away from the LORD, the God of Israel, who had appeared to him twice* (1 Kings 11:5–6, 9).

Looking at the issues from our human perspective, especially that of the politician, one may conclude that he would have done well initially in his strong alliance with neighboring nations through intermarriage. That strategy bonded Israel to the allied nations, thereby causing her to be considered by outsiders as a formidable force—not only in terms of Solomon's extraordinary wisdom, but also in the Davidic Kingdom's economic and political power. Nevertheless, since he didn't seek divine guidance in embarking upon those alliances through marital ties, what appeared politically glamorous and economically successful in human estimation eventually led to internal religious decay, apostasy and the eventual division of the formerly united kingdom of which he was made the monarch.

Solomon's experience, like that of many leaders today, confirms the truth that all the knowledge in the world doesn't offer insurance against missing the purpose of life (Eccl. 1:16–18). And it affirms the counsel of his father, David: "Unless the LORD builds the house, its builders labor in vain. Unless the LORD watches over the city, the watchmen stand guard in vain" (Ps. 127:1). Indeed, it was that experience coupled with several others that also brought Solomon, under the inspiration of the Holy Spirit, to write the following proverb as a sound warning to young people:

> **The truth is that all the knowledge in the world doesn't offer insurance against missing the purpose of life**

> *My son, do not forget my teaching, but keep my commands in your heart, for they will prolong your life many years and bring you prosperity. Let love and faithfulness never leave you; bind them around your neck, write them on the tablet of your heart…Trust in the LORD with all your heart and lean not on your own understanding; in all your ways acknowledge him, and he will make your paths straight. Do not be wise in your own eyes; fear the LORD and shun evil* (Prov. 3:1–3, 5–7).

Solomon's great wisdom in relation to the theme *Brains Are Not Enough* prompted Julie Ackerman Link to ask,

> Why do smart people do not-so-smart things? Time after time I hear sad stories about people with high IQs who fall short in the area of moral discernment, leading to tragic results. Obviously, a good brain isn't enough to keep a person from making bad choices. Ancient Israel's King Solomon, author of much of the book of Proverbs, wrote, "keep your heart with all diligence" (4:23) and "wisdom rests in the heart of him who has understanding" (14:33). Despite knowing the connection between the heart and wisdom, the King disobeyed God by marrying foreign women who turned his heart after other gods (1 Kings 11:4). As a result, the Lord said, "I will surely tear the kingdom away from you" (verse 11).

Ackerman concluded with the following insightful observation: "The ability to make good decisions demands a heart devoted to God."

To some degree, as a young, rich prince of Israel, Solomon's experience was rather exceptional for his time. But the spread and increase of wealth over the centuries has meant that in our own generation, we're seeing large numbers of men and women endowed with material wealth but never truly happy or satisfied. Elvis Presley, for instance, was one of the greatest musicians the world had ever known. In his book, *The Heart of Revival*, Nickie Gumbel wrote:

> In his heyday, [Presley] made $100 million in two years of stardom. He had three jets, two Cadillacs, a Rolls-Royce, a Lincoln Continental, Buick and Chrysler station wagons, a jeep, a dune buggy, a converted bus, and three motorcycles. His favorite car was his 1960 Cadillac limousine. The top was covered with pearl-white Naugahide. The body was sprayed with 40 coats of a specially prepared paint that included crushed diamonds and fish scales. Nearly all the metal trim was plated with 18K gold. Inside the car there were two gold-plated telephones, a gold vanity case containing a gold vanity razor and gold hair clippers, an electric shoe-buffer, a gold plated television, a record player, an amplifier, air conditioning, and a refrigerator. He had everything. Yet he was unfulfilled. These things do not fill the aching void within the soul. They always leave us wanting more. Hence, God asked, "Why spend money on what is not bread, and your labor on what does not satisfy?" (Isa. 55:2a). In His compassion, God invites us, "Come to me" (verse 3). For no one can satisfy our hungry soul but God alone [*Gye Nyame*] (p. 100).

Israel Indulged in Idolatry

Early in their journey through the wilderness, the Israelites camped in the land of Shittim, where the men indulged in immoral sexual liaisons with the local women, ate with the people and worshipped and sacrificed to local gods. Indiscriminate whoring compounded by acts of idolatry aroused such fierce anger in God that 24,000 of them died from a plague (Num. 25:1–9). This is a clear warning to everyone that God is the very source of our life: to leave Him for any other god brings nothing but disappointment, sorrow and catastrophe.

Roper of RBC Ministries put it this way: "We are born and we live for the express purpose of knowing and loving God. He is the source of our life" (*Daily Bread*, Friday, November 14, 2003).

After examining his lifestyle in the light of Holy Scripture, St. Augustine, one of the great pillars of the Roman Catholic Church, had a similar insight to offer about our human condition: "Thou hast made us for thyself, O Lord, and our hearts are restless until they find their rest in thee…" Like Solomon, Augustine honestly spoke from his personal experience.

He was born in the city of Thagaste in Numidia, North Africa, into a middle-class family of the mixed parentage of a pious and devout Christian mother, Monica, and a pagan father, Patricius. Through his love for learning, he became well-educated in the textual study of major Latin classics in Carthage. He sought out and tasted almost every religion and philosophy of his day, but none of them provided him with the inner satisfaction his soul needed most.

The Conversion of Augustine

It wasn't until Augustine turned 40 that he found the truth in the Christ's Gospel, the power to liberate every human being from sin and every other force that dominates human life. His conversion took place in a garden in Milan, where he overheard a child reciting a rhyme: "Take and read, take and read." Holding his Bible, he began to read Paul's letter to the Romans until he came to the text, "Let us behave decently, as in the daytime, not in orgies and drunkenness, not in sexual immorality and debauchery, not in dissension and jealousy. Rather, clothe yourselves with the Lord Jesus Christ, and do not think about how to gratify the desires of the sinful nature" (Rom. 13:13–14). He thenceforth began his new life in Christ under the guidance and power of the Holy Spirit.

Williston Walker wrote, "He was now able to see himself as a soul whose fulfillment lay in the knowledge and love of God; and not in himself or his ability." My friend, are you restless today, driven by discontentment and a longing for that elusive, unknown *something*? "Jesus Christ," says Roper, "is the source and satisfaction of all you seek."

Augustine was ordained a presbyter in 391 by Valerius, the bishop of the church in the city of Hippo in Numidia. When Valerius went to his eternal home four years later, Augustine was the one chosen to succeed him as Hippo's bishop. His teachings, writings (especially his *Confessions*) and devotional life—which helped immensely to guide and strengthen the church in North Africa—are still highly treasured among the great doctrines of the Roman Catholic Church today.

CHAPTER 12

Christians Are Part of the Problem

The question is: *If Christ is able to change sinful men and women into righteous people — whose new life of hard work and integrity can help lift a nation from deterioration to progress and from disgrace to honor — why is it that the majority of countries in Africa, including Ghana, are still lagging behind in terms of development?* "Righteousness exalts a nation, but sin is a disgrace to any people" (Prov. 14:34). This isn't by any means to suggest that Africans are the most sinful or backward people in the world. The Word of God applies to every nation under the sun that refuses God the first seat in the governing of their daily affairs and lives.

For example, Ghana's traditional chiefs, political leaders, preachers and tribal elders have known for years, through the popular African proverbial expression *Gye Nyame*, that unless God accompanies and assists you, life is in vain. As mentioned earlier, the sign *Gye Nyame* (☦) appears in many African artistic designs in clothes, clay and wood. Though it's a brief, idiomatic expression, it's pregnant with significant meaning and profound wisdom.

Worshipping God and Traditional Spirits

On the one hand, as members of the church who should have been God's instrument for change, we've distanced ourselves from the traditions of the people and have been largely unable to help or guide those outside the Church to find the way leading to salvation. On the other hand, the majority of those who don't isolate themselves but get involved with traditional religious practices, fail to discern the differences between the Christian faith and traditional religion.

We can find a typical example in the story of a certain rich Christian contractor hailing from the Central Region of Ghana. As related by Brother W.K. Idan, Sr., this man was instrumental in the building of a church as well as the erection of a shrine for the idol/god in his local community. The story continues as follows:

> Ironically, he put a cross of "Jesus" on the shrine similar to the one that he had erected on the front view of the church. While he served as an elder of the church and even had a special seating place in the church, he was also serving as *ɔsafohene* (chief of the tribal group), a position that involves idolatrous practices and rituals.
>
> After some years, the prominent man died and a struggle ensued between the church and the shrine over the body. The fetish priests and other *ɔsafohene* warned the church in question that on Friday, the wake-keeping day, the church should release this man's body to them at midnight to enable them to take it to their shrine for rituals to be performed over the body.
>
> True to their word on the wake-keeping day, when the town was filled with people from all walks of life—including a delegation from the church's headquarters—ministers from the various branches of the church and visitors, these idol worshippers—the fetish priests and priestesses and *asafohene* with their *asafo* companies—invaded the church grounds, demanded "their" body and took it to their shrine.
>
> While the church continued wake-keeping without the body, the idolatrous rituals and ceremonies also went on at the shrine. When it was time for the burial service to begin, they went to demand the body, but had to wait because the pagan rituals were not over. The body was later released and the burial service started (*Are You a True Christian?*, pp. 13–14).

In the face of such a critical situation, evangelist Idan poses the following challenging questions to you:

> Who owns the body by right; the church or the shrine? What will be the destination of the man's soul; heaven or hell? Why is someone called a Christian? Whose fault was it: the man, the church, ministers, the society, tradition, or the government? Do you worship the God of our Lord Jesus Christ or the god of our ancestors? You must decide and choose your stand before it is too late.

These are real, heart-searching questions that all readers need to ponder carefully to provide accurate answers for themselves. Let's take another instance, such as a naming ceremony, at which an elder of a Christian couple is called upon to pour libation as follows:

> O God, Almighty, we seek your approval for our libation [prayer]. We call on you this morning, for we know that you control our destiny. Ancestors of the clan, receive your drink. We call on you to bless this child who is being named this morning. Let him grow as strong and famous as the ancestor whose name he bears. Now, gods of the land, we pray you to protect this child from illness and untimely death. We pray you to make prosperous the work of the parents and all the families of the clan, and those abroad. Eguana [the name of a clan] *abosom* [gods], receive your drink.

After the libation, a church representative also prays to God on behalf of the couple. If we read the words of the above libation carefully, we find that the prayer is addressed to God, ancestors, other gods and spirits. This amounts to worshipping many gods (syncretism), infurating a holy and righteous God, jealous both of His people and His glory (Isa. 42:8). Holy Scripture warns us definitively against associating Him with other gods:

> *"I am the LORD your God, who brought you out of Egypt, out of the land of slavery. You shall have no other gods before me...You shall not bow down to them or worship them; for I, the LORD your God, am a jealous God, punishing the children for the sin of the fathers to the third and fourth generation of those who hate me, but showing love to a thousand [generations] of those who love me and keep my commandments"* (Exod. 20:2–3, 5–6).

Libation or prayer offered to ancestral spirits and lesser gods isn't the same as prayer made to God through the name of His Son; the two practices conflict with each other. A Christian prayer is offered to the Creator in the name of Jesus, Who died for the forgiveness of the world's sins, so that those believing in Him won't die but have everlasting life (John 3:16). Christ was resurrected and intercedes for all believers (Rom. 8:34), but as we're well aware, libation is offered to gods and ancestral spirits.

Therefore, the two types of prayer—that is, libation and Christian prayer—are *not* the same. Yet it's a commonplace in Christian homes and ceremonies because families and celebrants don't really know Jesus Christ or "the truth" that has the power to set one free (John 8:31–32). They assume they're adhering to tradition or ancestral religious values, but in reality, they're worshipping idols in ignorance of the Word of God.

The fact is, we can't serve Him through Christ and also bow to other gods or even make fellowship with idol worshippers (2 Cor. 6:14–16); in so doing, we provoke His anger. Jesus said, " 'No servant can serve two masters. Either he will hate the one and love the other, or he will be devoted to the one and despise the other…' " (Luke 16:13). There are a number of Christian leaders ensnared by this syncretic belief, and the following passage narrates one such example.

The Failure of Okomfo Damuah

The case of Rev. Father Damuah, who abandoned his Catholic faith for a position as a cultic priest intending to indigenize Christianity, illustrates to what extent we can be misled through false belief or religion. A cultic priest, in the Ghanaian or African sense, is called an *okomfo*, a fetish priest or diviner who worships idols, lesser gods and spirits, functioning primarily as the medium through whom the gods speak.

In this particular situation, as Victor Aquaah-Harrison wrote in his theses, "Damuah's role is the same as the medium at Endor, who was consulted by Saul (1 Sam. 28:7–25). Should the church have then worked with him?" He answers his own question with an emphatic, "No!" and then adds, "I believe he lost his hope in God, which brings joy and peace…so that one may abound in hope in the power of the Holy Spirit" (*Sankofa Yenkyi*, 2000, p. 42). The Church rejected him because the Scriptures denounce such pagan practices even if performed in the seemingly innocent guise of preserving African religious tradition and culture (Exod. 20:4; Deut. 32:16; 1 Cor. 10:14; 1 John 5:21).

The Problem with the African Culture of Silence

By definition, the African culture of silence is the supposed respect we hold for people in authority (e.g. kings, queens, etc.) or the elderly in the community or family, disallowing a public declaration of a leader's error. As Africans, we're forbidden by our culture to speak about the wrongs of elders, regardless of how detrimental they may be to the family, community or nation as a whole.

In every community, elders in their supposed wisdom have instituted a method for dealing with the chief of a clan or head of a family whenever he went astray. This was handled by a group of seven known as *basounfo* (the king's counselors), who are responsible for approaching the king quietly in his chambers when necessary to offer him crucial advice on the particular issue at hand. By so doing, the counselors are able to help the king straighten up his ways to avoid public disgrace. This is advantageous to the king, in that he's humbled himself before the elders and accepted their advice for the better. It's practiced in many countries to foster unity, stability, peace and economic prosperity.

Distoolment of a King or Chief

However, sometimes a king or chief may be too stubborn in taking advice from his counselors or elders. In such cases, the latter may be compelled to raise the issue in the court of elders. If the king still fails to give a satisfactory answer to them, the public is notified. Finally, the king is removed from office and a new one installed in his place.

Complications arise when the king bribes his elders in order to remain in power indefinitely, and these are instances when the culture of silence hardens, making it particularly difficult for anyone to speak his mind about what's transpired. If the situation becomes unbearable, the disgruntled group may break away to establish a separate society under a new leader, as was the case for Rehoboam, the king of Judah (1 Kings 12:6–10).

Those daring to vocalize their displeasure with harmful or misguided policies are branded disrespectful or opposed to harmony in the community, because they've broken the taboo, as it were—the ancient, traditional culture of silence. The situation worsens further when those boldly declaring the truth about a political issue in the country are threatened by the head of state or the ruling party with imprisonment without trial…or even death. When possible, a number of such people seek asylum in other countries, leaving the dictators to their own devices.

Unfortunately, this was the ugly ruling style of some African countries, like Ghana, Uganda, Liberia, Sierra Leone and others, in the past. It happened, for instance, during the later part of Kwame Nkrumah's tenure and the military regimes that followed. Aided by the culture of silence, Ghanaian leaders and their counterparts elsewhere caused more harm than good to the entire continent of Africa and the world as a whole. They're partly the cause of our beloved continent's slow progress.

Thanks to God, changes have taken place in various areas and improvements are continuing these days for the good of all, particularly in

Ghana, Liberia, Sierra Leone (with the first woman head of state) and other places in Africa. This must continue with vigor and reliance on God, from Whom all blessings flow.

Remedy for the Culture of Silence

What must be done to resolve the issue of the culture of silence? It has its merits and demerits. It does allow those in authority and other individuals to be advised in secret and to right the wrong. The offense is then forgiven and reconciliation established for the good of all in the family and community as a whole. Moreover, this accords with Scripture in its views on conflict resolution (Matt. 18:15–18), and Paul advised Timothy not to rebuke an elder in public (1 Tim. 5:1).

That being said, I've gleaned from careful observation of human nature that those of us in authority tend to abuse this privilege to the detriment of our families, churches, communities and the nation placed under our charge. For instance, Nana Osimasi, as the head of a clan and knowing that no one dares challenge or rebuke him publicly, may continue to misuse the family treasure entrusted to him: land, a large sum of money, etc. This may go on as long as he's in authority, to the disadvantage of the clan, demonstrating that the demerits of the culture of silence outweigh the merits.

To overcome this destructive practice, we need the power of the Holy Spirit to embolden us in lovingly speaking the truth, regardless of the consequences. Left to ourselves, we can do nothing, as when Peter regrettably denied the Lord when challenged outside Pilate's court during the trial of Christ (Mark 14:66–72). But after the experience of Pentecost—when he and his fellow apostles were filled with the power of the Holy Spirit—the same Peter courageously stated the truth without fear or favor when they were threatened by the high priest and the Jewish Supreme Court (Acts 4:1–21).

> To overcome this destructive practice, we need the power of the Holy Spirit to embolden us.

Jesus Reproves Religious Leaders Who Follow Tradition

In the following passage, Jesus vehemently rebukes religious leaders who had chosen tradition over God's Holy Word. He said,

"...' "These people honor me with their lips, but their hearts are far from me. They worship me in vain; their teachings are but rules taught by men." You have let go of the commands of God and are holding on to the traditions of men' " (Mark 7:6–8). Nevertheless, in hearing this from His lips, we shouldn't in any way conclude that He was against tradition. In another context, He declared, " 'Do not think that I have come to abolish the Law or the Prophets; I have not come to abolish them but to fulfill them' " (Matt. 5:17).

He proved the truth of His mission statement after healing a leper, sending him away with the following instructions: " '...show yourself to the priest and offer the sacrifices that Moses commanded for your cleansing, as a testimony to them' " (Mark 1:44). Contrary to His opponents, this is proof that He is not against the Law. However, He did reject vehemently any additions to the Commandments the scribes had formulated, which would have made it difficult or impossible for the people to obey God, as we've previously encountered in the Bible (7:6–8).

It's therefore crucial that committed Christians uphold the true teachings of Holy Scripture and be boldly determined to share the Gospel with others, whenever and wherever necessary to enlighten those in darkness and ignorant of the Bible. Unfortunately, there are some traditional elders, pastors and church leaders so steeped in tradition that they can't officiate at anything culturally significant—marriage ceremonies, funeral services, annual festivals, etc.—without pouring libation to the gods and ancestors.

They regard libation as a religious practice inseparably bound to our culture and necessarily to be dutifully followed. Any committed Christian's attempts to stop them or suggest alternatives are regarded as arrogant and offensive. They see such a bold stand for Christ as disrespect for the elderly, tradition or African culture. Although such reactions represent ignorance or a misunderstanding of the Holy Scriptures, we must hold fast to the truth that will set us free, never departing from it.

Doesn't God strictly warn His people—all who believe in Him and His Son—not to worship other gods?

> *"I am the LORD your God, who brought you out of Egypt, out of the land of slavery. You shall have no other gods before me...You shall not bow down to them or worship them; for I, the LORD your God, am a jealous God, punishing the children for the sin of the fathers to the third and fourth generation of those who hate me, but showing love to a thousand [generations] of those who*

love me and keep my commandments" (Exod. 20:2–3, 5–6).

What happened when the people of Israel disobeyed Him, engaging in syncretic, idolatrous practices? Moses, the leader of the Israelites wrote:

> *They made him jealous with their foreign gods and angered him with their detestable idols. They sacrificed to demons, which are not God—gods they had not known, gods that recently appeared…You deserted the Rock, who fathered you; you forgot the God who gave you birth. The LORD saw this and rejected them because he was angered by his sons and daughters. "I will heap calamities upon them and spend my arrows against them. I will send wasting famine against them, consuming pestilence and deadly plague…"* (Deut. 32:16-19, 23-24).

My dear reader, as evidenced in the Bible, as well as in our own individual, personal experiences, disobedience to God's commandments has always brought about lamentable consequences: "…The soul who sins is the one who will die" (Ezek. 18:4).

During the former military regime headed by Flt. Lt. J.J. Rawlings, foreign leaders and statesmen visiting Ghana were welcomed with the pouring of libation to the gods and ancestors. Prayers were offered to gods for the security and success of our guests, as if the gods and spirits of ancestors were the source of the country's peace, success and security. State functions were preceded by libation, indicating that the country as a whole depended upon such deities.

These spirits do truly exist, and when called they'll come, but "…only to steal and kill and destroy…" as Jesus cautioned (John 10:10). According to Scripture, these spirits are nothing but demons (1 Cor. 10:20, 22) without the power to save or benefit anybody. That's why God commands His people not to possess, bow down to or worship any other gods (Exod. 20:3–4). In disobeying this commandment, people everywhere invite the Devil and his demonic forces to take control, causing havoc in the country.

As a result of calling on these gods, demonic spirits gained access to the decision-making processes of the governing class, and thus succeeded in influencing thought processes and decisions on public policies for the nation. In fact, during that regime, many people, including women, died terrible deaths through torture in various places. Again, God said, "The thief comes only to steal and kill and destroy…" (John 10:10). I've repeated this text several times to warn everyone, because He is Lord and spoke the truth humans don't know in order to protect them from the Devil.

For instance, in his book *The Amazing Dictator*, John Westwood writes, "General F.W.K. Akuffo, General A. A. Afrifa, Air Vice-Marshal G. Y. Boakye, Rear Admiral Joy Amedume, Major-General R.E.A. Kotei and Col. R.J.A. Feli were also executed by firing squad. Their bodies, including those of Agyapong and Utuka, were put into crude coffins constructed with rough *wawa* wood and buried in the grounds of the prisons" (2001, p. 5).

Perhaps the cause of a lot of tension, fear and insecurity among Ghanaians during the past regime were the murders of Justices Cecilia Koranteng-Addow, Fred Poku Sarkodie, and Kwadwo Agyei Akyeampong and a retired army officer, Maj. Sam Acquah. They were taken from their homes under the cover of darkness and murdered in cold blood. "Each of them," writes Westwood, "was made to sit on a block and they were shot several times from behind. Their bodies were doused with petrol and set alight…" (p. 4).

As this state of affairs went from terrible to unbearable, the Makola market women courageously challenged the regime in a demonstration. They were protesting the brutal murders of innocent women in the streets of Accra, calling on the government and law-enforcement agencies to trace the killers and bring them to justice. Undoubtedly, those were ritual murders associated with demonic worship, confirming the words of Jesus concerning satanic activities (John 10:10).

According to Westwood, a legal team headed by Justice Azu Crabbe investigated the case, leading "to the trial and conviction of Amartey Kwei, Amedekah, Senya, Dzandu and Tekpor for murder" (*The Amazing Dictator*, p. 72). Though it was obvious those soldiers carried out orders issued by at least one superior officer, there wasn't enough evidence to convict the latter. But the Almighty God, through His *omnipresence* and *omniscience*, knows everyone who was involved in those heinous crimes: "The eyes of the LORD are everywhere, keeping watch on the wicked and the good" (Prov. 15:3; *also* Ps. 139:1–3, 7–12).

Any others involved and not yet apprehended must be aware that He will eventually bring every dark deed into the light of judgment, hidden or not, good or evil (Eccl. 14:13; Rom. 14:12). On that day, nobody can hide from the *omnipotence* of God in His roles as Maker and Governor of the world. God holds the whole world in His hands (Isa. 40:15–17; Dan. 4:34–35). My prayer, however, is that those involved might be led to repent of their sin and turn to Him for forgiveness and salvation through faith in His Son before it's too late.

The question bothering many Ghanaians is this: *What was the motive for the killing of General Afrifa, other army officers and the three judges?* According to one view, Rawlings was apparently fearful that Afrifa might lead other soldiers to intervene if the Provisional National Defence Council (PNDC) failed to fulfill its commitment to the nation. Others suspect a revenge for the overthrow of Kwame Nkrumah. The demise of the judges might've arisen from their daring stand against some of the policies initiated by the PNDC.

The overall underlying motive was possibly to keep the PNDC government permanently in power. Indeed, they reigned for 20 years—much longer than any other regime besides the British. However, they couldn't remain in power indefinitely. Did the brutal torture and senseless murder enable them to achieve their objectives and the nation's? The answer from many people is a big "No!" On the contrary, the PNDC government left Ghanaians much poorer spiritually, economically and emotionally than they were when they first took office in 1981.

For many Ghanaians, this was unlike the regime of the Armed Forces Revolutionary Council (AFRC) led by Rawlings in June 1979 and hailed by the masses. The cost of living had been so high that only the rich could afford three meals a day. But with him as the head of the AFRC government, we saw the following changes for the better in the living conditions of the people:

- Traders refrained from hoarding their commodities, and the prices of goods became affordable to the average Ghanaian.
- Accountability was required of those placed in authority or public office. Such awareness of accountability made office-bearers extra-careful in the use of public money or government property.
- Ghanaians came to realize that the natural resources of the nation (e.g., gold, cocoa, timber, etc.) were meant for the benefit of all, not only for those in authority. By these and other AFRC initiatives, "JJ" (as he was popularly called) sought to uproot *kalabule* (corruption), which had spread like cancer into every sector of Ghanaian society, hindering stability, integrity, economic progress and destroying precious lives.

Indeed, Rawlings was so popular with the masses, particularly students in the universities, that he was described by many as a man with a heart for the poor, viewed as a savior of some sort. Hence, "JJ" became the initials for "Junior Jesus," and he was hailed as such by citizens whenever he showed up to address them. Despite being in power for a little more than a year, he left the indelible impression on the minds of many as a selfless leader who staged the coup not for his personal gain, but for the poor in particular and for the good of Ghanaians in general.

These reasons and others too numerous to list here prompted Ghanaians to wholeheartedly welcome Rawlings when he appeared again in the 1981 coup d'état, toppling the Limann government. However, the outcome of the second round was less favorable than people had expected. By the year 2000, when Kufour's party took over the reigns of government, as I've mentioned earlier, the country entered the ranks of the HIPC. What happened to the gold, diamond, bauxite, manganese, cocoa, timber, etc. we exported during those 20 years? Where were the salutary qualities of compassion and selflessness that Ghanaians saw in Rawlings during his short reign in 1979? Only God truly knows the heart of a person!

Here I see the relevance of Herb V. Lugt's comment on Job, described in the Bible as " '…blameless and upright, a man who fears God and shuns evil' " (Job 1:8). Lugt said, "Yet after all his trials, Job said, 'I abhor myself, and repent in dust and ashes' (42:6). Even after reflecting on his own goodness (29:1–25), he knew the condition of his heart. From a human perspective, many people may be described as 'good,' but God sees the disobedience, selfishness, and hate that lie deep within all of us. He also knows that we have spiritual blind spots. And when He opens our eyes to see ourselves as He does, we understand why a 'good man' like Job said he abhorred himself." Lugt concluded with the following prayer and a poem by an unknown:

> Lord, help us to be good but never to lose sight
> of our sinfulness and unworthiness. Thank you
> for the forgiveness You offer us in Jesus Christ.
> —Herb Lugt
>
> Teach me, Lord, my true condition,
> Bring me, childlike, to Your side;
> May I never trust my goodness—
> Only in Your grace abide.

—Anon. (*Daily Bread*, January 24, 2005)

Hence, the Lord has rightly declared in His Word that as humans, we can't win the battle of life or save ourselves by our own might or power, but by His Spirit (Zech. 4:6). It's irrevocable and irrefutable that "Unless the LORD builds the house, its builders labor in vain…" (Ps. 127:1). That's to say, unless we allow God primacy in the governing of our individual lives and the nation as a whole, neither as leaders of the country nor as individuals can we make the best use of the gold, diamond, cocoa, food, etc. that He has richly bestowed on the land.

Because He is the Maker and Owner of everything in this world, nothing belongs to us, and we neither have the power to achieve our goals nor the capability to control anything. Jesus declared, " '…apart from me you can do nothing' " (John 15:5). But with Him, we can confidently say with Paul, "I can do everything through him who gives me strength" (Phil. 4:13). This must give us pause to closely examine people before conferring on them authority over us—in the Church, in business and in government.

Qualifications of People in Authority

What do we look for in those we put in authority—wealth, academic qualifications, divine wisdom? As we noted in Chapter 6, Joseph was appointed to high office in Egypt because Pharaoh saw in him the unique gifts of wisdom and discernment that God, through His Spirit, had bestowed on him. When we move into the New Testament, we find similar qualifications as the criteria for the selection of leaders of the Church. We may cite, for instance, the case of the seven deacons, whom the Apostles appointed to the office of Church administration, while they devoted themselves to "prayer and preaching of the gospel" (Acts 6:1–6).

We must take counsel from the Bible when we deliberate over choosing leaders to fill positions of authority in the Church and nation. We ought to exercise caution by prayerfully electing people who fear God and believe in Christ as their personal Savior and Lord. They should be men and women who depend on Him for wisdom, strength, direction and success in the exercise of their privileges and responsibilities. For "Righteousness exalts a nation, but sin is a disgrace to any people" (Prov. 14:34). And only He can lead a nation to success and prosperity.

Dear friend, let me remind you in all seriousness that our salvation lies solely in our humble obedience to God's call to salvation, by grace through faith in His Son. "For there is one God and one mediator between God and men, the man Christ Jesus, who gave himself as a ransom for all men…" (1 Tim. 2:5–6). Therefore, " 'Salvation is found in no one else, for there is no other name under heaven given to men by which we must be saved' " (Acts 4:12). He is God's answer to all our human problems.

Jesus said, "…'I am the way and the truth and the life. No one comes to the Father except through me' " (John 14:6). Earlier in John, He had declared to the world His incarnation's purpose: "I have come that they may have life, and have it to the full" (10:10).

It's therefore critical that we adhere to God's exhortation and not allow ourselves to be deceived by blind leaders groping in darkness as they rely on occult powers or spirits of the dead for assistance, or else we'll all be destroyed in the end (Matt. 23:16–17, 24, 26, 35–36). The legitimate question to ask here is: "Why consult the dead on behalf of the living?" (Isa. 8:19). In following blind leaders or depending on occultism, voodoo or ancestral spirits for success in life, we can expect disappointment, shame and, finally, condemnation before God.

Jesus unequivocally rebuked as "hypocrites," "blind guides" and a "brood of vipers" such leaders and those in authority who misled the people of Israel, because pride, greed and selfishness prevented their submission to His teaching and acceptance of Him as the Messiah, the Son of God (Matt. 23:15, 16, 30; John 8:42–47).

Paul characterized those opposed to the Gospel's truth as "those who are perishing." Why? Because, "The god of this age has blinded the minds of unbelievers, so that they cannot see the light of the gospel of the glory of Christ, who is the image of God." (2 Cor. 4:3–4).

When we look further back into the history of Israel, we find that the people of God fell into apostasy in Hosea's time, so His wrath singed the priests and elders, who had misled the people in their ignorance of His Word. Consequently, the people were led into all kinds of sin, the worst of which was idolatry against Him, finally resulting in the captivity or destruction of a great number of Israel's people. God's Word came to the prophet Hosea:

> *My people are destroyed from lack of knowledge. "Because you have rejected knowledge, I also reject you as my priests; because you have ignored the law of your God, I also will ignore your children…they exchanged their Glory for*

> *something disgraceful...They consult a wooden idol, and are answered by a stick of wood. A spirit of prostitution leads them astray..."* (Hosea 4:6–7, 12).

As in this prophet's days, there are in our own generation a number of leaders of nations, churches and tribal groups ignorant of the Truth (the Word of God), which if revered would free humanity from demonic forces and the seductive power of sin and its deadly consequences. Hence, through twisted teachings and maligned influences, many have been led astray or destroyed. When questioned by the religious leaders of the Jews—who didn't believe in the resurrection of the dead, "Jesus replied, 'You are in error because you do not know the Scriptures or the power of God' " (Matt. 22:29). As His followers, we must be on high alert for diviners and false teachers of the Holy Scriptures, or many will follow them into darkness, deceived. It's for this reason that Jesus warned Christians:

> *"Watch out for false prophets. They come to you in sheep's clothing, but inwardly they are ferocious wolves...Every tree that does not bear good fruit is cut down and thrown into the fire. Thus, by their fruit you will recognize them"* (7:15, 19–20).

Paul also alerted believers to evil days (Eph. 5:16). As always, false prophets and manipulative teachers are abundant, maneuvering with a variety of humanistic and New Age philosophies in misleading the innocent. It was with his customary fatherly concern that Paul warned his spiritual son, Timothy, to "...guard what has been entrusted to your care. Turn away from godless chatter and the opposing ideas of what is falsely called knowledge, which some have professed and in so doing have wandered from the faith..." (1 Tim. 6:20–21). Like his son, we pay heed to Paul's wise counsel for our own good.

God Does Not Want Anyone to Perish

I strongly believe that God is graciously showing His people, Israel and the whole world, especially Africa, the way to salvation, peace, love, and prosperity, which come with showers of blessings on all people who "...seek first his kingdom and his righteousness..." (Matt. 6:33).

It's noted throughout the Holy Scriptures that whenever God sends

His prophets with His Word to any people, it's a demonstration of His love for that particular group or nation indicating His willingness to save them from sin and its destructive consequences.

Nineveh's Repentence on Hearing Jonah's Message

When the ancient city of Nineveh, Assyria's capital, posed a great threat to Israel through its many acts of atrocities and wickedness, God sent Jonah to proclaim the imminent judgment on it. Guess what happened! The entire people, led by the king and his nobles, humbled themselves with prayer and fasting to sincerely repent from their sinful lives.

Jonah writes, "When God saw what they did and how they turned from their evil ways, he had compassion and did not bring upon them the destruction he had threatened" (Jon. 3:10). Did you know that he initially refused to go to Nineveh to preach God's Word? He was the type of selfish Christian who prefers that sinners be condemned by God and cast into hell rather than hear the Good News and turn to Him for salvation in His Son.

Are we also as self-centered and unconcerned for unbelievers as Jonah was? Aren't Christians supposed to illuminate the world in honoring Jesus as declared in His Sermon on the Mount? (Matt. 5:13–14). Aren't we willing to share His Father's Word with people, administer justice fairly, act out of selflessness, give generously to charity and exercise mercy? Aren't we capable of drawing others to Him so that they'll be saved by grace through faith in His name? (Eph. 2:8).

And finally, aren't we believers privilieged to be called " '…the salt of the earth…' " (Matt 5:13), a people endowed with divine qualities full of the potential to preserve a city from decay, corruption or destruction? There are modern cities like Nineveh throughout the world today, particularly Africa, filled to the brim with people led by wicked, selfish, greedy kings and nobles doomed to perish for their sins, unless they hear God's Word and repent.

I'll tell you what: the Lord sees them all and lays "…compassion on them, because they were harassed and helpless, like sheep without a shepherd" (9:36). Most certainly, it's not His will that anybody should perish. He desires the salvation of all, so that together we can enjoy the blessings awaiting us in His kingdom; but we must begin here and now, or it may be too late.

His question to us is: "…'Whom shall I send? And who will go for us?'…" (Isa. 6:8). Isaiah responded to His call, and through his prophetic ministry to Israel in three different phases of her history as His chosen people, His eternal purpose for the world was fulfilled in the birth, life, teaching, death and resurrection of Christ, the Savior of mankind. Paul thus wrote: "…God was reconciling the world to himself in Christ, not counting men's sins against them…" (2 Cor. 5:19).

Like this prophet, let ministers of the Gospel, together with our congregations, therefore lift high His banner, and proclaim His Word for all to receive His saving knowledge.

But wait—I'm afraid we can't exhalt Him or share His Word with others as boldly as we ought to if there's a question mark attached to our Christianity. That question is: *Are we truly believers and teachers of the Gospel of Jesus Christ, or are we false prophets, wolves in sheep's clothing* (Matt. 7:15), *intending to deceive others?*

If we're truly committed Christians, then we're "…not ashamed of the gospel, because it is the power of God for the salvation of everyone who believes…" (Rom. 1:16). Otherwise, we're no better than the carnal Christians described in the next chapter, or perhaps, at best the "…mere infants…" Paul addressed in his epistle (1 Cor. 3:1).

We must individually ask these questions soberly and answer them honestly toward assessing our own spiritual position in the faith and advancing our knowledge of the Scriptures. Only thereby will we become true witnesses to the world for the Lord, Jesus Christ.

Why didn't the Corinthian leaders take action on this serious matter before Paul issued instructions to them? Was it because the leaders themselves were walking in the flesh or lacking the moral courage to take disciplinary action against the member concerned? Whatever the reason might be, it does point to all of us who are leaders of a local church—or any organization—to take good care of the people entrusted to our charge. God will require us sooner or later to give an account of our stewardship at His judgment seat in heaven (Matt. 25:14–30; Heb. 9:27).

For my part, I hope to have some good answers ready ahead of time.

CHAPTER **13**

*C*arnal, or worldly, Christians are immature believers. Like children, they're easily deceived by the false teachers of every sort of doctrine, because they don't really grasp Scripture. They choose sides and bring about division in the Church, as happened to that of Corinth in Greece many lifetimes ago (1 Cor. 3:1–9). Since they're not strong in their faith, they often fall prey to the Devil's temptation and indulge in all sorts of immoral behavior.

A typical example of this can be found in the church of Corinth, where one such carnal Christian flirted with his father's wife. When Paul received such a disgraceful report, his primary reaction was to rebuke church leaders for the lukewarm attitude allowing this wanton, immoral conduct, "…and of a kind that does not occur even among pagans…" (5:1), to occur in the Church of Christ. His secondary reaction was to exhort the leaders of the Church to take immediate disciplinary action against that member: expulsion (3:1–9, 5:1–12 for the crux of the story).

Churchgoers

The term *churchgoers* refers to people attending church service for reasons having little to do with authentic faith in Jesus Christ. He said, " 'Not everyone who says to me, "Lord, Lord," will enter the kingdom of heaven, but only he who does the will of my Father who is in heaven' " (Matt. 7:21). Again, He describes them as "…people who honor me with their lips, but their hearts are far away from me" (Mark

7:6).

Individually, we need to ask ourselves: *What sort of Christian am I: a committed believer in Christ or a carnal Christian? Am I just an ordinary church-goer, not knowing exactly what the church is all about?* Querying ourselves and answering honestly will reveal who we truly are, leading us to repentance and durable faith in Him and finally yielding the fruitful results of salvation to the glory of His Father. Jeremiah was occupied with similar questions when the people of Judah began to live in repeated disobedience to God's covenant. He asked:

> *...From the least to the greatest, all are greedy for gain; prophets and priests alike, all practice deceit. They dress the wound of my people as though it were not serious. "Peace, peace," they say, when there is no peace...We hoped for peace but no good has come, for a time of healing but there was only terror....Is there no balm in Gilead? Is there no physician there? Why then is there no healing for the wound of my people?* (Jer. 8:10–11, 15, 22).

When the people of Judah refused to heed God's Word as proclaimed by the prophet Jeremiah, they fell miserably into the hands of the invading army of King Nebuchadnezzer of Babylon in 586B.C. That serves as a warning to all nations to accept His commandments. As vulnerable human beings, we've learned from the Holy Scriptures the sad but inevitable truth that disobedience to His Word often results in disgrace or death.

It's rightly been said that "choice determines destiny." On the one hand, if we choose God's Way, we have eternal life here and now; hereafter, we'll live eternally with Him and His Son in heaven. On the other hand, if we decide to strike out on our own or follow Satan's path, we'll live a mere *lifestyle* rather than a meaningful, fulfilling *life*. Then, of course, we'll face condemnation before His judgment seat after this earthly life (Rom. 14:12; 1 Cor. 5:10), finally to be cast into hell together with the Devil, as declared by Jesus (Matt. 25:41).

Dear friends, we need not remain carnal Christians. The good news is that even though we can't change our pasts, we can definitely do something positive about our destiny by trusting Jesus as

> **We can definitely do something positive about our destiny by trusting Jesus as our Lord and Savior**

our Lord and Savior. That means we take His Word seriously, meditate on it day and night, and pray without ceasing toward victorious Christian living. Thus, we become, as Paul put it, "…God's workmanship, created in Christ Jesus to do good works…" (Eph. 2:10). Conversely, you can choose to remain carnal, tossed about by every wind of doctrine and unable to bear fruit or lead a meaningful life. I want to encourage you to decide for Christ.

The Two Types of People in the World

There are people whom the scriptures classify either as the children of God or minions of the Devil. In other words, there are people living in the light and those in darkness. Does this surprise you? Let's find out from the words of Jesus Christ as He speaks to a religious group of Jews as follows:

> *"I know you are Abraham's descendants. Yet you are ready to kill me, because you have no room for my word. I am telling you what I have seen in the Father's presence, and you do what you have heard from your father." "Abraham is our father," they answered. "If you were Abraham's children," said Jesus, "then you would do the things Abraham did. As it is, you are determined to kill me, a man who has told you the truth that I heard from God. Abraham did not do such things. You are doing the things your own father does"…* (John 8:37–41).

Then the Jews vehemently protested, saying: "…'We are not illegitimate children…The only Father we have is God Himself' " (8:41). Jesus replied with the truthful words that would set them wild with rage:

> *"…If God were your Father, you would love me, for I came from God and now am here. I have not come on my own; but he sent me. Why is my language not clear to you? Because you are unable to hear what I say. You belong to your father, the devil, and you want to carry out your father's desire. He was a murderer from the beginning, not holding to the truth, for there is no truth in him. When he lies, he speaks his native language, for he is a liar and the father of lies. Yet because I tell the truth, you do not believe me! Can any of you prove me guilty of sin? If I am telling the truth, why don't you believe me? He who belongs to God hears what God says. The reason you do not hear is that you do not belong to God"* (8:42–47).

He made it clear to the Jews that in seeking to kill Him Who was telling the truth (the Good News) that would save them and the rest of humankind from sin and hell, they weren't only trying to prevent others from entering the Kingdom of God, but also doing exactly what the Devil always does: "…to steal and kill and destroy…" (John 10:10). Therefore, by plotting to kill Jesus, which they did anyway in the end, they had become indeed Satan's agents for destruction. God's children, on the other hand, are agents for righteousness in the world. "Righteousness exalts a nation, but sin is a disgrace to any people" (Prov. 14:34).

A Disciple of the Lord Becomes a "Devil"

What a shock to discover that Jesus finds a "devil" among His own close friends, I mean His own Disciples. Can you believe or imagine this? It's a conundrum to many Bible students to grasp Jesus' referring to Judas Iscariot as a devil in the following statement: " '…Have I not chosen you, the Twelve? Yet one of you is a devil!' " (John 6:70). John's explanation points to the person He was referring to, "(He meant Judas, the son of Simon Iscariot, who, though one of the Twelve, was later to betray Him)" (6:71).

All four gospels testify that Judas was one of the Disciples chosen by Jesus to be among His followers. For three-and-a-half years, they journeyed with their Master and had a closer relationship with Him than anyone else. They witnessed His miracles: the healing of the blind (9:1–7), the raising of Lazarus from the dead (11:38–44), the healing of lepers (e.g., Matt. 8:1–4), and the casting out of demons (Mark 5:1–20) and many others that space doesn't allow me to mention here.

The question vexing the minds of many is: *How did Judas become a "devil" at this point in Jesus' ministry?* The answer is that he had agreed to betray Christ to His enemies for a fee of 30 pieces of silver (Matt. 27:3). It had also become apparent that while following his Master for over three years, he didn't fully yield his heart to Him. In other words, he wasn't completely committed to Christ and His teachings as were the other eleven Disciples. Hence, "…the devil prowls around like a roaring lion looking for someone to devour" (1 Pet. 5:8), discovering and then entering a hiding place in Judas' empty heart (John 13:21–27; Matt. 12:43–45). From then on, he became Satan's vehicle to be used at the right time.

I see this as very troubling and a warning to all of us who avow our Christianity. There's a need for daily self-examination in making firm our stand in the Lord lest we fall (1 Cor. 10:13). We can't cheat or mock Him; our hypocrisy will eventually be exposed. As the Scripture declares:

> *Do not be deceived: God cannot be mocked. A man reaps what he sows. The one who sows to please his sinful nature, from that nature will reap destruction; the one who sows to please the Spirit, from the Spirit will reap eternal life* (Gal. 6:7–8).

My questions to you as you read these words of Scripture are: *Whose child are you? Are you on the Lord's side or on the Devil's? Are you bearing the fruit of the Spirit of God* — "…*love, joy, peace, patience, kindness, goodness, faithfulness, gentleness and self-control…*" (5:22–23) —*which identifies His true children? Or are you showing the Devil's traits* —*manifested in acts of wickedness:* "…*sexual immorality, impurity and debauchery; idolatry and witchcraft; hatred, discord, jealousy, fits of rage, selfish ambition, dissensions, factions and envy; drunkenness, orgies, and the like…*"? (5:19–21).

What is your answer to these questions? The main question you must consider is a simple one, but

It's not *What do you think of a certain religion?*

It's not *What do you think of Christians?*

It's not *What good works have you done lately?*

It's not *What are the traditions of your church?*

The main question that stands between every human and God is this: *What are you going to do with Jesus?*

He said, "…'I am the way and the truth and the life. No one comes to the Father except through me' " (John 14:6). Paul and Silas said, "…'Believe in the Lord Jesus, and you will be saved—you and your household' " (Acts 16:31). And Luke wrote, " 'Salvation is found in no one else, for there is no other name under heaven given to men by which we must be saved' " (4:12). Paul further said that "…God was reconciling the world to himself in Christ…" (2 Cor. 5:19).

The message is clear: faith in Jesus is the only way to His Father. *So what are you going to do with Him?* Will you permit a philosopher's deceptive words or a translator's semantic tricks to make you reject or mistrust the Savior? Will you let the musings of mere humans carry more weight than the message of Almighty God?

Please take Jesus at His word. Put your faith in His sacrifice for your sins on the cross of Calvary and you'll find the joy of being set free from the penalty of sin. *What will you do with Him?* That is the most important question you'll ever have to answer (*Daily Bread*, May 2007, adapted from *Who Is This Man Who Says He's God?* 1988, 2000, 2002, RBC Ministries).

This is the time for thorough and honest self-examination in the light of His Word, to discover where you truly stand in order to make a wise and concrete decision once and for all that will settle your destiny. You're either for God in heaven or Satan in hell. Jesus made it clear in Matthew's Gospel that hellfire was primarily "…prepared for the devil and his angels" (Matt. 25:41), but not for human beings.

What then must we do to get on the side of God, Whom to know means eternal life through His Son? The right answer may be found in the words of Pastor Scotty Smith of Christ Church in Nashville: "Instead of turning to lesser gods to fill a void, we must be willing to face our pain and trust the Lord for deliverance."

Now, brothers and sisters, as Smith experienced in his own spiritual journey, "healing begins with realizing that our hearts are bored, discontent, anxious, empty, or restless." According to him, God's ultimate purpose is "to win our hearts from things that hold no ultimate satisfaction." Therefore, the best way for us as individuals, regardless of our race, to restore our broken relationship with God and with one another, is to be honest among ourselves and before Him.

David's Sin with Bathsheba

Let's look briefly at the life of David, who as God's chosen king of Israel misused his authority. One evening, as he was strolling on the rooftop of his palace, he spotted the beautiful Bathsheba in the distance, invited her into his palace and committed adultery with her. Her husband, Uriah, one of Israel's most loyal soldiers, was with his fellow soldiers under the command of Joab, fighting against the Ammonites on the battlefield.

In an effort to conceal his sin, David sent orders to Joab to permit Uriah to come home. When Uriah arrived, the king tried to persuade him to go home to his wife, but he refused; his thoughts were with his fellow soldiers in battle. Since David couldn't get Uriah to do what he wanted, he finally sent him back with orders for Capt. Joab, requesting him to place the soldier in the fiercest part of the battlefront where he could be killed. Joab obeyed the king's orders and, as might be expected, Uriah was pierced by an enemy's arrow and died instantly.

Nevertheless, when God's Word came to the prophet Nathan to confront David with the sins of adultery with Bathsheba and the murder of her husband, the king instantly admitted it to them and said to him: "…'I have sinned against the LORD'…" (2 Sam. 12:13).

The following is part of David's classic prayer of confession and a plea for forgiveness, passionately sought before God:

> *Have mercy on me, O God, according to your unfailing love; according to your great compassion blot out my transgressions. Wash away all my iniquity and cleanse me from my sin. For I know my transgressions, and my sin is always before me. Against you, you only, have I sinned and done what is evil in your sight, so that you are proved right when you speak and justified when you judge* (Ps. 51:1–4).

Just as the king humbly acknowledged and confessed his sin before the Almighty and pleaded for forgiveness—and was indeed forgiven and restored—so must we come to Him to be saved.

CHAPTER 14

*J*ust as King David sincerely admitted his sins before God and humbly asked His forgiveness, so must we—irrespective of race, color, rank or sex—when convicted of sin, admit ours in His presence.

We Must All Acknowledge Our Sins to God

*L*ike David, we should, without hesitation, plead forgiveness for the sins of pride, idolatry, selfishness, greediness, etc. committed against God and our fellow human beings. The Bible declares in the prophecy of Isaiah, "We all, like sheep, have gone astray, each of us has turned to his own way; and the LORD has laid on him the iniquity of us all" (Isa. 53:6).

In his classic theological epistle to the believers in Rome, Paul reiterated the depravity of the human condition: " 'There is no one righteous, not even one…All have turned away, they have together become worthless…all have sinned and fall short of the glory of God' " (Rom. 3:10, 12, 23). Then and now, it serves as a timely warning to those relying on their own righteousness for salvation.

A good example of such people is the rich, young ruler who came to Jesus with a question: " 'Good teacher, what must I do to inherit eternal life?' " (Luke 18:18). He answered him unequivocally, saying:

"Why do you call me good?" Jesus answered. "No one is good—except God alone. You know the commandments: 'Do not commit adultery, do not murder, do not steal, do not give false testimony, honor your father and mother.' " "All

these I have kept since I was a boy," he said. When Jesus heard this, he said to him, "You still lack one thing. Sell everything you have and give to the poor, and you will have treasure in heaven. Then come, follow me." When he heard this, he became very sad, because he was a man of great wealth. Jesus looked at him and said, "How hard it is for the rich to enter the kingdom of God!" (Luke 18:19–24)

As you might've observed from the context, despite his desire to follow the path toward the Kingdom of God, he was unwilling to relinquish the "one thing" that was an obstacle in the way: his wealth. This isn't to say that Jesus condemned riches or wealth, for "Every good and perfect gift is from above..." (James 1:17). We know that "...it is [God] who gives you the ability to produce wealth..." (Deut. 8:18).

But if material things become the life-and-death objects of our love, then surely we've chosen the way that leads to evil and destruction (Prov. 14:12). Thus, wealth becomes our god, an idol we worship instead of our Creator. Such devotion to things He created—whether the moon, stars or angels—is a rebellion against Him and His commandments (Exod. 20:2–6; 1 Tim 6:10).

Jesus further illustrated a similar self-righteous attitude with the following story:

"Two men went up to the temple to pray, one a Pharisee and the other a tax collector. The Pharisee stood up and prayed about himself: 'God, I thank you that I am not like other men—robbers, evildoers, adulterers—or even like this tax collector. I fast twice a week and give a tenth of all I get.' But the tax collector stood at a distance. He would not even look up to heaven, but beat his breast and said, 'God, have mercy on me, a sinner.' I tell you that this man, rather than the other, went home justified before God. For everyone who exalts himself will be humbled, and he who humbles himself will be exalted" (Luke 18:10–14).

He is teaching the religious Jews—as well as all of us—the need to show humility in the presence of His Father. Therefore, we must come before Him, not with a high opinion of ourselves, but with a spirit of humility and a penitent heart and, like David, ask Him for forgiveness:

Have mercy on me, O God, according to your unfailing love; according to your great compassion blot out my transgressions. Wash away all my iniquity and cleanse me from my sin...The sacrifices of God are a broken spirit; a broken and contrite heart, O God, you will not despise (Ps. 51:1–2, 17).

Conversely, Scripture warns us, "If we claim to be without sin, we deceive ourselves and the truth is not in us." But God's promise is that "If we confess our sins, he is faithful and just and will forgive us our sins and purify us from all unrighteousness" (1 John 1:8–9).

The hymn writer William Cowper puts it this way:

> There is a fountain filled with blood
> Drawn from Immanuel's veins;
> And sinners, plunged beneath that flood,
> Lose all their guilty stains.
>
> The dying thief rejoiced to see
> That fountain in his day;
> And there may I, though as vile as he,
> Wash all my sins away.
> (*MHB*, 201, verses 1–2)

Just as expressed in the above hymn, Ghanaian ancestors echoed the same Biblical truth illustrated in the Adinkra patterns on page 19, declaring that "the Son of God offered Himself as a sacrificial lamb for the salvation of the household."

In the days before the dawn of Christianity, our fathers offered either a sheep, goat or cow to pacify the gods whenever someone in the community had been found guilty of a wicked act. The Jews, too, offered animal sacrifices when they sought God's forgiveness through the priests in the temple, according to the Old Testament law or tradition in Leviticus 17:11.

But the great difference is that their sacrifice was offered to God — the Supreme Being, the Creator — and not to lesser gods or spirits of the dead, as in the manner of our African ancestors. Still, as pointed out by the writer to the Hebrews, "…it is impossible for the blood of bulls and goats to take away sins" (Heb. 10:4). The next section shows us the sacrifice perfectably acceptable to God toward the forgiveness of our sins.

Christ's Sacrifice for Our Sins Was Perfect

Since Jesus was conceived by the Holy Spirit and not by the seed of man (Luke 1:35–38; John 1:1, 14), He did not inherit the depravity, natural characteristics or tendencies of humanity to sin, which all human beings inherited from Adam and Eve. For He was mysteriously fully human and fully God. Hence, the Bible speaks of Him as "…one who has been tempted in every way, just as we are—yet was without sin." (4:15). Concerning His sacrificial death for our redemption, He Himself declared :

> ..."*Sacrifice and offering you did not desire, but a body you prepared for me; with burnt offerings and sin offerings you were not pleased. Then I said, 'Here I am—it is written about me in the scroll—I have come to do your will, O God'*" (Heb. 10:5–7).

By setting aside the Old Covenant—with its ritual sacrifices and offerings that couldn't remove sins—He willingly offered the body prepared for him. "And by that will," the writer continues, "we have been made holy through the sacrifice of the body of Jesus Christ once for all...because by one sacrifice he has made perfect forever those who are being made holy" (10:10, 14). Paul explains this further in his letter to the Romans:

> *Consequently, just as the result of one trespass was condemnation for all men, so also the result of one act of righteousness was justification that brings life for all men. For just as through the disobedience of the one man the many were made sinners, so also through the obedience of the one man the many will be made righteous* (Rom. 5:18–19).

Let me remind you that just as in the African traditional religion—wherein an elder of the family or clan offers a chicken/lamb/goat/cow as sacrifice to the gods in the belief that the ritual will atone for *musu/musuo* (sin or calamity)—so did the priests on behalf of Israelites. However, the Scriptures declare emphatically to us all—whether we're white or black, Jew or Asian—that "the blood of bulls cannot take away sins." It cannot deliver us from either Satan or eternal condemnation in hellfire on the Day of Judgment (Eccl. 12:14; Matt. 25:41–46). What then must we do to escape God's judgment of eternal fire awaiting the impenitent heart or the hardened criminal?

Come with a Penitent Heart and Mind

What is repentance? As I understand it, it's more than "feeling sorry for wrongdoing." It's an act of actually turning away from error, confessing sin, forsaking our own wrongful way of life and taking the hand of Jesus Christ. It's believing in Him as our Savior: "God made him who had no sin to be sin for us, so that in him we might become the righteousness of God" (2 Cor. 5:21).

Paul puts it this way: "Do not conform any longer to the pattern of this world, but be transformed by the renewing of your mind..." (Rom. 12:2). True and sincere repentance therefore inevitably results in a transformation of life, as we find, for example, in the parable of the prodigal son (Luke 15:11– 24).

According to Jesus, the young man first acknowledged his sin and didn't blame anyone for it or its consequences. Second, he remembered his father's generosity, mercy, hired ser-vants and the abundance of provisions he had made available for his household. Third, believing in the loving kindness of his father, he arose from his miserable situation and returned home with a pen-itent heart. Then, as the story unfolds, we are told that " '...while he was still a long way off, his father saw him and was filled with compassion for him; he ran to his son, threw his arms around him and kissed him' " (15:20).

> **Believing in the loving kindness of his father, he arose from his miserable situation and returned home**

Guess what happened to this prodigal son! He was completely for-given and clothed with "the best robe;" a ring was put on his finger and a pair of new sandals on his feet.

The best robe he received was a practical demonstration of the hon-or that the father accorded his son. Spiritually speaking: "...he has clothed me with garments of salvation..." (Isa. 61:10), referring to the gift of new birth or life that God freely gives to all who turn to Him with repentance and faith in His Son.

"The ring on his finger" was symbolic of the father's acceptance of his son, while "the sandals on his feet" indicated that he had been whol-ly reinstated as an equally beloved and worthy family member, not "like one of your hired men," as the son had previously proposed on his way home (Luke 15:19).

We need to understand that the story of the prodigal son depicts what God does for any sinner turning to Him with repentance. The joy-ful reception and celebration attending his homecoming indicates that " '...there is rejoicing in the presence of the angels of God over one sin-ner who repents' " as Jesus declared in Luke 15:10. It's an assurance of the complete salvation His Father graciously offers everyone —black or white, young or old, man or woman—truly repenting of sins in seeking His forgiveness and the change of life through faith in Jesus.

Similarly, when King David came before God to confess his sins, he did so with "…a broken and contrite heart…" (Ps. 51:17), seeking a complete renewal of life. He didn't come with a lamb as sacrifice for his sins. The following is a portion of his prayer of confession:

> *Create in me a pure heart, O God, and renew a steadfast spirit within me…You do not delight in sacrifice, or I would bring it; you do not take pleasure in burnt offerings. The sacrifices of God are a broken spirit; a broken and contrite heart, O God, you will not despise* (Ps. 51:10, 16–17).

In response to God's invitation, let's come with true, penitent hearts in sincerely confessing our sins to the Lord, asking not only for forgiveness and cleansing from sin, but also a complete change of life through the transforming power of His Holy Spirit, through faith in His Son:

> *"Come now, let us reason together," says the LORD. "Though your sins are like scarlet, they shall be as white as snow; though they are red as crimson, they shall be like wool. If you are willing and obedient, you will eat the best from the land; but if you resist and rebel, you will be devoured by the sword." For the mouth of the LORD has spoken* (Isa. 1:18-20).

Christ's Death on the Cross Is the Greatest Miracle of God in the Redemption of Humanity from Sin

Through this vision, the Holy Spirit has taught me to understand that Christ's death on the cross was the means by which God wrought the greatest miracle on earth: humankind's salvation by grace through faith in His Son. In that one single event, the Almighty redeemed for Himself all human beings—white or black, men or women, adults or children, bound or free—who truthfully repent and confess their personal faith in Jesus as their Lord and Savior.

His crucifixion proved to be our substitute sacrifice, redeeming humankind from its sins and consequences (Rom. 6:23). As His Father's sacrificial lamb (Heb. 10:12; John 1:29), He also removed the original sin's curse inherited from our first parents in Eden. By purging our sins through His precious blood, Christ has both justified and perfected forever those coming to His Father through Him, as declared in Hebrews 10:14.

That's why I deem it such significant and insightful artistry that our ancestors could intuitively design each of the Adinkra patterns on page 19 to contain the symbol of a cross. I believe that whether they realized it or not, it was the Holy Spirit Who led them to produce such wonderful workmanship speaking so eloquently about Him (*Nyame*) and the sacrifice of His Son—the Lamb of God—for the redemption of humankind. Isn't that amazing?

Paul wrote as follows to the Colossians concerning the miracle-working power of the cross:

> *When you were dead in your sins and in the uncircumcision of your sinful nature, God made you alive with Christ. He forgave us all our sins, having canceled the written code, with its regulations, that was against us and that stood opposed to us; he took it away, nailing it to the cross. And having disarmed the powers and authorities, he made a public spectacle of them, triumphing over them by the cross* (Col. 2:13–15).

It follows that all who truly believe in Christ are no longer slaves to sin. As Paul writes, "For sin shall not be your master, because you are not under law, but under grace" (Rom. 6:14). Through this grace, believers are empowered to lead a new life of righteousness, made possible by the indwelling power of the Holy Spirit. Hence, Paul boldly stated, "Therefore, if anyone is in Christ, he is a new creation; the old has gone, the new has come! All this is from God, who reconciled us to himself through Christ and gave us the ministry of reconciliation" (2 Cor. 5:17–18).

In Christ, the sinner is thus changed into a saint, while the spiritually dead person is quickened and made alive, the afflicted healed (Isa. 43:19–21, 53:4–5; Matt. 8:17). These were some of the miracles foretold signifying the Messianic Age (e.g., Isa. 11, 35:1–10). If we don't consider these as the greatest miracles God has performed—and continues to do among humankind—then I don't know what else can appeal to us as the greatest miracle people can experience. And who else is capable of making it happen? No one has power to do these things except Him. Hence, Nicodemus recognized Christ's divine power and rightly admitted: "…'Rabbi, we know you are a teacher who has come from God. For no one could perform the miraculous signs you are doing if God were not with him'" (John 3:2).

Again, Paul emphasized the same truth when he wrote to the converts in the city of Ephesus about the new way of life into which believers had entered by virtue of their faith in Jesus Christ. He declared:

> *You were taught, with regard to your former way of life, to put off your old self,*
> *which is being corrupted by its deceitful desires; to be made new in the attitude*
> *of your minds; and to put on the new self, created to be like God in true right-*
> *eousness and holiness* (Eph. 4:22–24).

From these two references above, Paul underscores the undeniable fact that true believers really have a new life quite different from the previous, a rebirth created and controlled by the indwelling Holy Spirit. Hence, the Bible declares that "those who are led by the Spirit of God are sons of God" (Rom. 8:14), because their new life reflects the fruit of the Spirit (Gal. 5:22), similar to the character of the Creator. Thus, believers are privileged to be indwelt by the Holy Spirit and classified as partakers of the Kingdom of God.

The concept of a new life in His Kingdom was the primary goal of His Son's ministry. All the miracles He performed were signs of His claim to be God, thereby establishing in the midst of humanity the presence of His Kingdom.

Anyone in the U.S. who's seen Mel Gibson's film *The Passion of the Christ* bears witness to the power of its appeal to moviegoers. According to *People* magazine, *The Passion of the Christ* had earned an astounding $300 million at the box office as of this writing, defying all expectations. According to a March Gallup poll, nearly 45% of Americans have either seen the film or say they intend to—evidence that its draw extends far beyond evangelical Christians (April 5, 2004, p. 95).

There have been several testimonials of healing and conversions after experiencing the film's powerful message. For instance, a man who had murdered his girlfriend and kept the crime secret for a decade could no longer hide his sin after watching how much pain Jesus had to endure at Calvary. On leaving the theater, he confessed to the slaying and handed himself over to the police. Surely, there's power in the cross, and it works unimaginable wonders.

It was anticipated that by the end of the following few week or so, the film would have brought in a record amount of more than $500 million. Thanks be to God for the marvelous gift of His Son for the redemption of humankind.

The Purpose of the Miracles of Christ

He did other wondrous things to encourage men and women everywhere to "…believe that Jesus is the Christ, the Son of God, and that by believing you may have life in his name" (John 20:31). For instance, at the wedding ceremony in Cana, during which He turned water into wine, John wrote: "This, the first of his miraculous signs, Jesus performed in Cana of Galilee. He thus revealed his glory, and his disciples put their faith in him" (2:11).

The New Testament Gospel writers recorded several other miracles performed during the course of His ministry. He made a bed-ridden man completely whole to demonstrate His authority to both heal the sick and forgive sins. With a young boy's meal of five loaves and two fish, He fed 5,000, not counting women and children, and still had 12 baskets of food left over (6:1–13). Thus, He fulfilled His claim as "…the bread of life…," (6:35) and having "…streams of living water…" (7:38).

He walked on water and stilled the raging seas to affirm His power over nature (Mark 4:35–41). He cast out demons to set captives free, healed the sick and restored paralyzed limbs. He cleansed lepers and opened the eyes of the blind. He enabled the deaf to hear and the dumb to speak. All this was done to fulfill what had been said about the Messiah through the prophet Isaiah: "Surely he took up our infirmities and carried our sorrows…" (Isa. 53:4; *also* Matt. 8:17).

Above all, He raised a man named Lazarus from the dead after he had been buried four days in a tomb. This confirmed His claim to be "…the resurrection and the life…" (John 11:25).

As I've already pointed out, these wonders were done to fulfill Christ's claim to be the Son of God, the Messiah—"…that this man really is the Savior of the world," as even the Samaritans admitted (4:42). Surely, no one can claim the power to save humanity except God, through the miracle of His Son's death on the cross.

The beloved apostle John concluded his Gospel with the following: "Jesus did many other miraculous signs in the presence of his disciples, which are not recorded in this book. But these are written that you may believe that Jesus is the Christ, the Son of God, and that by believing you may have life in his name" (20:30–31).

The salient point here is that Christ provides healing and new life to all confessing faith in Him. That's why John emphatically stated in the last chapter of his epistle: "And this is the testimony: God has given us eternal life, and this life is in his Son. He who has the Son has life; he who does not have the Son of God does not have life" (1 John 5:11–12)

What does he mean by "life" in this context? Surely, he's not talking about our temporal existence on earth. As in many passages in his

Gospel, he's certainly referring not only to everlasting life, but also one of personal, spiritual relationship with God the Father, Son and Holy Spirit. This quality of life is supernatural, one that He alone has the power to give those turning their back to the world and coming to Him for salvation through faith in His Son. This is the eternal life the Holy Spirit creates in us the moment we receive Jesus into our lives as our Savior and Lord.

Everlasting life, therefore, begins here and now in this earthly life, with Christ in us, and continues beyond death for evermore with His Father in heaven. According to the Scriptures, nothing—not even death—can separate believers from that bond of eternal life. With un-flinching conviction, Paul thus writes in his epistle to the Romans:

> *Who shall separate us from the love of Christ? Shall trouble or hardship or persecution or famine or nakedness or danger or sword? As it is written: "For your sake we face death all day long; we are considered as sheep to be slaugh-tered." No, in all these things we are more than conquerors through him who loved us. For I am convinced that neither death nor life, neither angels nor demons, neither the present nor the future, nor any powers, neither height nor depth, nor anything else in all creation, will be able to separate us from the love of God that is in Christ Jesus our Lord* (Rom. 8:35–39).

That's the great assurance of the security Christianity offers to all be-lievers in Him—that He died to save us from our sins and, lives again to preserve forever those He has saved. For example, in the commis-sioning of His Apostles after the resurrection, Jesus's last words were, "…All authority in heaven and on earth has been given to me. There-fore go and make disciples of all nations, baptizing them in the name of the Father and of the Son and of the Holy Spirit, and teaching them to obey everything I have commanded you. And surely I am with you al-ways, to the very end of the age." (Matt. 28:18–20).

Always with You

With these words of Christ's promise in mind, Cindy Hess Kasper tells the following family story:

> The highway that winds around the southern shore of Lake Michigan can be treacherous in the winter. One weekend as we were driving back to Grand Rapids from Chicago, a buildup of snow and ice slowed traffic, caused numerous accidents, and almost doubled our drive time. We were relieved as we eased off the expressway

onto our final road. It was then that my husband said out loud, "Thanks, Lord. I think I can take it from here."

Just as he finished saying the words, our car spun around 180 degrees. As we came to a stop, hearts pounding, we could just imagine God saying: "Are you sure?"

Why do we sometimes try to go it alone in life when at every moment we have access to God? He said: "I am with you and will keep you wherever you go" (Gen. 28:15). And He assures us: "I will never leave you nor forsake you" (Heb. 13:5).

Scottish mathematician, theologian, and preacher Thomas Chalmers (1780–1847) wrote: "When I walk by the wayside, He is along with me. When I enter into company, amid all my forgetfulness of Him, He never forgets me…Go where I will, He tends me, and watches me, and cares for me."

What a comfort to know that God is always with us—we don't need to go through life alone!

> As I travel down life's pathway,
> Jesus keeps me day by day;
> And although the road is winding,
> Yet, with Him I need not stray.
> —Bradshaw

(*Daily Bread*, January 2, 2010)

With the Cross, the Bitter Turns Sweet

Whenever believers focus on the cross, they receive extraordinary grace from God to overcome their problems through the ever-abiding presence of Christ with His people. In David Roper's view, this was exemplified in the Israelites' lives as they journeyed to the Promised Land. Commenting on Israel's wilderness experience, Roper said,

> Joy and sorrow are often close companions. Just as the Israelites went from the thrill of victory at the Red Sea to the bitter waters of Marah just 3 days later (Exod. 15:22-23), our rejoicing can quickly turn into anguish.
>
> At Marah, the Lord told Moses to throw a tree into the water, which made it "sweet" and drinkable (verse 25). Another "tree," when "cast into" the bitter circumstances of our lives, can make them sweet. It is the cross of Jesus (1 Pet. 2:24). Our outlook will be transformed as we contemplate His sacrificial death and His submission to the will of God (Luke 22:42).
>
> Our pain may come from the ill-will of others, or worse, from their neglect. Nevertheless, our Lord has permitted it. We may not

understand why, yet it is the will of our Father and Friend, whose wisdom and love are infinite.

When we say yes to God as His Spirit reveals His will to us through His Word, the bitter circumstances of our lives can become sweet. We must not grumble against what the Lord permits. Instead, we must do all that He asks us to do. Jesus said that we are to take up our cross daily and follow Him (Luke 9:23).

When we remember Jesus's cross and submit to the Father as He did, bitter experiences can become sweet.

I completely agree with Roper in concluding that, "God uses our difficulties to make us better—not bitter" (*Daily Bread*, January 27, 2004).

At this point, it's quite appropriate for us to turn our focus to the next chapter for a brief discussion of yet another miracle, perhaps the greatest miracle about which the most has ever been written: the resurrection of Jesus Christ and its implications for believers and non-believers alike.

CHAPTER 15

The Resurrection of Jesus Christ

*T*he rising of Jesus Christ from death on the third day after His burial is a critical event and one of the most remarkable dimensions of His life and mission. The resurrection impacted His early followers, the Disciples, and ultimately, of course, the rise of Christianity. Indeed, without His resurrection, the purpose of His sacrificial death on the cross at Calvary would have been incomplete: sin would otherwise have triumphed over righteousness, and evil overcome virtue in the world.

There would have been no ultimate moral standard for humanity to follow, and our behavior would have been relative, depending on our own human judgment, which differs one from the other. There would have been no hope in this life or in any future existence. It profoundly changed the course of history.

As Paul put it, "Then those also who have fallen asleep in Christ are lost. If only for this life we have hope in Christ, we are to be pitied more than all men" (1 Cor. 15:18–19). Hope is what we expect for the future; for without it, guess who would have rejoiced and reigned as *king* and *lord* over humanity and the entire universe? It certainly wouldn't have been one of the patriarchs or prophets, not Abraham, Isaac, Jacob, Moses, Elijah; not a god or ancestor of any earthly race, but the enemy of God and of humankind, the Devil. "But thanks be to God!..." (15:57) that in His divine wisdom, He used the death of "...his one and only Son..." (John 3:16), Jesus Christ, to defeat forever His enemies and Satan's wicked plot. It's written:

...."Death has been swallowed up in victory. Where, O death, is your victory? Where, O death, is your sting?" The sting of death is sin, and the power of sin is the law. But thanks be to God! He gives us the victory through our Lord Jesus Christ (1 Cor. 15:54–57).

Jesus, the Great Overcomer

Commenting on the resurrection of Jesus, Mart De Haan of RBC Ministries described Him as The Great Overcomer. In addition, he said, "Jesus made the most amazing comeback the world has ever seen. After being humiliated, insulted, spit upon, whipped, beaten and nailed to a cross, His executioners claimed victory and declared Him dead. A military guard secured His tomb. How could anyone be more down and out than that?

"Yet the struggle was not over; it was only the beginning. Three days later, He rose from the grave and reappeared as the victor over sin, death, and hell—a comeback like no other in all of history. No one has overcome like our Lord." De Haan concluded with the following poem by Branon:

> The great example is our Lord
> Of overcoming power;
> The strength that brought Him from the grave
> Gives hope in life's dark hour

What the Resurrection Means to Believers

In God's plan of salvation, the death and resurrection of His Son have one purpose: to redeem humankind from the Devil's dominion of sin's power and deadly consequences. This was necessary so that all who believe in Christ might live in a new life of righteousness, joy, peace and hope (Gal. 5:22). The rebirth imparted by the Holy Spirit in every believer is made possible by the power of Jesus' presence: "…'I am making everything new!'…" (Rev. 21:5). "Therefore," said Paul, "if anyone is in Christ, he is a new creation; the old has gone, the new has come!" (2 Cor. 5:17).

For example, let's take a look at Peter's life before the crucifixion. We know from Scripture that Jesus appointed him to be the leader of the Disciples (Luke 22: 31–32) and was given " '…the keys of the kingdom of heaven…' " (Matt. 16:19)—authority to win souls into the Church of Christ—after he had made his great confession of Christ in Caesarea Philippi.

We all know how woefully Peter denied Him three times during His trial before the rooster crowed, just as He had predicted (26:69–75). Realizing how much he had failed his Master, he wept bitterly with shame and sorrow. Nevertheless, after Jesus had risen from the dead, He appeared to Peter and six other Disciples by the Sea of Tiberias. Knowing they had caught no fish, He compassionately directed them to make a big catch. When they had drawn the net to the shore where He was, He prepared some of the fish and said to them, "…'Come and have breakfast'…" (John 21:12). The beloved disciple John continues:

> *…None of the disciples dared ask him, "Who are you?" They knew it was the Lord. Jesus came, took the bread and gave it to them, and did the same with the fish. This was now the third time Jesus appeared to his disciples after he was raised from the dead* (21:12–14).

Having dined with them to regain their trust that He truly was Jesus, He gave Peter the second chance to affirm his faith in Him by asking the same question three times: "…'Simon son of John, do you truly love me…?' " When he answered in the affirmative, Christ said to him: "Feed my sheep" (21:15–18). He indicated by these words His forgiveness and acceptance of Peter into His fold as a leader of His flock, thus affording him a second chance to affirm his loyalty to Him and the Church, regardless of his failure to stand the test of discipleship.

Following are a few of the Resurrection's lessons I would like to share with you. First, the risen Christ brings joy and peace to replace sorrow and weeping. Mary Magdalene, overcome with grief at the crucifixion, stood in the graveyard weeping. But when Jesus appeared and gently called her by name, she turned toward Him and responded in Aramaic "Rabboni!" (Teacher) (20:13–16). In the presence of the risen Christ, her sadness and tears instantly vanished like vapor, replaced by an unspeakable contentment no one could take from her.

Furthermore, without His resurrection, there would have been no Peter of the sort we read about in the Acts of the Apostles, let alone his first and second Epistles. Jesus had previously cautioned the Disciples: " '…apart from me you can do nothing' " (15:5). Therefore, Simon Peter became a person with whom the first-century world could reckon—the leader of the Apostles and of the Church in Jerusalem. Why? By His resurrection, Jesus had overcome death and given His follow-

> **The Apostles had not only the courage to pursue the mission of Jesus, but also hope for eternal life**

ers, led by Peter, the power to be His witnesses " '…in Jerusalem, and in all Judea and Samaria, and to the ends of the earth' " (Acts 1:8; *also* Mark 16:15; Matt. 28:18–20).

With His resurrection and the assurance of His abiding presence among them, the Apostles no longer feared death or persecution. They had not only the courage to pursue His cause, but also hope for eternal life (John 14:1–3, 11:25–26; Luke 18:29). Indeed, the resurrection brought transformation in His followers' lives, and they remained bonded together in one spirit, "constantly in prayer, along with the women and Mary the mother of Jesus, and with his brothers" (Acts 1:14).

How about Paul? Without the resurrection, there would have been just " '…a man from Tarsus named Saul…' " (9:11), but no Paul, the Apostle to the Gentiles (26:16–18). As you may remember, he wasn't one of the followers of Christ.

After Pentecost, Saul appeared as a young man watching over the garments of those who stoned Stephen, "…giving his approval to his death" (7:58–8:1). With that, he obtained the high priest's permission to go to Damascus to arrest and imprison any Disciples he might apprehend in the cities and towns. While traveling, he encountered Jesus in a vision and fell to the ground, converted and commissioned with the anointing of the Holy Spirit as an Apostle to the Gentiles.

Thus, Paul boldly began to proclaim His Good News throughout the Gentile world, the defender of a faith he once sought to destroy (9:4–6, 11–12, 16–18, 26). What a wonderful power of God that can transform a killer into a vessel for the salvation of souls! "The LORD has done this," says the Psalmist, "and it is marvelous in our eyes" (Ps. 118:23).

All these transformations in His followers' lives happened because He truly rose from the dead, never to die again. He is seated at the right hand of God, ever-present to intercede for all believers. Saul had pursued salvation in Judaism, failing miserably until Jesus finally revealed Himself and pointed the right way. For " '…apart from me you can do nothing' " (John 15:5).

Why does He make such a claim? He is certainly aware of the

worldly presence of our "…enemy the devil[, who] prowls around like a roaring lion looking for someone to devour" (1 Pet. 5:8). But through belief in Christ, He comes to dwell within us as our Lord and Savior through the power of the Holy Spirit. He becomes our Teacher, Guide, Strength and Wisdom. We become winners over Satan, because "I have overcome the world," says the Lord. Again, He has promised us, saying, "…'Never will I leave you; never will I forsake you' " (Heb. 13:5), and " '…no one can snatch them out of my hand' " (John 10:28). We must believe His promises, because "The one who calls you is faithful and he will do it" (1 Thess. 5:24).

Peter faltered in his walk with Christ, gathered courage, humbly repented and turned to Him. Don't abandon *your* divinely appointed position. No amount of your difficult situation, a sense of failure in your family relationships, obligations or job can be rectified in following Peter's example. "Come near to God and he will come near to you…" (James 4:8), because He is much closer to you than you can imagine.

Even if you've blasphemed against Him, persecuted a number of His followers or hurt members of your family, it's still not too late to turn to Him and ask forgiveness (1 John 1:9). Remember, the chief purpose He was anointed to accomplish here on earth was " '…to preach good news to the poor. He has sent me to proclaim freedom for the prisoners and recovery of sight for the blind, to release the oppressed' " (Luke 4:18). He said, "…I have come that they may have life, and have it to the full" (John 10:10).

Be reminded that Christ's purpose is still being fulfilled in our generation by anointed preachers of the Gospel throughout the world. Right now, He is calling you—especially those of you who, like Peter, are facing difficult situations and temptations in your lives:

> *"Come to me, all you who are weary and burdened, and I will give you rest. Take my yoke upon you and learn from me, for I am gentle and humble in heart, and you will find rest for your souls. For my yoke is easy and my burden is light"* (Matt. 11:28–30).

Dear reader, in case you consider yourself too sinful to come to Jesus, listen to His promise to all who respond to the call, "…whoever comes to me I will never drive away" (John 6:37). Therefore, don't hesitate in surrendering to His open arms—He stands right where you are to receive you as a newborn child in His Father's kingdom. I be-

lieve it was in the light of the encouraging message of Christ to all believers that the Hebrew writer was inspired to pen the following:

> *Since the children have flesh and blood, he too shared in their humanity so
> that by his death he might destroy him who holds the power of death—that is,
> the devil—and free those who all their lives were held in slavery by their fear
> of death…Because he himself suffered when he was tempted, he is able to help
> those who are being tempted* (Heb. 2:14–15, 18).

Always conscious that Jesus had overcome every temptation, suffering and even death, Christians are assured of salvation, hope and the
courage to pursue their daily lives, working diligently in whatever form
of employment or situation they find themselves. They know that
Christ will surely bless and reward them accordingly and that their
good works in Him won't be in vain. It was with similar motivation that
Paul wrote to the Corinthian Church: "Therefore, my dear brothers,
stand firm. Let nothing move you. Always give yourselves fully to the
work of the Lord, because you know that your labor in the Lord is not in
vain" (1 Cor. 15:58; *also* Eph. 6:8).

> What was the power that sustained Peter in accomplishing the task his Master entrusted to him?

The questions to ask are: *How can we stand firm and unmovable in Christ? What was the power that sustained Peter and the other Apostles in accomplishing the task their Master entrusted to them?* In answer, I'm reminded of the following final instructions Jesus gave to His Disciples before ascending into heaven.

> *"All authority in heaven and on earth has been given to me. Therefore go and
> make disciples of all nations, baptizing them in the name of the Father and of
> the Son and of the Holy Spirit, and teaching them to obey everything I have
> commanded you. And surely I am with you always, to the very end of the age"*
> (Matt. 28:18–20).

He was fully aware that the Disciples couldn't carry out the task of
what has since come to be known as the Great Commission until they
were filled with supernatural power. Therefore, He assured them, " 'I
am going to send you what my Father has promised; but stay in the city
until you have been clothed with power from on high' " (Luke 24:49).

Now that you're excited, let's turn quickly to the next chapter to discover how the Disciples were empowered by the Holy Spirit in accomplishing the Master's task: the Great Commission.

CHAPTER 16

*T*he work of the Holy Spirit in our lives as Christians will be taken very seriously if we understand Who the Spirit is and the importance of His role in our lives.

Who Is the Holy Spirit?

He is God. He is the Third Person of the Trinity, co-eternal and co-equal with God the Father and God the Son, and worshipped together with the Godhead. He is the Christian's source of power in living a consistent life of the love and obedience that reflect His glory. The work of the Apostles was made possible by the power of the Holy Spirit Jesus Christ had promised them. Among His final words to the Disciples just before leaving them for His throne in heaven was the following: " '…you will receive power when the Holy Spirit comes on you; and you will be my witnesses in Jerusalem, and in all Judea and Samaria, and to the ends of the earth' " (Acts 1:8). This promise was duly fulfilled on the day of Pentecost, as Luke reported:

> …they were all together in one place. Suddenly a sound like the blowing of a violent wind came from heaven and filled the whole house where they were sitting. They saw what seemed to be tongues of fire that separated and came to rest on each of them. All of them were filled with the Holy Spirit and began to speak in other tongues as the Spirit enabled them (2:1–4).

The Holy Spirit Is for All Believers in Christ

There are people in various churches holding the view that the Holy Spirit is God's gift to special people in the church's leadership positions. They base their argument on the way God's Spirit came upon people called to the prophetic ministry in the Old Testament period (e.g., 1 Sam. 3:10–14; Isa. 6:1–8; Jer. 1:5). It's true that during that era, the Holy Spirit equipped some people for special service to God, yet He had plans to make His gift of the Spirit available to all people. This is evidenced in the prophecy of Joel:

> *"And afterward, I will pour out my Spirit on all people. Your sons and daughters will prophesy, your old men will dream dreams, your young men will see visions. Even on my servants, both men and women, I will pour out my Spirit in those days"* (Joel 2:28–29, also 32; Acts 2:17, 21).

The obvious question to ask here is, *How do we receive the Holy Spirit?* The answer *won't* be found in calling upon other gods or ancestral spirits through libation, but from Peter's anointed message to the large audience listening on the day of Pentecost, as follows:

> *...*"*Repent and be baptized, every one of you, in the name of Jesus Christ for the forgiveness of your sins. And you will receive the gift of the Holy Spirit. The promise is for you and your children and for all who are far off—for all whom the Lord our God will call"* (Acts 2:38–39).

Scripture bears witness that after Peter's sermon, as many as 3,000 converts were added to the company of believers in Jerusalem. Thus, we can confidently say that Pentecost marked the birthday of the Church there. As the Church began to expand, the exclusivity of the Jews as the elect of God began to disintegrate, yielding to His universal evangelism, because it pleased Him to graciously give the Holy Spirit to the Gentile believers, as declared in Peter's message to Cornelius:

> *...*"*I now realize how true it is that God does not show favoritism but accepts men from every nation who fear him and do what is right"...While Peter was still speaking these words, the Holy Spirit came on all who heard the message. The circumcised believers who had come with Peter were astonished that the gift of the Holy Spirit had been poured out even on the Gentiles. For they heard them speaking in tongues and praising God. Then Peter said, "Can anyone keep these people from being baptized with water? They have received the Holy Spirit just as we have." So he ordered that they be baptized in the name of Je-*

sus Christ... (10:34–35, 44–48).

Cornelius and his household were thus incorporated into the universal Church, much to the displeasure of the circumcised believers in Jerusalem (11:1–3). However, Peter's response to their objection clearly pointed out to them that "the LORD has done this, and it is marvelous in our eyes," because " '...what God has joined together, let man not separate' " (Ps. 118:23; Matt. 19:6). His work continues unabated, and no one can stop it until all His purposes are fulfilled.

Since God is just and there's no partiality in Him, His gifts to humanity—Jesus Christ, salvation, the Church, the Holy Spirit and His attributes (1 Cor. 12:4–11; Rom. 12:6–8; Eph. 4:11–13)—are truly meant for all believers, regardless of race, color, rank or sex. This is affirmed by Scripture as follows:

> *You are all sons of God through faith in Christ Jesus, for all of you who were baptized into Christ have clothed yourselves with Christ. There is neither Jew nor Greek, slave nor free, male nor female, for you are all one in Christ Jesus. If you belong to Christ, then you are Abraham's seed, and heirs according to the promise* (Gal. 3:26–29).

It's the work of the Holy Spirit to bring men and women together with our children into one fellowship or family under Jesus Christ, and it can't be achieved by any other god, ancestral spirit, human power, wisdom or scientific knowledge except the Spirit of the Living God.

The Work of the Holy Spirit

The Kingdom of God preached by His Son is universally present and dynamically active through the Holy Spirit. Hence, before Peter—under the guidance of the Holy Spirit (Acts 10:10–15)—could reach the house of Cornelius, the Holy Spirit had already prepared the entire household to receive the Good News.

The Spirit functions in the Church in various forms, such as preaching, healing, worship and sacraments. Nevertheless, I've come to realize through God's revelation that the Spirit appears covertly in secular structures. The Holy Spirit—the presence of God active in time and space—poured out on the believers at Pentecost to create the body of Christ: the Church. Simultaneously, the Spirit was poured forth on the world, " '...on all people...' " (Joel 2:28), to draw everyone to Christ and His Church (Acts 2:17–21). Hence, before an individual's encounter with Him through the preaching of the Gospel, the Spirit operates in the person unconsciously, speaking through personal needs, hungers and questions.

John Wesley calls this Prevenient Grace—the gracious, active work of God through His Spirit to move a sinner toward Christ for salvation. In other words, He takes the initiative to bring lost humanity to Himself through the work of His Holy Spirit (John 3; Rom. 5:8). Here is a vivid testimony related by Agnes Sanford affirming the work of the Spirit to draw people to Christ in the world. She writes:

> The Holy Spirit of Jesus Christ having entered into this world can enter and move everything! A successful and prosperous businessman once came to me in great perplexity. He had received a baptism of the Spirit and was troubled about his business. He left it and went into the ministry. We prayed for guidance—for, indeed, there are times when the Lord invites a man to do just this, as He invited the rich young man in the Scriptures. But our guidance was that he should remain in his business, but give it to the Lord and asked the Holy Spirit to bless it and use it according to His will.
>
> Last winter, I saw this man again, after a number of years. He had only one trouble: His income had doubled and trebled in a manner that embarrassed him, and he could not stop it. But the joy that he felt in his business was tremendous, for there he testified to the glory of God. He and his staff pray for the guidance of the Holy Spirit in every decision. No man was hired except at the Word of God. His factories were places of peace, for the Holy Spirit through the love of Christ so pervaded them that the heartbreak of quarreling did not enter in. Strangers entering his factories would stop and look around in surprise, as one sometimes does when entering a church, sensing a power, which can be seen with the eyes. "What is it?" they would ask. "I feel something here that I have never felt before…"
>
> How strange that we have tried to keep God out of our creativity and the work of our hands, when He is a creator and a worker, and when every factory and every school and every garden is of interest to Him!" (*The Healing Gifts of the Spirit*, Harper, San Francisco, 1966, pp. 167–168).

In addition to drawing people to Christ, directing their businesses and fashioning their handiwork to the glory of God, the Spirit also functions in secular culture to actualize the commission in concrete forms, as He moves history towards its fulfillment of His Kingdom. It's dawned on me that as the Spirit impacts human spirits universally, they're drawn toward the truth, a movement that occurs continuously in secular society. For example, I believe the Holy Spirit leads or moves the spirit of scientists in their quest for truth, inspiring their imagination and illumining their minds to leap from the known to the unknown.

Once in a while, physicians, herbalists and other specialists discover a remedy for a particular disease. A few years back, cancers, for instance, had no cure, but today, many are curable if reported and treated early. This is indicative of the continued work of Christ by God through the Holy Spirit to bring healing and wholeness to humankind. It goes to affirm the truth of this book, *Gye Nyame (Except for God): Without God, We Cannot Make It*, because we live by the power of God.

Were it not for His power sustaining us, we would surely have dropped dead and become dry bones by now. All that we are, have, can do and hope to be is altogether wrapped up in a beautiful package from Him Who created the world and everything in it. He has graciously made us stewards of His creation (Gen. 1:28–30).

Paul put it this way: "All things are yours…the world or life or death or the present or the future—all are yours, and you are of Christ, and Christ is of God" (1 Cor. 3:21–23). Therefore, as custodians of God's wonderful creation, we have to acknowledge Him in every aspect of life—at worship, prayer, work, play, etc., because He is a Spirit and present everywhere. He cannot be limited by space, time, or any thing, saying, " '…I am with you always…' " (Matt. 28:20). We have to learn to be conscious of His abiding presence with us every moment of the day. For instance, Charles Stanley, an accredited preacher of the Gospel in Atlanta, Ga., cited the following story to illustrate the truth of His omnipresence with believers:

> In the 1600s, there lived a monk named Brother Lawrence, whose job was to wash dishes. He learned the profound truth that God's presence could be experienced even in the grind of daily work. "For me," he wrote, "the time of activity does not differ from the time of prayer… in the noise and clatter of my kitchen, while several persons are calling together for as many different things, I possess God in as

great a tranquility as when upon my knees at the blessed Sacrament." He found no urgency for retreats, because in his mundane tasks, he met the same God he loved and worshipped in the stillness of prayer and devotions.

Thus, Stanley declares that "You may be called to be a mechanic, a doctor, a secretary, or a CEO. Know that your calling is equal to that of the pastor or vocational Christian worker. The key is to be where God has called you and to live for His glory in that place. You are a servant of the Living God, functioning [by the power and guidance of the Holy Spirit] in the world as a mechanic, a doctor, a secretary, or CEO." This leads us to realize the awesome responsibility of the Church in how we fulfill our mission in the world, to which I now turn.

The Mission of the Church

We've come to realize that God's Kingdom incarnated in His Son is now being actualized in people by the mysterious work of the Holy Spirit. While the realization of the Kingdom depends on God, we know that He uses human beings to bring it into fulfillment, for example through evangelism. As the body of Christ, the Church is the spearhead in this endeavor, and thus the primary agent intentionally seeking to make the Kingdom a reality in the world.

The mission of the Church in furthering the Kingdom is to create a community of God's people, to bear corporate witness to the action of the Holy Spirit in the world and to resist evil in all its forms: selfishness, greed, alienation, oppression, war, waste, disease, racism and dehumanization. In addition, this mission includes doing good, witnessing for righteousness and seeking new members; not for itself, but for God's larger purpose. Through the witness of the Church, family members still adhering to the worship of other gods and ancestors will yield to the Gospel truth, making them free, indeed (John 8:32).

As in any human organization, the Church requires a healthy body as the preparatory ground for its effective witnessing in the world. Hence, outsiders will join the Church only when they hear about the transforming and healing power of God at work there. The Apostles, John Wesley, George Whitefield, Billy Graham and other renowned evangelists undertook their ministerial tasks under the anointing power of the Holy Spirit. We, privileged successors to these spiritual giants, can't expect ourselves to do without the Holy Spirit. Otherwise, we'll be like the Disciples Paul met at Ephesus: they preached God's Word but hadn't received the Holy Spirit or heard about Him, until Paul had borne witness and prayed for them (Acts 19:1–7).

It's our responsibility as pastors and leaders of the Church to ensure that converts to Christianity mature in Christ. Let me illustrate this point with the following testimony of Chip Ingram, president of "Walk Through the Bible," who visited Africa recently: "During my journey in Africa," Chip wrote, "I also heard Christian leaders say that many in their congregations are still caught in traditional, demonic religions. These people believe in Jesus, but they have a mixed-up, warped theology. They accept the gospel, but they add the ancestor worship and other beliefs to it—and they have no power to live the Christian life. As I traveled throughout Africa, I thought of Jesus's words in John 8:32: 'Then you know the truth, and the truth,' He said, 'will set you free.' " Chip concluded his testimony with the following:

> Sadly, many of the people who have heard the gospel in Africa are not yet free. They have heard bits and pieces of the truth, but no one has taught them how to walk in the truth and live by the power of the Holy Spirit (*Walk Through the Bible*, letter to John Bonful, dated May 25, 2006).

Being Gospel communicators, we too must have a personal experience of the Holy Spirit's indwelling in order to be well-equipped, thus helping our congregations overcome their problems. As William G. Mclaughlin once declared:

> No man can urgently plead the joy of salvation through Christ, who has not experienced that joy in his own heart. The secret of success in the preaching of the gospel is that the preacher himself shall have felt the power of that gospel (*The American Evangelicals*, 1968, p. 133).

The mission of the Church is comparable to that of an army's general. Just as a general depends on soldiers in warfare, so does the Church depend on the Holy Spirit for its life and mission. The Holy Spirit comes with power: power to proclaim the good news of the kingdom, heal the sick, raise the dead, cast out evil spirits, give peace to troubled hearts and make the crooked straight. What we need today, as in the early Church, is a demonstration of that power in our own churches.

Jesus said, " '...you will receive power when the Holy Spirit comes on you; and you will be my witnesses…' " (Acts 1:8). How did the Apostles do it? They prayed and preached His message under the anointing power of the Holy Spirit, proving to both Jews and Gentiles alike that Christ—whom they had crucified—was risen indeed, and was actively present in His Church. For instance, the miraculous healing of the lame man at the Beautiful Gate of the Temple in Jerusalem led to a series of events that brought the membership of the local Christian community up to 5,000 (4:4).

The Fruit of the Spirit

The major work of the Holy Spirit in the believer's life is to transform his or her character into Christ's image. Such a person no longer exhibits a wayward lifestyle, characteristic of the old, sinful nature, but begins to bear the fruit of the Spirit, which Paul described in Galatians 5:23: "But the fruit of the Spirit is love, joy, peace, patience, kindness, goodness, faithfulness, gentleness and self-control…" Vernon Grounds of RBC refers to this inner life as "the beauty of holiness." Here is what he says:

> When you look in a mirror, what do you see? Do you see a lovely reflection—a handsome face? Or do you see a plain or unattractive countenance? We want to give those who behold us what my friend called an aesthetic blessing. But what about the beauty of holiness? Are others blessed by the beauty that flows through us from Christ? When Stephen was brought before the Jewish council for interrogation, "they were not able to resist the wisdom and the Spirit by which he spoke." (6:10). As he was being accused, "they saw his face as the face of an angel" (verse 15). By God's transforming grace, we too, can have a daily beauty in our lives. As we walk prayerfully in the Spirit, our faces increasingly reflect the beauty of Jesus.

Grounds concluded his comment with this short poem by Albert Osborn:

> Let the beauty of Jesus be seen in me,
> All His wonderful passion and purity;
> O Thou Spirit divine, all my nature refine
> Till the beauty of Jesus be seen in me.
> (*Our Daily Bread*, June 7, 2006)

For this reason, Paul emphasized that, "Those who belong to Christ Jesus have crucified the sinful nature with its passions and desires" (Gal. 5:24). He could state further to the Corinthians, "Therefore, if anyone is in Christ, he is a new creation; the old has gone, the new has come!" (2 Cor. 5:17). The best criterion by which to identify a true Christian among others is to look at his or her life. Hence, Jesus stated, " 'By their fruit you will recognize them...' " (Matt. 7:16).

Let's take a practical example in the life of 13-year-old Amy, who lived with her single mother. Growing up without a father figure and discipline, she didn't respect Mom. She wouldn't make her bed, clean up the mess in her room or do the dishes after meals. Her school performance was poor, because she wouldn't stay around to do her homework. Her mother nearly gave up on her.

However, during one summer, her mother succeeded in persuading her to attend a summer camp. She agreed to go because some of her classmates would attend, and she thought it would just be fun to join them. A Christian camp organized by a church group, this was no place for her idea of fun. Each morning began with a Bible story and devotion, with each participant memorizing a verse of Scripture. Every activity was under the control and discipline of the camp leaders, a school chaplain and a youth leader.

When the camp was over, Amy, the wayward teenager, was never the same again. *Why? What had happened?* She told her mom that everyone at the camp was nice and kind to her, especially the leaders. "So I began to hate my bad habits," she confessed to her mom, "and I told my chaplain to help me change for the better. He told me how God loves me through Jesus Christ, Who died for my sins and rose again to justify those who believe in Him. He then asked me if I do believe in Jesus Christ. I said, 'Yes.' He then prayed with me to receive Jesus into my life as my Lord and Savior. That prayer was answered, and Jesus changed my life. Mom, I'm a new person!"

Amy concluded her testimony in a loud voice, and her mom could see in her daughter's eyes a light shining as bright as the rays of the sun, coupled with unspeakable joy and peace in her heart. Isn't that wonderful? Yes, it is, indeed! This young girl's a new creation in Christ now, bearing the fruit of the Spirit, thus revealing to her mom her inner beauty—that of a Christ-like character imparted by the Holy Spirit. Surely, nothing can dim the beauty that shines from within. Praise the Lord! *Hallelujah!*

CHAPTER 17

Transformed Life for Believers in Christ

*W*ith the Good News of the mighty working of the Holy Spirit in the world, there's hope for a new life for all who sincerely turn to Jesus Christ by faith for salvation. Though He died for the forgiveness of our sins, without the work of the Holy Spirit in our hearts, there would have been no transformation of believer's lives. Furthermore, there would have been no hope in exchanging evil for goodness and sin for righteousness. Then, of course, we would still be living in darkness, that is, in sin, not in the light and new life of the Spirit (Gal. 5:22). Let's refresh our minds with a few biblical examples.

Case Stories of People Who Came to Jesus

Case 1

In His discourse with the Samaritan woman by the well, Jesus alluded to the new life those coming to Him would receive: "…'Everyone who drinks this water will be thirsty again, but whoever drinks the water I give him will never thirst. Indeed, the water I give him will become in him a spring of water welling up to eternal life.' " (John 4:13–14). Those familiar with the story will remember that on hearing Him talk about this special water, the woman asked, "…'Sir, give me this water so that I won't get thirsty and have to keep coming here to draw water' " (4:15). When He finally realized how much she wanted to see the promised Messiah, He revealed Himself to her, saying, "…'I who speak to you am he' " (4:26).

Upon this thrilling, face-to-face-encounter with the Messiah, the woman ran to Samaria, testifying to everyone her experience. " 'Come, see a man who told me everything I ever did. Could this be the Christ?' " (4:29). Her testimony led to the conversion of many Samaritans, who then came to listen to Him. Hearing the good news, they joyfully invited Him to be their guest in Samaria. Those who believed said to the woman afterward: "… 'We no longer believe just because of what you said; now we have heard for ourselves, and we know that this man really is the Savior of the world' " (4:42).

It's very important to observe here that Jews traditionally had nothing to do with Samaritans, yet Jesus broke down this barrier and accepted their invitation to stay among them for two days. What was the outcome of His visit with them? "And because of His words many more became believers" (4:41). By believing in Him, the Samaritan woman was saved, and through her testimony, others too came to know Jesus. By inviting Him to Samaria, they had opened the way for their neighbors to become believers. It began with one person, then a group and finally the city or community.

It sadly dawned on me that many people have heard the Good News but haven't come to believe in Jesus. By rejecting Him on religious, racial or traditional grounds, they're lost, together with their families and a whole community.

Due to tradition, no Jew—particularly a religious leader, such as a rabbi, teacher or scribe, or any Pharisee—would have even bothered to speak with the Samaritan woman at the well in the first place, let alone live among her people for a while. Nevertheless, Jesus obliged her so that many lost souls there might have new life through faith in Him. He did not allow the traditions of His time to hinder His divinely appointed task: "…to seek and to save the lost" (Luke 19:10). As David Egner observed: "He crossed all kinds of traditional barriers to talk with tax collectors, sinners, non-Jews, people of mixed races, the poor as well as the rich. He came to identify with each of us, and to pay the price for all our sins" ("The Underbird," *Our Daily Bread*, Monday, October 27, 2003).

I consider Christ's evangelistic strategy worthy of emulation by all soul-winners. There are well-meaning pastors and evangelists seeking to garner sinners for Him, but they find it difficult and at times impossible to share the Good News with some ethnic groups because of prejudice or the color of their skin. That's unfortunate—and uncharacteristic of Christ, Who crossed barriers of race, religion, rank, sex and wealth with the Good News of the Kingdom of God. He had only one aim: " '...to seek and to save the lost' " "...that they may have life, and have it to the full" (Luke 19:10; John 10:10).

If we claim to be His true disciples, we soul-winners need to humble ourselves and learn to follow our Master and His strategy for drawing sinners into the Kingdom.

Case 2

Another interesting story about new life in Jesus is recorded in Luke 19:1–10 concerning Zacchaeus, a wealthy chief tax collector. People in his position were employed by Rome to extract money from their fellow Jews, and thus not particularly well-liked as a group. Jesus was going to pass his way on His journey to Jerusalem, so Zacchaeus climbed a tree in order to have a clear view of Him over the crowd, on account of his short stature.

Upon His arrival, Jesus looked up and said, "...'Zacchaeus, come down immediately. I must stay at your house today' " (19:5). After gladly welcoming Him, they headed home and the crowd began to murmur, "...'He has gone to be the guest of a "sinner" ' " (19:7). Hearing their gossip, Zacchaeus said to Him, "...'Look, Lord! Here and now I give half of my possessions to the poor, and if I have cheated anybody out of anything, I will pay back four times the amount.' Jesus said to him, 'Today salvation has come to this house, because this man, too, is a son of Abraham. For the Son of Man came to seek and to save the lost' " (19:8–10).

Yes, indeed! Jesus knew what He was about and would not be deterred in the least by His sinful opponents' criticism. Zacchaeus had humbly repented and publicly confessed his sin of extortion, so Jesus declared His acceptance of him as a child of God by virtue of his faith in Him. His new convert had captured the essence of the moment and made a decision to commit his life to Him. Zacchaeus also refused to be discouraged by his enemies, who had sought only his downfall, not his salvation. He didn't depend on his wealth or allow pride to hinder his decision to accept Jesus as his Lord and Savior when the hour struck. He simply received Him into his heart when he heard Him knocking at its door.

What about you, my friend? Have you received Jesus into your heart as your personal Savior and Lord of your life? There are a lot of people who hear the Good News, yet allow riches, pride, criticism, spouses, relatives, friends and enemies to prevent them from coming to Him. Zacchaeus, like the Samaritan woman, seized the opportunity without delay. As the saying goes, "Opportunity comes but once." With that in mind, he seized the chance to meet his Savior when He randomly passed his way, regardless of his own sinfulness or opposition from his enemies or critics.

Case 3

A third vivid example of one who broke through all ranks of opposition to get to Jesus was the case of Bartimaeus, recorded in Mark 10:46–52 (*also* Matt. 20–29; Luke 18:35–43). Mark informs us that as Christ was leaving Jericho to continue His journey to Jerusalem followed by a large crowd, blind Bartimaeus was sitting by the roadside begging. But when he heard that it was Jesus of Nazareth, he began to shout: "Jesus, Son of David, have mercy on me!" Even though it is recorded that, "many rebuked him and told him to be quiet," he wouldn't pass up his chance for healing. So he kept on shouting all the more "Son of David, have mercy on me!" (Mark 10:48).

He rose above all these hindrances and cried out to Christ for the healing he very much needed

On hearing his cry, Jesus stopped and said, "Call him." Throwing his cloak aside, Bartimaeus jumped to his feet and came to Him. " 'What do you want me to do for you?' Jesus asked him. The blind man said, 'Rabbi, I want to see' " (10:51). To the surprise of everybody, including His disciples, He said to him, " 'Go…your faith has healed you'…" (10:52). Bartimaeus received his sight instantly and followed Jesus on the way.

Like the individuals in the two previous stories, Bartimaeus didn't allow himself to be overcome by life's obstacles, in his case, the rebuke from the crowd, the blindness that had made it difficult for him to find his way to Christ, and the cloak that got in his way. He rose above all these hindrances and cried out to Christ for the healing he very much needed, believing that apart from Him, no other person would be able to heal him—and he was right.

Bartimaeus also sensed that Jesus might not pass his way again, resolving to press courageously forward in obtaining what he needed from Him. Clearly, he wasn't denied the request. In this story and many others, Jesus fulfilled His promise: "All that the Father gives me will come to me, and whoever comes to me I will never drive away" (John 6:37).

Many individuals like Bartimaeus had failed to come to Jesus to be saved, healed or delivered from a particular situation because they yielded to certain stumbling blocks in their paths. It's important for us to remember that nothing can be achieved without effort. As someone said, "Life is war." Similarly, we ought to struggle hard to relinquish our pride and turn a deaf ear to our enemies' criticism — including that of the Devil, who always seeks our downfall and destruction. Acknowledging our need for a Savior, we must turn to Him for deliverance from our sinful condition with bravery and humility. We come to Him just as we are, armed with only one assurance: that He will never turn anybody away.

See how beautifully hymnist Christina Georgina Rossetti writes about this:

> None other Lamb, no other Name,
> None other hope in heaven or earth or sea,
> None other hiding place from guilt and shame,
> None beside Thee.
>
> My faith burns low, my hope burns low;
> Only my heart's desire cries out in me,
> By the deep thunder of its wants and woe,
> Cries out to Thee.
>
> Lord Thou art life, though I be dead;
> Love's fire Thou art, however cold I be:
> Nor heaven have I, nor place to lay my head,
> Nor home, but Thee.
> (*M.H.B.* 94: verses 1–3).

Before going any further from where you are at the moment, you may find it beneficial to put aside this book for a little while and ponder your life and God's love for you. If you haven't already given your life to the Lord Jesus, count this as your day of salvation. Even if you're a Christian, taking a moment to rededicate your life afresh to Him would yield greater blessings in your life and family than not doing anything at all with this anointed message of salvation.

This enables us as believers to look to the future with high expectations from our God. Full of power and love, He has redeemed us from the dominion of sin and demonic forces. Now, having the Lord Jesus Christ as our Refuge and Strength—our Guide and Provider of all our needs—there's the natural tendency to assume that, henceforth, life will flow on smoothly without any trouble or hindrance; but this is a fallacy and inconsistent with the Scriptures. " '…In this world you will have trouble. But take heart! I have overcome the world' " (John 16:33). It's thus very important that we believers understand why we face afflictions in life and how to cope with them. We'll discuss this subject fully in the next chapter.

CHAPTER 18

Why Do the Righteous Encounter Suffering?

*T*he ancient problem bothering the minds of many Bible scholars down the centuries has been the question of why righteous people endure suffering in a world that's under the control of a loving God. *If indeed God is almighty, as well as full of love and compassion, then why does He not protect His children from suffering, but allow them to pass through the fire of affliction?*

Unable to find answers to these difficult questions, some preachers avoid them altogether by resorting to what's called "Prosperity Gospel" or "Health-and-Wealth Gospel." They promote the false belief that once you become a Christian, all will be well with you; but little time passes before the varied experiences in life prove them wrong—allegiance to Christ is soon reduced or withdrawn entirely.

In a lesson chosen from John 12:12–19, Dennis J. De Haan had this to say about such shallow loyalty: "Some preachers proclaim a clear-cut gospel message. Others, however, pace before an enraptured audience, telling them that Jesus will heal all their diseases and make them rich. 'He wants you well! Poverty is of the devil!' shouts the preacher. People love the 'gospel' of prosperity and deliverance from sickness."

Now turn back the calendar to a Sunday morning around 33A.D. in Jerusalem. For three years Jesus has been healing the sick, feeding the hungry and even raising the dead. Now He rides into the city on a colt, receiving the acclaim of the crowd. But those who shout "Hosanna!" are accepting Him for what they think He will give them, not for who He is and what He came to do. They want an earthly Messiah who'll provide for their material welfare, not a suffering Messiah whose death on the cross will eventually expose their sin, provide forgiveness and call for a lifetime's commitment. He did not promise release from all the suffering in the world, but instead died to offer forgiveness, peace, eternal life and a cross to bear. "Anything less than taking up that cross in serving Him," De Haan emphasizes, "is shallow allegiance."

Of course, there's a sense in which the Lord graciously meets "…all your needs according to his glorious riches…" (Phil. 4:19), yet they're not inseparable from the world's troubles. The fact of the matter is that our sinful human condition in a fallen, sin-cursed world is inseparably bound up with sickness and health, crying and laughter, poverty and prosperity. Nevertheless, with the Sovereign Lord in control, whatever happens in the lives of those who love Him is designed for their good—whether it makes sense to them or not.

In his book *Broken Things*, M.R. De Haan, M.D., wrote: "The greatest, deepest truths of God's Word have often been revealed not by those who preached as a result of their seminary preparation and education, but by those humble souls who have gone through the seminary of affliction and have learned experientially the deep things of the ways of God." Such people had learned to depend upon Him as the only source of power by which they could live, and they grew stronger in faith in the end.

The purpose of this chapter isn't only to explain why Christians face tribulations here and there in this life, but also to demonstrate—with examples from both Scripture and the testimonies of other believers—how to deal with such inevitable, dark situations when they cloud our horizon.

Suffering Silences Our Adversary, Satan

The first reason God permits the Christian to suffer is that He uses the experience of His faithful children to silence the enemy of the Word of God and the Lord Jesus Christ. The story of the patriarch Job is probably our best example. The Bible informs us that he wasn't only wealthy, but also a blameless and upright man who feared God. When He drew Satan's attention to this untainted life, the Devil retorted that it was for the resulting material benefits that Job feared Him.

God then permitted Satan to afflict him with both the loss of material possessions and family. Instead of becoming morose and angry at Him, Job praised Him, saying: " '…The LORD gave and the LORD has taken away; may the name of the LORD be praised' " (Job 1:20) By his affirmative response, God was able to close Satan's mouth. It's quite amazing to realize that in His own mysterious way, He could use his children—however frail we might be—to silence the chief adversary of humanity, the Devil, through the hardships that we encounter in our lives.

I recall that a few years ago—while taking the Clinical Pastoral Education Course at the National Institutes of Health (NIH)—each of the student chaplains was assigned to one or two particular units, where we went from bed to bed, visiting and praying with patients. Though some of these patients were wracked with pain for years, they greeted us with smiles never worn by healthy people on the streets. As Dr. De Haan put it: "Those smiles, which indicate gratitude and praise to God, belong only to those who have been trained in the school of affliction. If you are one of God's 'Satan-silencers,' praise Him for it."

The Story of Horatio G. Spafford is another fitting example here. As a result of the Great Chicago Fire, which consumed the beautiful city in 1871, Spafford, an attorney with a heavy investment in real estate, lost his entire fortune. In the midst of this calamity, his only son of 4 died of scarlet fever. Undaunted by this adversity, he nevertheless helped to rebuild the city, housing about 100,000 people rendered homeless.

According to the author, Robert Morgan, "in November 1873, Spafford decided to take his wife and daughters to Europe. Horatio was close to D.L. Moody and Ira Sankey, and he wanted to visit their evangelistic meetings in England, then enjoy a vacation. When an urgent matter detained Horatio in New York, he decided to send his wife, Anna, and their four daughters, Maggie, Tanetta, Annie, and Bessie, on ahead. As he saw them settled into a cabin aboard the luxurious French liner *Ville du Havre*, an unease filled his mind, and he moved them to a room closer to the bow of the ship. Then he said good-bye, promising to join them soon."

In the early hours of "November 22, 1873, as the *Ville du Havre* glided over smooth seas, the passengers were jolted from their bunks. The ship had collided with an iron sailing vessel, and water poured in like Niagara…Screams, prayers, and oaths merged into a nightmare of unmeasured terror. Passengers clung to posts, tumbled through darkness, and were swept away by powerful currents of icy ocean. Loved ones," says, Morgan, "fell from each other's grasp and disappeared into foaming blackness. Within two hours, the mighty ship vanished beneath the waters. The 226 fatalities included Maggie, Tanetta, Annie, and Bessie, but Anna was found nearly unconscious, clinging to a piece of the wreckage. When the 47 survivors landed in Cardiff, Wales, she cabled her husband: "Saved alone."

Spafford immediately booked passage to join his wife. En route, on a cold December night, the captain called him aside and said, "I believe we are now passing over the place where the *Ville du Havre* went down." Spafford went to his cabin but found it hard to sleep. He said to himself, *It is well; the will of God be done.* He later wrote the famous hymn "It Is Well with My Soul" based on those words. (*Then Sings My Soul*, p. 185). The following is the hymn:

> When peace like a river, attended my way,
> When sorrows like sea billows roll;
> Whatever my lot, Thou has taught me to say,
> It is well, it is well, with my soul.
>
> *Refrain:* It is well, it is well, it is well, with my soul.

Dear friend, this story contains seemingly unbelievable, unbearable suffering, yet it happened to a real man and his family at one time in Chicago. He was a philanthropic Christian, one who gave his best—in money and in kind—to improve the lot of many, yet his faith in God did not wane. Like Paul and Silas, beaten and cast into prison in Philippi, rising at midnight to sing praises to the Lord, Spafford, in the midst of his grief over such tremendous loss, composed a soothing hymn sung at funeral services everywhere to bring comfort to other bereaved families.

Suffering Enables Us to Glorify God

Recorded in John 11, the death of Christ's very dear and precious friend Lazarus shows us the second reason believers endure suffering: it gives them the opportunity to glorify God. When the news of Lazarus' ill-condition reached Jesus, He knew His friend needed immediate attention and could have healed him from the distance by just speaking a Word, as He had done in the case of the centurion's servant. Nevertheless, He deliberately awaited his death and burial for four days in order to reveal the power and glory of His Father, which couldn't otherwise have been taught to Lazarus and his sisters Mary and Martha.

Hence, Jesus said to His disciples: "…'This sickness will not end in death. No, it is for God's glory so that God's Son may be glorified through it" (John 11:4). The next verse says with assurance, "Jesus loved Martha and her sister and Lazarus." Yet He deliberately permitted his death in order to be glorified by it, and furthermore, that the joy of resurrection—which can't come to any family except those who've lost loved ones—might be the most exhilarating experience of Christ's blessed friends.

Suffering Makes Us More Like Jesus

The third reason God allows His people to suffer is to enable Him to fulfill the ultimate purpose for which He has called and saved us. The following is how De Haan illuminates our call: "The Lord is not interested in saving you, keeping you out of hell, and taking you to heaven when you die. His purpose is much wider and deeper than providing salvation merely as a means of escaping punishment and entering into bliss at the end of life." We read in Romans 8:29:

> *For those God foreknew he also predestined to be conformed to the likeness of his Son, that he might be the firstborn among many brothers.*

This is a great, irrevocable truth from the Word of God that we must etch deeply into the tablets of our hearts, because "...people are destroyed from lack of knowledge..." of the Bible (Hosea 4:6). Knowing such a truth sets us free as believers to serve the Lord, no matter what we face, knowing that suffering is inextricably tied to our calling as Christians. Those who He foreknew were all in His plan from eternity.

Being made like the Lord Jesus Christ means that we remain faithful to Him in every circumstance of life. De Haan put it this way: "This means not only on the mount of Transfiguration, but also the mount of Calvary, and the garden of Gethsemane; it means darkness and suffering." Hence, the chief of all the Apostles, Paul, could boldly say in Philippians 3:10:

> *I want to know Christ and the power of his resurrection and the fellowship of sharing in his sufferings, becoming like him in his death.*

Therefore, if we're to be like Him, then we can't go our own way but must certainly be willing to follow Him wherever He leads us. Let's read what Peter, too, has to say:

> *Dear friends, do not be surprised at the painful trial you are suffering, as though something strange were happening to you. But rejoice that you participate in the sufferings of Christ, so that you may be overjoyed when his glory is revealed. If you are insulted because of the name of Christ, you are blessed, for the Spirit of glory and of God rests on you* (1 Pet. 4:12–14).

This implies that not only will we be like Him in His suffering, but we'll also have the privilege of being glorified together with Him. That's why Thomas O. Chisholm wrote the following poem:

O to be like Thee! O to be like Thee,
Blessed Redeemer, pure as Thou art;
Come in Thy sweetness, come in Thy fullness;
Stamp Thy own image deep on my heart

Suffering Teaches Dependence on God

Many Christians have discovered that the fourth reason the Lord allows suffering, pain and sorrow to try His children is to learn to rely on Him and not depend on their own strengths or any other nation's. For instance, in the days of Isaiah, when the people of Israel were threatened by surrounding enemies, they forged an alliance with strong nations, such as Egypt or Assyria. At that point, God spoke through His prophet to Israel: "…'In repentance and rest is your salvation, in quietness and trust is your strength…'" (Isa. 30:15). The Lord told them that their strength was neither in nations nor armies.

Perhaps you're a businessman/woman—maybe even in a responsible position, such as pastor, administrator, executive, chairperson of the board of directors—who's often had the experience of feeling indispensable. Your ability to transact the business in a meticulous manner has convinced you that without your input, the company would collapse. You had to be there by hook or crook in order for things to get done right. You wouldn't take time off for vacation, family or to be peaceful. You see yourself always fretting and hurrying around your business.

Suddenly, stress broke into your busy lifestyle and as a result, you are laid aside with an illness. What became of your business? You realized, to your utter amazement, that the business, your family and close associates were able to get along as well without you as with you.

This reminds me of the story of Matthew Edusei (not his real name), who was a popular businessman, a local preacher and the accountant/ society steward of one of the big churches in Ghana. Edusei's business often took him away from home, so he traveled extensively across Africa and Europe to keep in touch with his business associates. His church work suffered and was often taken over by his assistant. One day, he had a stroke rendering him bedridden and unable to use both legs, only his upper body. The strange thing I noticed about him whenever I visited was that he would be reading his Bible or working on the church's accounting books.

One day, he said to Charlie, his eldest son, "You know what, my son? God has been merciful to me, in that He did not take me away or make me completely useless. He graciously spared my upper body. I'm able to exercise my brain, hands, mouth and tongue. Don't you ever imitate my busy lifestyle, which almost paralyzed me but for God's grace. Learn to do better than I've done. I've learned from my mistakes. Now, I look to God and thank Him daily for every opportunity He gives me to do something worthwhile, however little, for His kingdom." Charlie thanked his dad for the timely advice.

Edusei's and several others' experiences can teach you that the Almighty God has the power to sustain and guide you down some difficult paths in life you never dreamed you had the endurance for walking. The greater lesson we all learn from this is that He can manage His business with or without us, and that we must learn to depend on Him as the source of all that we possess spiritually, emotionally and physically.

We may recall the story of the journey of the Israelites in the wilderness, standing before the Red Sea, the Egyptian army coming fast behind them, a vast expanse of deserts and mountains on each side. They were terrified and cried out to the Lord. He said, "...'Do not be afraid. Stand firm and you will see the deliverance the LORD will bring you today...' " (Exod. 14:13). True to His word, He fought for them.

I pray we learn fast the precious lesson that He teaches us: He is able to take over our business and perform wonderful things far beyond our wildest imagination and understanding. "...'Not by might nor by power, but by my Spirit,' says the LORD Almighty" (Zech. 4:6). In simple terms, He is saying to all hu-

He is saying to all humanity that we can't succeed in life by relying on our human capabilities

manity that we can't succeed in life by relying on our human capabilities. We need to acknowledge and count on Him in every aspect of our lives if we really want to achieve our goals.

Suffering Leads to Faith in Christ

The fifth reason God visits us with various trials and tribulations is to test the stuff of which we're made—the unflinching faith in Christ that overcomes the world's strife and the Devil's manipulation (1 John 5:4–5; 1 Pet. 5:8–9).

In my teenage years in Bibiani, I had some friends whose parents were goldsmiths, trading in trinkets, jewels, necklaces, earrings, rings, etc. My mother would occasionally buy some of their wares when they called on the house. Each time I visited one of my friends, I took particular interest in observing the way the goldsmith would pick a copper wire from the fire, hit it several times on the anvil and put it back into the fire's heat once again. When it had turned red-hot, he brought it onto the anvil again, hammering and pounding it until he was able to shape the copper into the particular form he wanted. The metal was further soaked in a bowl of hot gold dust, finished and polished in order to become a high-quality golden jewel—beautiful, shining, and worth a tremendous amount of money.

I hope to illustrate the point that as Christians, we exercise more faith in God and draw much closer to Him in prayer than we do in the ordinary circumstance of life. Like that gorgeous jewel plucked from the fire, we become better Christians than we had been previous to that experience. As it's been proven in life, "Experience is the best teacher." The best example that comes to mind is Job, who declared, "But he knows the way that I take; when he has tested me, I will come forth as gold" (Job 23:10).

We must bear in mind that like the goldsmith, the farmer doesn't waste his time tilling sandy soil that has no value for his crops. He concentrates his time and energy on the field he believes has the greatest potential for producing a worthy harvest. Similarly, God in His divine wisdom, spends His precious time economically on issues that have eternal value. Out of the school of suffering, someone has said, "Sunshine all the time only makes a desert." Certainly, we need the clouds, dark days, storms and rain just as much as we need the sunshine.

What ultimately keeps us clinging to God by faith is the assurance that He Who is molding our lives after the likeness of His Son knows what's best for each of us. Hence, Job could boldly say, "...he knows the way that I take...,"capping it all with a great declaration of his mature faith in Him: " 'I know that you can do all things; no plan of yours can be thwarted' " (Job 42:2).

He was convinced that God had power and complete control over his circumstances and that He would ultimately fulfill the purpose for his life, no matter what. That kind of faith didn't come to him overnight but through a long period of suffering, which by God's intervention ended in abundant blessing much greater than anyone could imagine (42:12–16).

Paul and his companions suffered greatly while spreading the Gospel, listing their outward trials, their inward pains and their spiritual resources (2 Cor. 6:4–7). Let's try to imagine the circumstances in which all these things interacted: beatings, patience, imprisonment, kindness, distress and love. Although broken physically, depleted emotionally and tested spiritually, the authenticity of their faith in Christ shone through, crowning them with the light of victory in the end.

Suffering Makes Us Humble

God is Almighty and there's none like Him in power, majesty and honor; heaven and earth are full of His glory. Nevertheless, He humbled Himself and sent His Son among us—not to be served, but to serve and give His life as a ransom for us. Hence, the Lord wants His children to be humble: He sends His invitation to all: " 'Come to me, all you who are weary and burdened, and I will give you rest. Take my yoke upon you and learn from me, for I am gentle and humble in heart, and you will find rest for your souls' " (Matt. 11:28–29).

It was the sin of pride that caused Lucifer, the angel of light thrown down from heaven, to become the Devil. And so it was that Adam and Eve, our first parents, were forever turned out of Eden. And yet again, it was pride that caused confusion and the failure to build the Tower of Babel. God resists the proud but exalts the humble in heart.

Therefore, the sixth reason God allows us the pain of numerous tribulations and suffering is that we may learn one of the most important lessons for mature Christians: humility. Perhaps the best biblical example illustrating this principle is found in the account of the great Apostle Paul. He tells us of a tormenting physical affliction, "...a thorn in my flesh, a messenger of Satan..." (2 Cor. 12:7).

There are many schools of thought concerning the source of his torment. Some have suggested that it was a painful eye disease resulting from the blinding vision on the day of his conversion on the road to Damascus. Others posited that he might be suffering from a hunchback, while some point to a speech impediment. Whatever the nature of Paul's suffering, we don't need to analyze what really troubled this great man of God, except to be certain that it caused him tremendous physical pain and extreme anguish. Our interest lies in finding out why the Lord would permit a faithful servant like him to go through such torture at the hands of Satan.

According to his own narration, Paul recounts a particular transformation in his Christian experience, wherein he was caught up into paradise, the third heaven. There he received a wonderful revelation from God that hadn't been made known to any other person. In spite of this amazing and thrilling spiritual experience, the Apostle—who describes himself as "the chief of sinners"—certainly knew that this heavenly revelation could easily become the source of vainglory and fleshly pride. But he explains as follows:

> *To keep me from becoming conceited because of these surpassingly great revelations, there was given me a thorn in my flesh, a messenger of Satan, to torment me. Three times I pleaded with the Lord to take it away from me. But he said to me, "My grace is sufficient for you, for my power is made perfect in weakness." Therefore I will boast all the more gladly about my weaknesses, so that Christ's power may rest on me. That is why, for Christ's sake, I delight in weaknesses, in insults, in hardships, in persecutions, in difficulties. For when I am weak, then I am strong (2 Cor. 12:7–10).*

Thus, we learn from his testimony that he received definite assurances from the Lord that the thorn in his flesh had been placed purposefully to keep him from becoming proud, inflated with pomposity and to remain humble. In other words, if he were to lose his humility, he would no longer be useful to God, because He hates pride.

What do believers learn from this truth in relation to our own experiences? It explains to us the reason the Lord does not grant us the long-prayed-for promotion, simply because it might lead us into the pride and subsequent disgrace that easily beset us. Perhaps in your case, He has not answered your prayer for healing and restoration. Certainly, He answers His children's every prayer, but the answer probably wasn't what you wanted. That could mean that you didn't pray in His will, that you haven't learned to utter the prayer of our Savior in the Garden of Gethsemane: " 'Father, if you are willing, take this cup from me; yet not my will, but yours be done' "(Luke 22:42). Our prayers must be in the will of God, knowing for certain that He has our best interests at heart.

We can demonstrate this from our own parental experiences. As Christian parents, we know how much we love our children; but will you give a loaded gun to your five-year-old son if he pleads with you and even cries for it? I believe the answer will be: "No, my son. It's too dangerous for you, for the simple reason that it could kill you or others." He has neither the slightest idea about its danger to his life nor does he understand why he can't have a gun that attracts him. He may pester you for weeks or months with the same request, yet, no matter how often he pleads for the weapon, you'll never give in to his petition, because you know better as a parent.

Fellow Christians, we're very much like this child: as God's offspring, we're very much limited in our knowledge of the eternal plans and purposes He has for us. But we can be secure in knowing that our Father knows what's best for us and will not deny us anything that brings glory to Him and blessings upon us. Jesus said to His disciples after washing their feet, "...'You do not realize now what I am doing, but later you will understand' " (John 13:7).

Lincoln's Testimony

Dennis Fisher of RBC Ministries tells the following story to illustrate how suffering, affliction or tragedy can be used by God to bring someone to give his life to Christ. "Abraham Lincoln," according to Fisher, "was a backwoods man who rose from humble beginnings to the heights of political power. During the dark days of the U.S. Civil War, he served as a compassionate and resolute president. Depression and mental pain were his frequent companions. Yet the terrible emotional suffering drove him to receive Jesus Christ by faith."

Lincoln told a crowd in his hometown Illinois: "When I left Springfield, I asked the people to pray for me; I was not a Christian. When I buried my son, the severest trial of my life, I was not a Christian. But when I saw the graves of thousands of our soldiers, I then and there consecrated myself to Christ. I do love Jesus."

Fisher continues, "Life's most painful tragedies can bring us to a deeper understanding of the Savior. When two men walked the road to Emmaus, they were dumbfounded by the senseless murder of Jesus of Nazareth. Then a stranger joined them and gave a scriptural insight about the suffering Messiah (Luke 24:26–27). The stranger was Jesus Christ Himself, and His ministry to them brought comfort. Heartache has a way of pointing us to the Lord Jesus, Who has shared in our sufferings and can bring meaning to seemingly senseless pain." Fisher concludes with a poem by Dennis J. De Haan:

> Though tragedy, heartache, and sorrow abound
> And many a hardship in life will be found,
> Just put all your trust in the Savior of light,
> For He can bring hope in the darkest of night.
> (*Our Daily Bread*, February 18, 2009)

Due to their relevance in our daily Christian lives, there's much more to say on these matters; but insufficient space in this chapter only allows me to mention them without comment. Suffering brings us to pray more to God than we would under the more usual circumstances of life. Again, suffering helps us learn patience, leading us to trust and hope in God. Finally, the Scriptures assure us that there's much reward for those suffering patiently for the Lord.

"If we endure, we will also reign with him. If we disown him, he will also disown us" (2 Tim. 2:12). Jesus says to His followers: "Do not be afraid of what you are about to suffer. I tell you, the devil will put some of you in prison to test you, and you will suffer persecution…Be faithful, even to the point of death, and I will give you the crown of life" (Rev. 2:10). He is our best example here, saying to the two Disciples on the road to Emmaus, " 'Did not the Christ have to suffer these things and then enter his glory?' " (Luke 24:26).

Hymn writer Horatius Bonar (1808-1889) wrote:

> Go, labor on; spend and be spent,
> Thy joy to do thy Father's will;
> It is the way the Master went;
> should not the servant tread it still?
> (*MHB* 589: verse 1)

Now, the final questions are these: *In their various situations of suffering, how were these faithful Christians able to endure such difficult conditions without collapsing under the weight of affliction, depression and pain? And by what means can we cope with misfortunes when they happen to us?* According to the Scriptures, "…God did not give us a spirit of timidity, but a spirit of power, of love and of self-discipline" (2 Tim. 1:7).

Furthermore, we know that "…in him we live and move and have our being…" (Acts 17:28). Believers thus live by His power, and it's this power that keeps us from burning when we walk through the fire of affliction or drowning when we pass through the waters of strife, flames or waves rising high above our heads. In the same vein, King David wrote:

> *Even though I walk through the valley of the shadow of death, I will fear no evil, for you are with me; your rod and your staff, they comfort me. You prepare a table before me in the presence of my enemies. You anoint my head with oil; my cup overflows. Surely goodness and love will follow me all the days of my life and I will dwell in the house of the LORD forever* (Ps. 23:4–6).

My wife and I are both living testimonies to God's power in sustaining the believer in his weakness as he holds on firmly to Him during the storms of life. When we're weak, we're supplied with His power so that we can do all things through Him Who strengthens us. We're kept by His power, having hope not only in this life, but also in the future life eternally with Him in heaven promised to all awaiting the return of His Son. It's by giving that we receive, by losing that we find and by being broken that we're made whole. It's by dying for His sake that we're born again in His Father's Kingdom.

In this connection, even if the storms of death take us away, He still holds the souls of the faithful departed—including those of our little ones—to His bosom, covered by His mighty hands, so that no one is lost. That's why Christians never lose hope: no matter how dark the night may be around us, we still have the light of hope. We'll discuss in detail the subject of Christian hope in the next chapter.

CHAPTER 19

*B*efore dealing with the subject of *Christian Hope* let's first discuss what *hope* is in its ordinary sense.

What is Hope?

According to the dictionary in the *New Century Version of the Holy Bible, hope* in the general sense may be defined as "looking forward to something you really expect to happen" (p. 1537).

In its common usage, we often put less emphasis on the "expectation" component of hope. For instance, one may say: "I hope my college team wins the championship this year, but I've been hoping that for the past five years." Although we still look forward to a desired end, we don't stake our lives on whether or not it happens, because the thing hoped for is uncertain at best. In other words, being human, we don't have the power or absolute control to enable us change or prevent the daily events or circumstances that come our way.

As a matter of fact, hope always carries the idea of "looking forward to the desirable," but with varying degrees of probability, as in the following example: "I hope my husband wins $25,000 playing *Wheel of Fortune* tonight, but I'm aware his chance of winning is less than that of receiving a surprise visit from his mom this weekend." In practical experience, we realize that our hope always tends to be feeble and desperate. The simple reason for this is that the basis of our hope is so flimsy that it can't stand the test of time, stress and strain that come our way to cause a change in our situation.

As ordinary humans in society, we may thus be likened to those Paul describes: "...separate from Christ..." and, consequently, "...without hope and without God in the world" (Eph 2:12). In other words, real hope is a divine virtue that we can receive from no one else except Him through faith in His Son. Now, let's examine the type of hope that we can have in Christ.

The Christian Hope

Hope in the Biblical or Christian point of view is quite different from *hope* in the human or general perspective. In the Scriptures, hope is a certainty: a confident expectation of what God will do in the future based on His past faithfulness and promises. Its certainty exists because of Who He is: He is faithful and His Word is trustworthy. He is a reliable reason for and source of our hope. For instance, it was on the basis of His own integrity and ability that He made the promise to bless Abraham and give him many descendants (Gen. 12:1–3, 22:16–18; Heb. 6:13–15).

> Indeed, God's promise is the kind of hope on which we can stake our lives right from the very beginning

Abraham and his wife, Sarah, were long past their natural, child-bearing years, yet their hope in God's promise was not wishful thinking, but a confident trust in the One who could deliver. Biblical/Christian hope is thus hope in God and His promises, even though we haven't yet seen their complete fulfillment. This kind of hope is solid and dependable, "...an anchor for the soul, firm and secure..." (Heb. 6:19). To the Jews exiled in Babylon, for example, God's promise of hope came through the prophet Jeremiah, vowing, " 'For I know the plans I have for you,' declares the LORD, 'plans to prosper you and not to harm you, plans to give you hope and a future' " (Jer. 29:11).

Indeed, this is the kind of hope on which we can stake our lives right from the very beginning. The people of God have been a people of hope, thus the Holy Bible is His message of hope for a hopeless world. All who trust in and cast their hope on Him won't be ashamed or disappointed.

Beginning from God's promise that Adam and Eve's descendant would crush the head of the serpent (Gen. 3:15), to His promise of the land of Canaan to Abraham's descendants (12:7), to the promise that David's descendants would rule forever (1 Chron. 17:11–14), to the promise of Jesus' return (1 Thess. 4:16; Rev. 22:7, 12:20), His people have believed Him and waited in hope for the day of fulfillment.

Let's take as a practical example the days of the Jewish captivity in Babylon. God's Word came to them through the prophet Jeremiah:

> *This is what the LORD says: "When seventy years are completed for Babylon, I will come to you and fulfill my gracious promise to bring you back to this place. For I know the plans I have for you," declares the LORD, "plans to prosper you and not to harm you, plans to give you hope and a future. Then you will call upon me and come and pray to me, and I will listen to you. You will seek me and find me when you seek me with all your heart. I will be found by you," declares the LORD, "and will bring you back from captivity. I will gather you from all the nations and places where I have banished you," declares the LORD, "and will bring you back to the place from which I carried you into exile"* (Jer. 29:10–14).

This promise was fulfilled during the days of Ezra and Nehemiah, but Israel didn't become a sovereign nation until 1948. Since then, she has become a world actor, a strong nation to reckon with among the other powerful nations of the world.

It's important to note that while many who first received the promises didn't see their fulfillment (Heb. 11:39), their willingness to walk in God's promise and not their own circumstances kept them faithful to the end. Those privileged to see the realization of their cherished hope in Him experienced His faithfulness to all His promises. As Jesus said, " '...blessed are those who have not seen and yet have believed' " (John 20:29). It's a vivid example of hope in God's promise—and also an inspiration to us as we live in the latter days of the Holy Spirit's dispensation—to persevere in hope, as declared in the following Scripture:

> *Therefore, since we are surrounded by such a great cloud of witnesses, let us throw off everything that hinders and the sin that so easily entangles, and let us run with perseverance the race marked out for us. Let us fix our eyes on Jesus, the author and perfecter of our faith, who for the joy set before him endured the cross, scorning its shame, and sat down at the right hand of the throne of God. Consider him who endured such opposition from sinful men, so that you will not grow weary and lose heart* (Heb. 12:1–3).

Now, you may raise the question, *How can we practice living in hope in our daily lives?* For a detailed discussion, let's turn to the following.

Living in Hope as Faithful Disciples of Christ

In what way does Biblical/Christian hope help us live as Christ's faithful followers in our time? Psalm 39:7 helps us understand that to hope in God is to make Him the object of our hope; it means placing our trust in His promises and His ability to fulfill them. This will, among other things, include:

- Trusting God to raise us from the dead and give us eternal life (Acts 23:6; 1 Cor. 15:19; Titus 1:2);
- Trusting Him to grant us a share in His glory (Rom. 5:1–5); and
- Trusting Him to redeem all of creation from ruin (Rom. 8:18–25).

This trust in Him isn't passive; it's demonstrated in a life of perseverance and faithful obedience to Him (Heb. 12:1–3). This trust leads us to act on His Word (Matt. 7:21). Our hope in Him surely means that we take His commands seriously, becoming doers of His Word and not simply hearers in deceiving ourselves (James 1:22).

In order to keep our hope unmovable in Christ, we must be deeply rooted, structured and established in the Holy Scriptures, through which God revealed Himself and spoke to the prophets. They in turn proclaimed the Word to His people, reminding them of His covenant relationship and commandments. Under that constant reminder—and the reading and studying of Torah—most of the people of Israel managed through the help of the Holy Spirit to keep their identity as His people. It's the responsibility of all parents to teach their children the Scriptures, as follows:

> *Hear, O Israel: The LORD our God, the LORD is one. Love the LORD your God with all your heart and with all your soul and with all your strength. These commandments that I give you today are to be upon your hearts. Impress them on your children. Talk about them when you sit at home and when you walk along the road, when you lie down and when you get up. Tie them as symbols on your hands and bind them on your foreheads. Write them on the doorframes of your houses and on your gates* (Deut. 6:4–9).

Reading through this passage carefully, we observe the priestly writer's unique recommendation as to how the Scriptures should be taught to our children: from the rising of the sun to its setting, and in whatever situation we find ourselves—whether we're at home or elsewhere, we should be alert to the Word of God.

Jesus Taught the Religious Leaders the Holy Scriptures

Careful study of the Gospels reveals that Jesus knew the Old Testament and often quoted from it to His critics in support of His claims or actions. For example, in Satan's temptation in the wilderness, He used Scripture as His only successful weapon.

On another occasion, one of the experts in the Law tested Him, asking: " 'Teacher, which is the greatest commandment in the Law?' " In answer, Jesus rightly quoted from Deuteronomy, as mentioned in the above passage: " 'Love the Lord your God with all your heart and with all your soul and with all your mind.' This is the first and greatest commandment. And the second is like it: 'Love your neighbor as yourself.' All the Law and the Prophets hang on these two commandments" (Matt. 22:36–40).

When the lawyer demanded further to know, "Who is my neighbor?" Jesus narrated the now-popular story in the Bible, "The Good Samaritan" (Luke 10:30–36). In turn, He asked the questioner to identify who was a real neighbor to the wounded man. He replied, " 'The one who had mercy on him.' " Jesus finally told him, " 'Go and do likewise' " (Luke 10:37).

In His response to the lawyer, Christ summed up what life is all about in terms of the love relationship with God, our neighbors and ourselves. You can't transmit love to someone unless you've personally tasted His love first for yourself. From that loving perspective you can practice the same toward your neighbor.

Rebecca Manley Pippert wrote: "Our sociology reveals our theology. The way we treat others reveals what we think God is like. The way we treat others is critical. People will understand as much of the love of God as they see in our lives. The first Bible people will read will be your life."

For instance, I recently listened to the powerful testimony of a man who had converted as a result of the prayers and exemplary life of his Christian wife. When they had first married, according to the man's testimony, neither followed Christ, but his wife gave her life to Him later on. What they now describe as *spiritual mismatch in marriage* then began to disturb their previously "happy" union. He testified that whenever his wife went to church, he stayed home or hung out with friends. However, his wife loved him unconditionally, always exercising compassion, patience, gentleness, restraint and forgiveness toward him for his wrongdoing. He called his marriage "a spiritual mismatch," but his wife pinned her trust on God's promise, declared in Ezekiel:

> *I will sprinkle clean water on you, and you will be clean; I will cleanse you from*
> *all your impurities and from all your idols. I will give you a new heart and put*
> *a new spirit in you; I will remove from you your heart of stone and give you a*
> *heart of flesh. And I will put my Spirit in you and move you to follow my de-*
> *crees and be careful to keep my laws* (Ezek. 36:25–27).

This Christian woman constantly interceded for her husband, hoping and trusting that one day he would yield his heart to God's love, as revealed in Jesus Christ, Who died for our sins. An accredited journalist, the husband finally converted, answering His call to the ministry. Today, both husband and wife are conference speakers, experienced marriage counselors and authors of various Christian books.

Pippert continues, "We are called, therefore, to mirror the love of God—a love that is so extravagant that we must never keep it to ourselves. We must spread it around. It is not a mushy love, all sentiment and no action. Jesus' love drove him deeply into the lives of people. He cared for their wholeness. When He went out into a day, He did not ask himself, 'Is this my social action day or do I give them the salvation message?' Jesus cared for people as He found them. So must we care for their wholeness—spiritual, social, psychological, you name it."

> **We must spread Jesus' love around. It is not a mushy love, all sentiment and no action**

Concluding, Pippert states, "Our love for God, others and ourselves, and all the actions that the Law entails, mirrors what the Law is all about and what it is preparing us for. We do not try to prove our own righteousness by obeying the Law as some of the Pharisees tried to do. Rather we accept the Law's verdict on us: we are sinners. Moreover, we acknowledge that only when we live 'according to the Spirit' can we fulfill the Law's righteous requirements. By living in Christ's Spirit, we joyfully submit to God's Law, because it tells us what is pleasing to God, what the things of the Spirit are and what it means to walk in the Spirit" (*Out of the Saltshaker*, pp. 76–77).

Realizing that Jesus had given the right answer, the court's questioner had nothing more to say and agreed with Him. On many occasions, religious leaders came to test Him with questions concerning the Law or the Scriptures in terms of the Sabbath or marriage and divorce. There was no way Jesus could make them understand His ministry except by teaching or reminding them of the Scriptures, i.e., the Law. Law in this context refers not only to the Ten Commandments, but the whole of God's moral plan in the Old Testament, to which His people, especially, the Pharisees held dearly (John 5:39).

The Sadducees' Ignorance of God's Word

Let's take another example from the case of the Sadducees, who didn't believe in the doctrine of resurrection. They came to Jesus with a question:

> *"Teacher," they said, "Moses told us that if a man dies without having children, his brother must marry the widow and have children for him. Now there were seven brothers among us. The first one married and died, and since he had no children, he left his wife to his brother. The same thing happened to the second and third brother, right on down to the seventh. Finally, the woman died. Now then, at the resurrection, whose wife will she be of the seven, since all of them were married to her?"* (Matt. 22:24–28).

Again using the Scriptures, Jesus easily outwitted them with an answer proving their ignorance:

> *…"You are in error because you do not know the Scriptures or the power of God. At the resurrection people will neither marry nor be given in marriage; they will be like the angels in heaven. But about the resurrection of the dead — have you not read what God said to you, 'I am the God of Abraham, the God of Isaac, and the God of Jacob'? He is not the God of the dead but of the living"* (22:29–32).

Living by the Word of God

These are but a few of many examples of Scripture's use in answer to many tricky questions put to Jesus by His critics the Pharisees and the Sadducees. Without knowing God's Word or the Holy Scriptures, we won't know His character and holiness, or Him, Who made us in His own image. And without knowing Him through the study of His Word, we *won't* be able to even know or value ourselves as human beings worthy of moral conduct.

Without moral judgment, we would find ourselves living and dying like beasts. As humans made in God's image, we're to measure our lives by the moral standards and principles laid down by Him in the Bible for guidance in our daily conduct. Just as carpenters or masons use plumb lines to check whether a wall being erected is square with the floor, we gauge our lives in accordance with His principles to find our alignment.

For instance, when Israel backslid in turning away from following His commandments, His Word came to the prophet Amos in a vision. He saw the Lord standing beside a straight wall holding a plumb line, meaning that since Israel's conduct did not match His Word, she had suffered His severe judgment (Amos 7:6–8). Commenting on His judgment, Dave Egner of RBC Ministries had this to say:

> As followers of Jesus Christ, we have a plumb line by which we can evaluate our lives. It is the word of God with its principles and commands. When faced with moral choices, we see what the Scriptures teach. When we follow the Lord's directives, we need not fear what His plumb line will reveal in our lives (*Our Daily Bread*, December 17, 2002).

It follows, therefore, that knowing the Scriptures and living by them is the wisest thing we can do to enjoy real peace and happiness in this life through Christ. It is "...in [his] light we see light" (Ps. 36:9). The Psalmist knows for certain that this is God's world, that humans can't live and work successfully in it without guidance from the Bible; otherwise, all our efforts end in total defeat. King David wrote from the experience of his walk with Him:

> *Your word is a lamp to my feet and a light for my path. I have taken an oath and confirmed it, that I will follow your righteous laws. I have suffered much; preserve my life, O LORD, according to your word...The wicked have set a snare for me, but I have not strayed from your precepts. Your statutes are my heritage forever; they are the joy of my heart* (119:105–107, 110–111).

Thus God's Word is very precious to David; indeed, it's "more precious to me than thousands of pieces of silver and gold" (119:72). So he made his desire for God's Word his first priority, investing his hope and trust in the Scriptures. He never made a move or went to battle without first consulting the prophet for God's counsel and guidance, because he knew that victory was impossible unless He was with him.

With Him, David could say, "All the nations surrounded me, but in the name of the LORD I cut them off... I was pushed back and about to fall, but the LORD helped me. The LORD is my strength and my song; he has become my salvation (118:10, 13–14). Consequently, he never lost a battle (1 Sam. 30:3–8; 2 Sam. 5:17–21).

Like the king, if the heads of nations, tribes and families throughout the world—especially in Africa—sought the Lord and loved His Word more than anything else, there would be fulfillment of peoples' hopes and aspirations—spiritually, psychologically, politically and materially. If the Lord becomes our leaders' Shepherd, Guide, Wisdom and Strength, as a people under God, all of us would surely succeed and prosper in whatever we set our minds to do, regardless of the problems that come our way. " 'With man this is impossible, but not with God; all things are possible with God.' " (Mark 10:27).

However, you may ask, *How will God make all things possible for me?* Well, here's how He may work in your life. Irrespective of your rank in family or community, it is a certainty

> *That if you confess with your mouth, "Jesus is Lord," and believe in your heart that God raised him from the dead, you will be saved. For it is with your heart that you believe and are justified, and it is with your mouth that you confess and are saved. As the Scripture says, "Anyone who trusts in him will never be put to shame." For there is no difference between Jew and Gentile—the same Lord is Lord of all and richly blesses all who call on him, for, "Everyone who calls on the name of the Lord will be saved"* (Rom. 10:9, 11–13).

Whenever anyone accepts Jesus into his or her life, at that very moment, the Lord takes His rightful place in the heart by means of His Holy Spirit. This enables the believer to submit to the teachings of Christ as told in the Holy Scriptures. King David testified, "The LORD is my shepherd, I shall not be in want" (Ps. 23:1). Henceforth, He takes the reins in your life, to "guide[you] in paths of righteousness for his name's sake" (23:3).

The Bible underscores the truth that "Righteousness exalts a nation, but sin is a disgrace to any people" (Prov. 14:34). It follows that any country whose people live righteously in obedience to God will be blessed with peace and prosperity,

> **Proverbs reminds us that righteousness exalts a nation, but sin is a disgrace to any people**

while one living in sin or ignorance of Him will inevitably find no peace, but instead turmoil, poverty, disaster and death. Jeremiah's prophecy is relevant:

This is what the LORD says: "Cursed is the one who trusts in man, who depends on flesh for his strength and whose heart turns away from the LORD. He will be like a bush in the wastelands; he will not see prosperity when it comes. He will dwell in the parched places of the desert, in a salt land where no one lives. But blessed is the man who trusts in the LORD, whose confidence is in him. He will be like a tree planted by the water that sends out its roots by the stream. It does not fear when heat comes; its leaves are always green. It has no worries in a year of drought and never fails to bear fruit" (Jer. 17:5–8).

For instance, as a result of Israel's disobedience to God's commandments, He made " '...the sun go down at noon and darken the earth in broad daylight...religious feasts into mourning, and...singing into weeping...' " (Amos 8:9–10). Conversely, obedience to Him comes with His promise of providence, as declared by the prophet Isaiah to Israel: "If you are willing and obedient, you will eat the best from the land" (Isa. 1:19).

By faith you've made the Almighty—who lives in you with fullness of love, goodness, and mercy—not only your Savior, but also your Provider, Shepherd, and the Source of all your needs, as He was to King David. Thus, you can humbly and confidently join your voice with his: "The LORD is my shepherd, I shall not be in want...He guides me in paths of righteousness for his name's sake...Surely goodness and love will follow me all the days of my life, and I will dwell in the house of the LORD forever" (Ps. 23:1, 3, 6).

> **This isn't to suggest believers are always able to please God or fulfill the Law's demands on us**

This isn't to suggest that believers are always able to please God or fulfill the Law's demands on us. "We in the twentieth century," says Pippert, "tend to neglect God's Law too much. But we must not abandon the Law as having meaning for the people of the Old Testament...Our love for God, others and ourselves, and all the actions that the relationship entails, mirrors what the Law is all about and what it is preparing us for. We do not try to prove our own righteousness by obeying the Law, as some Pharisees tried to do. Rather we accept the Law's verdict on us: we are sinners. We are what we are by the grace of God, because God's love is unconditional" (*Saltshaker*, p. 77).

That is why this book constantly echoes loudly and clearly to all its readers the irrevocable, irrefutable and eternal truth: *Gye Nyame: Without God, We Cannot Make It.*

CHAPTER 20

The Benefits of Knowing the Holy Scriptures

At this juncture, I think it's appropriate to share with you some of the benefits we can derive from a serious study of the Bible. This is of prime importance, because from our human experience, we know that we can't have a close relationship with a person unless we really know his or her character; neither should any two thinking people enter into a contract unless they have mutual trust. Jesus said, "You diligently study the Scriptures because you think that by them you possess eternal life. These are the Scriptures that testify about me" (John 5:39). Thus, by studying them, we get to know the Lord in an intimate way and thus are richly blessed. Now, let's explore some of the benefits accruing to us by studying the Scriptures.

The Word Leads to Success and Prosperity

After the death of Moses, the mantle of Israel's leadership fell on the shoulders of young Joshua, the son of Nun. Though he naturally felt quite inadequate for the great task entrusted into his hands, God promised to be with him as devotedly as He was with Moses, with the following injunction:

> *Be strong and very courageous. Be careful to obey all the law my servant Moses gave you; do not turn from it to the right or to the left, that you may be successful wherever you go. Do not let this Book of the Law depart from your mouth; meditate on it day and night, so that you may be careful to do everything written in it. Then you will be prosperous and successful (Josh. 1:7–8).*

Before going any further, I want to make it clear here that God's promise of *success* and *prosperity* isn't merely that of material wealth. It embraces spiritual and physical well-being concerning the quality of life, bearing the fruit of love, "…righteousness, peace and joy in the Holy Spirit" (Rom. 14:17), and reaching out to others in need, so that He is glorified in all things. So long as the people of Israel under Joshua remained obedient, He would neither fail nor forsake them (Heb. 13:5), but would meet in abundance their "needs according to his glorious riches in Christ Jesus" (Phil. 4:19).

This promise stands for the total well-being and wholeness of life. Take, for instance, John's prayer for his fellow believers: "Beloved, I wish above all things that thou mayest prosper and be in health, even as thy soul prospereth" (*KJV*, 3 John 2). Commenting on this, Charles Stanley wrote:

> The prayer of John was that the people would prosper in all things—their material, social, natural, financial, outer lives—just as they would prosper in their personal health and their spiritual lives. The prosperity he desired for them covered their entire lives. It was prosperity that might be described as "wholeness in action" (*Success God's Way*, pp. 14–15).

In saying to Joshua, "then you will be prosperous and successful," God desired the prosperity of His people to embrace every aspect of their lives if they lived in obedience to His Word. Inspired by His Spirit and under His guidance, Joshua took courage and led the Israelites victoriously to the Promised Land, crossing the great River Jordan with the Ark of God ahead of them. Just as the Lord empowered Moses to cross the Red Sea, so did He shepherd young Joshua over the Jordan. He won for his people their battles and overcame every obstacle, including the walled city of Jericho, for "…The commander of the LORD's army" was with him (Joshua 5:15). He had promised to be with him for victory and faithfully delivered.

Joshua didn't rely on his military expertise or the years of experience serving under Moses, but depended completely on the Lord through obedience to His Word. He understood clearly that without obedience to His Commandments, he could do nothing. Hence, he made the Word his Guiding Light, Principle, Strength, Salvation, Refuge, Defense, Wisdom and his All in All—and the Lord never failed or forsook him. Similarly, those who take His Word seriously and obey

Him will never be disappointed, because He Who spoke the heavens and the earth into being by His Word is faithful and will always keep His promise to the obedient. Otherwise, if we choose our own way, we encounter defeat and worse.

Neglecting the Word Results in Defeat

After the Israelites' complete victory over Jericho, they had to attack Ai, a much smaller country. Instead of seeking counsel from the Lord, their leader, Joshua, took advice from spies who had supposedly gathered information about Ai. They said to him, "…'Not all the people will have to go up against Ai. Send two or three thousand men to take it and do not weary all the people, for only a few men are there.' " Complying with their counsel, he sent three thousand of his men, "but they were routed by the men of Ai," says Scripture, "who killed about thirty-six of them. They chased the Israelites from the city gate as far as the stone quarries and struck them down on the slopes…" (7:3–5).

Why was Israel defeated and thirty-six of them killed? I can think of two main reasons. First, Joshua didn't seek counsel from God, as expected of him as a leader of His people.

Second, Achan had sinned against God's commandment by stealing some of the devoted things and hiding them in his tent. When he was found out, he and his entire family were stoned to death, in accord with the Scriptures in Deuteronomy 17:2–7; "For the wages of sin is death…" (Rom. 6:23). In this episode, we see the proof of His faithfulness to His Word: "…'Not by might nor by power, but by my Spirit'…" (Zech. 4:6), for the Lord says, " '…apart from me, you can do nothing' " (John 15:5).

As leaders and individual followers of Christ, we learn a great lesson from Israel's mistake, seeking God's mighty power and guidance in all our endeavors in order to win the battle of life. This is imperative, because we've learned that human effort alone is no match against evil forces assailing us on our upward journey to heaven. "For our struggle," as Paul rightly points out, "is not against flesh and blood, but against the rulers…against the powers of this dark world and against the spiritual forces of evil in the heavenly realms" (Eph. 6:12).

Now, let's take a cue from Jesus as He faced the Devil's temptation.

Jesus Defeated Satan with the Word of God

In His encounter with Satan in the wilderness, Jesus used the Scriptures to defeat him. Let's take the second temptation as an example. The Devil led Him to the peak of the temple and said to Him:

> *… "If you are the Son of God," he said, "throw yourself down from here. For it is written: 'He will command his angels concerning you to guard you carefully; they will lift you up in their hands, so that you will not strike your foot against a stone.' " Jesus answered, "It says: 'Do not put the Lord your God to the test' "* (Luke 4:9–12).

It's interesting to observe here that Satan also knows the Scriptures, and so he could quote them to Jesus. Doesn't that warn you and me to take Holy writ more seriously than ever before, and to master its application accordingly to our daily lives, especially in times of temptation? My friend, if Satan dared to tempt the Son of God and wanted to trick Him into misapplying His Father's Word to His life, he will surely come to tempt us, even in our moments of serious prayer and worship.

Ignorance of the Bible will inevitably lead to defeat by the Devil, who "…prowls around like a roaring lion looking for someone to devour" (1 Pet. 5:8). Our only secure hope for victory lies in meditating on and memorizing the Scriptures as our weapon against our archfoe, Satan.

The Key to Victorious Christian Life

Christ's victory over Satan didn't happen automatically, but through prayer, fasting and the right application of His Father's Word; it's the greatest ammunition in the arsenal of every Christian. We must learn to maintain and make use of it in our war against our own sinful inclination and the Devil's. This is how the writer of Hebrews describes the Word of God:

> *For the word of God is living and active. Sharper than any double-edged sword, it penetrates even to dividing soul and spirit, joints and marrow; it judges the thoughts and attitudes of the heart. Nothing in all creation is hidden from God's sight. Everything is uncovered and laid bare before the eyes of him to whom we must give account* (Heb. 4:12).

Hence, mastering His Word and using it rightly for every situation in which we find ourselves is the key to victorious Christian life in this world of sin and woe. In his second epistle to young Timothy, Paul explains to him how the Scriptures are able to equip believers in becoming useful citizens in the community: "All Scripture is God-breathed and is useful for teaching, rebuking, correcting and training in righteousness, so that the man of God may be thoroughly equipped for every good work" (2 Tim. 3:16–17). It's clear from this passage that believers are the best people to hire, because we're hard-working, honest and trustworthy.

> **Mastering God's Word and using it rightly is the key to victorious Christian life in this world of sin and woe**

A few years ago, I worked as a cashier at CVS (Customer, Value, Service), one of the biggest pharmaceutical stores in the Washington Metropolitan Area. Once a week, we received a consignment of goods that needed to be unloaded from a truck. The manager would leave me alone at the cash register to handle the customers, while he and the rest of my colleagues would unload the goods from the truck. One day, when he was asked why he let me alone serve the customers, he replied, "Because John is able to handle the customers and the register better than any of you." Though my colleagues probably weren't happy with his response, they knew what he had said was true.

This continued until I left the store for another job in a medical office, where I was put in charge of medical records. My success as a cashier or office clerk depended on God's Word, on which I meditated early each morning before going to work. It enabled me to get on well, not only with my fellow workers, but also with customers, some of whom were troublesome. But with patience and gentleness through the working of the Holy Spirit within me, I was able to handle every situation to His glory and for the blessing of my employer and the community I served.

The Word Equips Us for Spiritual Warfare

The benefits derived from equipping ourselves with God's Word are seen not only in our encounters with difficult situations, but particularly in spiritual warfare. Our archenemy sometimes attacks us in our unguarded moments and our victory over the Devil depends solely on how we can apply the Word against him. Paul explains it further in this way:

> *For though we live in the world, we do not wage war as the world does. The weapons we fight with are not the weapons of the world. On the contrary, they have divine power to demolish strongholds. We demolish arguments and every pretension that sets itself up against the knowledge of God, and we take captive every thought to make it obedient to Christ (2 Cor. 10:3–5).*

You may ask, *Why are "our weapons not the weapons of this world?"* The answer is simple:

> *For our struggle is not against flesh and blood, but against the rulers, against the authorities, against the powers of this dark world and against the spiritual forces of evil in the heavenly realms. Therefore put on the full armor of God, so that when the day of evil comes, you may be able to stand your ground, and after you have done everything, to stand (Eph. 6:12–13).*

What is this "full armor of God" that we need to don in ensuring victory over Satan? Let's look for the answer to this question in the next chapter, where I discuss the subject in detail in the light of Paul's letter to the Ephesians, chapter 6:10–18. There, we'll discover the Christian's weapons for warfare.

CHAPTER 21

Equipping Ourselves with "the Full Armor of God"

From Paul's observations of the Roman soldier guarding him while in a Roman prison, he prescribes for believers a set of powerful weapons, described as "the full armor of God," in Ephesians 6:11–18, as follows:

"The Belt of Truth" (Ephesians 6:14)

Knowing that Satan and his cadre of demons use deceit and tricks to gain dominion over humans, the Holy Spirit revealed to Paul that our first weapon of defense should always be to speak the truth. Under no circumstances must we, as followers of Christ—Who is the Truth—distort or misrepresent the truth, regardless of whatever advantage we might gain by so doing, or we become victims of the Devil, "…for he is a liar," says Jesus, "and the father of lies" (John 8:44). Speaking the truth, therefore, keeps us abiding in Him, and with Him, "…we are more than conquerors… " (Rom. 8:37).

"The Breastplate of Righteousness" (Ephesians 6:14)

Since Satan lives and thrives in sin, any sin in our lives makes us vulnerable to demonic influence. Though we have received the *imputed* righteousness of Christ (2 Cor. 5:21), we must steadfastly maintain holy living by the power of His Father. It means our daily submission to His Power in order to be compelled by the Holy Spirit in thought, word and deed. King David wrote, "…He guides me in paths of righteousness for his name's sake" (Ps. 23:3). We know from the Scriptures that the Shepherd will never leave or forsake the sheep who listens to His voice

(John 10:28).

"The Shoe of the Gospel of Peace" (Ephesians 6:15)

Holding fast to the Good News that "...we have peace with God through our Lord Jesus Christ" (Rom. 5:1), we can stand firm against any satanic maneuvers. This emphasizes, once again, the importance of grasping the Scriptures—especially the Gospels—and applying them to our day at home or workplace. For instance, if a soldier loses his shoes on the battlefield, he becomes immobile and unable to stand and fight against the enemy; nor can he run, inevitably falling victim to the enemy.

Just as the shoes of a soldier protect his feet from being wounded and enable him to move about with his weapon to fight the enemy to victory, so do the Christian's "shoes of the Gospel of peace" shield him from Satan's attacks and allow him to go everywhere in security, sharing the Good News with others that Christ might save them from sin and the Devil's dominion.

Thus shod, you have "...authority to trample on snakes and scorpions and to overcome all the power of the enemy; nothing will harm you" (Luke 10:19). "...'How beautiful are the feet of those who bring good news!'" (Rom. 10:15).

"The Shield of Faith" (Ephesians 6:16)

Paul goes on further to teach us that in order to quench the fiery darts of the enemy, we must believe wholeheartedly whatever God's Word says about our life. That's to say, we don't doubt the Bible. We should take Him at His Word, stand by it, depend on it and faithfully apply it in our daily lives. According to James, "...faith without deeds is dead" (James 2:26).

What is a shield? In this context, a shield is a Roman soldier's steel plate, worn to protect mainly his chest (his heart) from being hit or wounded. A Christian who similarly holds fast to his or her faith will strongly resist the Devil in all his temptations or attacks, not allowing any force or circumstance to overcome faith in the Lord. This is the faith that John describes as "...victory that has overcome the world..." held by "...Only he who believes that Jesus is the Son of God" (1 John 5:4–5).

It's the unflinching faith of a person knowing without a shred of doubt that his God has the power to deliver—no matter what the circumstances surrounding him or her. Just believe that He is able.

A typical example of this kind of faith was demonstrated by Daniel's three friends in defying King Nebuchadnezzar's orders to bow down to the image in Babylon, declaring:

> *Shadrach, Meshach and Abednego replied to the king, "O Nebuchadnezzar, we do not need to defend ourselves before you in this matter. If we are thrown into the blazing furnace, the God we serve is able to save us from it, and he will rescue us from your hand, O king. But even if he does not, we want you to know, O king, that we will not serve your gods or worship the image of gold you have set up"* (Dan. 3:16–18).

Surely, their God was able to deliver them from the blazing furnace. Their miraculous deliverance proved the overarching nature of His power over the kingdom of men. With this experience, the king made a new decree in favor of the faithful friends' Kingdom of God and promoted them in the province of Babylon (3:28–30). Thus, with strong faith in Christ, we, too, will overcome our adversary.

"The Helmet of Salvation" (Ephesians 6:17)

This has to do with the confidence that there'll be a great victory celebration in the future, coupled with the "...hope of salvation..." (1 Thess. 5:8). In this instance, Paul compares the Word of God to a helmet, usually worn to shield the head from anything that might hurt or destroy it. Thus, with the helmet always in its rightful place, we're protected by the power of God, Who has saved us from sin and the dominion of Satan. We must always be conscious of our salvation through His Son's precious blood. This constant awareness promotes confidence and empowers believers to look to Him, clinging to His promise: " '...surely I am with you always, to the very end of the age' " (Matt. 28:20).

"The Sword of the Spirit" (Ephesians 6:17)

Knowing the Holy Scriptures as the sure foundation of our faith, we learn how to use them with authority as our best offensive weapon against the Devil. Jesus defeated him with the Word of God (Matt. 4:1–11). Had He not known the Bible and used it with authority, Satan would have been reigning supreme now, and we would have continued to be his victims. Thanks be to God Who gives us the victory through our Lord Jesus Christ, Who overcame Satan, not only with the Word of God in His temptation in the wilderness, but finally on the cross at Calvary. *Hallelujah!*

However, we must be reminded that the Devil hasn't been bound yet; he's still on the loose and "...prowls around like a roaring lion looking for someone to devour." Therefore, Peter warns us to "Resist him, standing firm in the faith, because you know that your brothers throughout the world are undergoing the same kind of sufferings" (1 Pet. 5:8–9). With the Word of God used in the name of Jesus Christ, John testifies to its power in defeating the enemy when he wrote:

> *Then I heard a loud voice in heaven say: "Now have come the salvation and the power and the kingdom of our God, and the authority of his Christ. For the accuser of our brothers, who accuses them before our God day and night, has been hurled down. They overcame him by the blood of the Lamb and by the word of their testimony; they did not love their lives so much as to shrink from death"* (Rev. 12:10–11).

Remember, dear friend, that there's no other person in heaven, on the earth or beneath the earth who's overcome Satan except God's Son. That's why Paul testifies in his epistle to the Philippians His pre-eminence:

> *Therefore God exalted him to the highest place and gave him the name that is above every name, that at the name of Jesus every knee should bow, in heaven and on earth and under the earth, and every tongue confess that Jesus Christ is Lord, to the glory of God the Father* (Phil. 2:9–11).

> **After learning to wear the full armor of God, against the Devil, we must get to know who our enemy is**

After learning to wear the full armor of God to ensure victory over the Devil, we must get to know who our enemy is in order to become more committed than we've ever been to our lives, staying close to our Master so that through Him, we too might have an edge over our arch-foe. This is very necessary, because there are people everywhere in denial or ignorance of his existence: they contend he's only an idea in the mind, something unreal and intangible.

Those holding this view haven't yet encountered the dark side of life and live it day-dreaming. It shouldn't surprise you, my friend, because there are self-satisfied people of upper and middle incomes disbelieving in the existence of God, let alone the reality of Satan. Notwithstanding their doubt, we clearly know otherwise. Moreover, there are those who believe in the existence of Satan, yet don't know how to face and defeat him on the battlefield.

This being the case, in the following pages I'll discuss the enemy of both God and His Son's flock, examining who he is from the biblical point of view. It's my hope that such study will help readers draw closer to Christ than ever before and thus join His faithful soldiers in keeping watch over His Father's city, in protecting themselves and the Church from Satan through the mighty resources provided for us in the Holy Scriptures.

CHAPTER 22

*T*he greatest enemy of humanity is the Devil, who's also called Satan (Job 1:6; Zech. 3:2; Matt. 12:26, 16:23; Luke 10:18). He was the cause of our first parents' downfall, and his evil goes on unabated, stealing, killing and destroying precious human beings (John 10:10). His enmity for God and His creation began thousands of years ago in heaven.

According to the Scriptures, Satan was originally one of God's precious angels, known as Lucifer, "…morning star, son of the dawn!…" (Isa. 14:12). He had had a leadership role among the angelic beings in heaven, who worship Almighty God in the beauty of holiness.

The Duty of Angels
They worship God.

The primary duty of angels is to worship Him in heaven. We catch a glimpse of their worshipfulness through six winged angels (seraphs) standing in His presence and calling to one another,

> …*"Holy, holy, holy is the LORD Almighty; the whole earth is full of his glory." At the sound of their voices the doorposts and thresholds shook and the temple was filled with smoke (6:3–4.*

In the New Testament, John also writes vividly about the exalted Christ seated upon His throne in heaven:

> *Then I looked and heard the voice of many angels, numbering thousands upon thousands, and ten thousand times ten thousand. They encircled the throne and the living creatures and the elders. In a loud voice they sang: "Worthy is the Lamb, who was slain, to receive power and wealth and wisdom and strength and honor and glory and praise!"* (Rev. 5:11–12).

They serve as God's messengers.

Another important service that angels perform on God's behalf is to serve as ministering spirits to His people according to His instructions. It's asked rhetorically in the epistle to the Hebrews: "Are not all angels ministering spirits sent to serve those who will inherit salvation?" (Heb. 1:14).

We're very familiar with the wonderful story of the angel Gabriel, who brought to the Virgin Mary the Good News of the miraculous conception and birth of Jesus Christ (Luke 1:26–38). All believers in Him are His Father's children, those who'll inherit salvation (Rom. 8:17). There are several instances in the Bible when angels were sent by God to minister to human beings at critical times in their lives (1 Kings 19:5–9; Dan. 6:21; 12:7–10; Rev. 4:6–8).

They offer deliverance and protection from danger.

A vivid example of deliverance through the ministration of angels can be seen in the story of the leader of the Apostles, Simon Peter. During the Church's early years in Jerusalem, King Herod, after killing James, went further to arrest Peter, putting him in custody with the intention of having him beheaded the following day. But as the Church kept praying earnestly for his deliverance, God—by His gracious, timely intervention—dispatched His angelic messenger to save Peter from the king's hands (Acts 12:1–17).

Furthermore, of course, we mustn't forget the interesting and dramatic story of Jacob's wrestling match with an angel of God (Gen. 32:24–29).

They bring believers protection, guidance and the message of salvation.

In Psalm 34:7, David speaks of the protection believers enjoy in the hands of God by means of His angels, who not only surround our houses but also guard us on our way, protecting us from our enemies (*also* 91:9–16; Judg. 6:11–23).

They offer divine guidance.

Joshua's victory over the great walled city of Jericho would have been utterly impossible but for the divine guidance offered by the " '...commander of the army of the LORD...' " (Josh. 5:14). Similarly, Philip was guided in his evangelistic outreach by an angel of God in preaching Christ to the Ethiopian Eunuch, who gladly believed the Good News and was saved (Acts 8:26–39).

God neither changes nor is He a respecter of persons. Hence, we have the assurance that He Who provided the needs of His servants through His angels in the past is able to offer similar supernatural care in our day to all serving Him faithfully in various ways according to His purpose.

Lucifer's Rebellion in Heaven

The Scriptures inform us that on one occasion, Lucifer and a third of the angels rebelled against God, resulting in their being cast down from heaven. Though the Scriptures originally refer to the king of Tyre, the descriptions go beyond an earthly monarch to Lucifer, as follows:

> ..."*You were the model of perfection, full of wisdom and perfect in beauty. You were in Eden, the garden of God...You were anointed as a guardian cherub, for so I ordained you...You were blameless in your ways...till wickedness was found in you...Your heart became proud on account of your beauty, and you corrupted your wisdom because of your splendor. So I threw you to the earth...You have come to a horrible end and will be no more*" (Ezek. 28:12–15, 17, 19; *also* Rev. 12:1–12).

Thus, Lucifer was no longer called "morning star" or "son of the dawn," but Satan, "adversary of God, and lord of evil in Judaism and Christianity. He is full of extreme cruelty, wickedness and viciousness" (*Webster's New Collegiate Dictionary*). He's called by several names in the Scriptures, as for instance: the serpent (Gen. 3:1); the thief, the prince of this world (John 10:10, 14:30); the great dragon, the ancient serpent, the Devil/Satan, the accuser (Rev. 12:9–10). The Akans of Ghana—including the Gas and others—call him Abonsam or Sasambonsam.

Satan and those angels who teamed up with him in his act of rebellion made a bad decision on that day. By rejecting their divinely appointed position and purpose in heaven, they eternally forfeited the honor and purpose for which they were created. They didn't have the opportunity to repent of rebellion's sin: it was obvious that pride had made it impossible for Satan to do so. Masterminded by the Devil, hell was created for the entirety of demonic spirits.

Now, let's look at a little of their subterfuge and learn how to resist them.

Activities of Satan and Evil Spirits

As we've learned from the Bible, Paul speaks of Satan and his demonic team as "…the rulers…the powers of this dark world…" (Eph. 6:12). They operate in darkness, invisible to us, because their deeds are evil and wicked. John echoed the same message when he said, "…Light has come into the world, but men loved darkness instead of light because their deeds were evil. Everyone who does evil hates the light, and will not come into the light for fear that his deeds will be exposed" (John 3:19–20).

Thus, Peter counsels believers to beware of the Devil: "Be self-controlled and alert. Your enemy the devil prowls around like a roaring lion looking for someone to devour" (1 Pet. 5:8). He points out here the cunning manner in which Satan operates: in his anger, he roams about watching and waiting, only to attack anyone chancing his way.

It was to keep all earth-dwellers, especially believers, on the alert against the attacks of the Devil that a voice from heaven sounded the following warning through John:

> *"…But woe to the earth and the sea, because the devil has gone down to you! He is filled with fury, because he knows that his time is short"…Then the dragon was enraged at the woman and went off to make war against the rest of her offspring—those who obey God's commandments and hold to the testimony of Jesus* (Rev. 12:12, 17).

This reminds me of the story of a teenaged girl possessed by a spirit on her father's farm the very day she came of age (i.e., when she reached puberty). After several months of the spirit's torment, she became so seriously ill that she was hospitalized for many days. During one of my early morning visitations to patients in the hospital, her mother told me about her daughter's condition.

Realizing that "…'This kind can come out only by prayer' " (Mark 9:29), I devoted the following day to my assignment: interceding for this young girl and helping her to fast. I visited her toward evening at the hospital. After about half-an-hour of intensive prayer to the Holy Spirit in the mighty name of Jesus, the girl was delivered from the evil spirit that had victimized her for more than six months.

My friend, without Christ living in you as your Savior and Lord, you don't have power over Satan and his demonic forces. And if you're a believer, are you so fully committed to Christianity that you're filled with the Holy Spirit and wearing "the whole armor of God?" We need to remind ourselves that it's only Christ who defeated the Devil in the encounter with him during His earthly ministry. He routed him completely and finally on the cross (Col. 2:13–15). Therefore, without Him, people can't "escape from the trap of the devil, who has taken them captive to do his will" (2 Tim. 2:26).

Therefore, I seriously counsel you to yield to Jesus, whom to know garners for you eternal life and perfect freedom. The hour of decision is now—tomorrow may be too late! Please read further on to know much more about the works of evil spirits.

They Slander God and Believers

With Satan as their leader, demons deceive and create doubt in believers concerning the character of God, as they did to Eve in the Garden of Eden (Gen. 3:1–5)—as well as Job and others (Job 1:9–11; Acts 5:3, 26:18; 2 Cor. 12:7, Rev. 12:10–12). It takes a man of God filled with the Holy Spirit to discern the cunning voice of the Devil, who whispers into our ears to deceive or manipulate us into disobeying the Lord.

Haven't you occasionally heard a voice instructing you to retaliate after someone's insulted or mistreated you? Those are Satan's words, and usually contrary to God's Word. That's why it's very important for every true child of the Lord to study and equip himself with the Scriptures. There's no other way by which we can know God's Word, let alone to use it against the enemy. Jesus's sheep hear His voice, and they follow Him. If we sincerely study, meditate on and keep God's Word, the Holy Spirit will always guide us to obey His voice and reject Satan's.

They Plant Evil Thoughts in People's Minds

It was Satan who moved King David to take a census of the people of Israel at a time when it wasn't appropriate in God's view. David was doubtless motivated by pride in boosting his ego, to prove his greatness as the leader he had been since enthronement (1 Chron. 21:1).

Selfish pride was the exact cause of Lucifer's downfall, and he always tempts people in high positions with its allure, so they'll stumble just as he did. For instance, he caused Judas, the treasurer of Christ's ministry, to harbor the malicious thoughts that steadily led to the betrayal of his Master and subsequent suicide (Luke 22:3; John 13:2, 6:70).

There's a huge lesson for Christian leaders, especially ministers, to learn from Judas' experience and its repercussions. We sometimes become so engrossed in the ministry—serving the needs of our members, attending meetings here and there—that we don't seem to find the time to minister to our own spiritual and physical needs and those of our families, leaving a gap for the enemy to enter and attack the Church and our loved ones. That's the chief reason Jesus cautioned His followers: " 'Watch and pray so that you will not fall into temptation. The spirit is willing, but the body is weak.' " (Matt. 26:41).

They Negatively Influence National Leaders

In an engagement with His disciples, Jesus speaks about the Devil: "...the prince of this world is coming. He has no hold on me" (John 14:30). Indeed, this was because though fully man, He was also fully God. Unlike any of us, He was not conceived by the seed of man but by the power of the Holy Spirit (Luke 1:26–38). Therefore, since He Who is in Jesus (God, the Holy Spirit) is greater than the Devil, who's in the world, Christ overcame Satan in all the temptations he directly or indirectly placed in His earthly ministry's path (Matt. 4:1–11; Col. 2:1–15).

Satan Blinds the Minds of Unbelievers

Writing to the Corinthian Church, Paul also refers to one of the Devil's activities as follows: "The god of this age has blinded the minds of unbelievers, so that they cannot see the light of the gospel of the glory of Christ, who is the image of God" (2 Cor. 4:4). This and other references clearly suggest to us that Satan has the power to coerce any pagan king, head of state or other authority figure to commit such acts of wickedness as torturing to death or killing by firing squad all who dare to oppose his policies.

Some national leaders in Africa and other parts of the world are guilty of these diabolical acts in their attempts to pursue their own political agendas. Adolf Hitler of Germany killed millions of Jews in gas chambers. Idi Amin of Uganda gunned down many of his opponents. There remain other vicious leaders who liquidate their opponents out of hatred and not for the love and progress of their countries.

> Satan has the power to coerce kings and heads of state into atrocities such as torture and murder

A fitting biblical example is the case of Haman in the Book of Esther. In a high position under Xerxes, Haman hated Mordecai because he wasn't willing to bow to him for religious reasons (Exod. 20:3–6). This created hatred for the whole Jewish race in Xerxes' Persian kingdom, and a wicked plot to annihilate them completely from the face of the earth developed (Esther 3:6). By God's intervention through the prayers of Queen Esther and the Jews, Haman was hung from the very gallows prepared for Mordecai (8:9–10). "If a man digs a pit, he will fall into it; if a man rolls a stone, it will roll back on him" (Prov. 26:27). Thus, the "stone" that Haman rolled to fall on Mordecai instead fell on himself.

In other words, Paul says, "Do not be deceived: God cannot be mocked. A man reaps what he sows. The one who sows to please his sinful nature, from that nature will reap destruction; the one who sows to please the Spirit, from the Spirit will reap eternal life" (Gal. 6:7–8). *What are we of this generation sowing—and what do we expect to reap in return?* This is a question you must ponder carefully and honestly answer for yourself. Surely, Haman's attempt to destroy the Jews could be likened to the labors of the Antichrist (Rev 13:2, 4) and all who work for the Devil in hindering God's work in this world.

Under the influence of an evil spirit, King Saul of Israel twice threw a sword at David, intending to pin him to the wall, but he cleverly eluded him in both incidents (1 Sam. 18:10–12). Saul and his son Jonathan ultimately both died in Israel's battle against the Philistines at Mount Gilboa (2 Sam. 1:4).

There's another instance when Satan used "a lying spirit," this time leading King Ahab to his death (1 Kings 22:20–23, 37–38). He also assigned another demonic spirit to control the king of Persia (Dan. 10:10–21). It's a prophecy recorded by John that through evil spirits, Satan will finally gather "the kings together to the place that in Hebrew is called Armageddon" (Rev. 16).

Now, having known these concrete examples of the havoc that the Devil and his demonic allies can wreak throughout humanity, we must ask the next question: *How can we overcome him?* Honestly speaking, I regret to say that there's no human being able to face the devil and overcome him, except the Lord, Jesus Christ, empowers Him.

If Satan succeeded in deceiving Adam and Eve, thereby creating death for human beings in their disobedience to God, it's no wonder that he's called, "…the prince of this world…" (John 14:30) and "…the ruler of the kingdom of the air, the spirit who is now at work in those who are disobedient" (Eph. 2:2). Since the fall of our first parents, humanity has abdicated its God-given authority and privilege as overseer and steward of His creation (Gen. 1:27). However, by His gracious intervention, there's Good News. As Prof. Charles Paul Conn puts it: "The tree of Eden became the tree of Calvary."

That's only part of the Good News. Let's be reminded that just as Haman perished in the gallows of his own home, so will Satan be cast down and destroyed in the lake of fire prepared for him and his angels, as will those who help to carry out his wicked plans. Furthermore, Jesus "…was raised on the third day according to the Scriptures" (1 Cor. 15:4) and thus "…has destroyed death and has brought life and immortality to light through the gospel" (2 Tim. 1:10). *Hallelujah and amen!*

Gordon Lindsay connects Christ's victory over Satan with His prayer and fasting in the wilderness and declares:

> As Adam and Eve's disobedience by eating the forbidden fruit was the original cause of man's losing his God-given dominion in the Garden of Eden, so Christ's fasting forty days and nights in the wilderness, there overcoming the fiercest onslaughts of the enemy, made possible the restoration of man's dominion. (*Prayer and Fasting: The Master Key to the Impossible*, Ohiseyi Press Ltd., Ibadan, 1990, p. 1).

This then leads us to the answer to the question: *How can we resist and overcome Satan and his demonic forces?* It comes from Jesus' response to the disciples when they wanted to know why they weren't able to cast out a demon from a young boy, whose father had approached them for help. They said to Him, " 'Why could not we cast him out?' " Christ replied:

" 'This kind can come forth by nothing, but by prayer and fasting' " (*KJV*, Mark 9:28–29).

In other translations of the Bible, such as *NIV*, the word *fasting* is omitted. Nevertheless, having personally experienced the benefits of fasting, I strongly recommend it to mature believers, who can practice it as discipline in their prayer life. Since the Son of God and the Apostles found it necessary to fast and pray in the pursuit of their faith and the fulfillment of their ministries, we can't do otherwise. It's only by so doing that we can also be truly faithful stewards of the legacy entrusted to our charge.

CHAPTER **23**

*I*want to begin this chapter with the sound counsel offered to all believers by James, the brother of Jesus, and presiding elder of the first Christian Council of the Church in Jerusalem. He stated, "Submit yourselves, then, to God. Resist the devil, and he will flee from you" (James 4:7). That's to say, we should have the desire to do God's will and the humility to obey Him. It implies counting ourselves as dead to sin but alive to God in His Son. "Therefore do not let sin reign in your mortal body so that you obey its evil desires" (Rom. 6:12).

We must refuse to yield to the Devil's tricks or temptations in the name of the Lord Jesus Christ by the power of the Holy Spirit. The way to go about this task is *prayer.* "More things are wrought by prayer than this world dreams of," wrote Alfred Lord Tennyson several ages ago; it's just as true in our day.

The importance of prayer was underscored by Jesus in His statement to the merchants who had turned the Temple into a marketplace: "…'Is it not written: "My house will be called a house of prayer for all nations"? But you have made it "a den of robbers" ' " (Mark 11:17). In saying this, He rebuked the leaders of temple worship for the following reasons: They had

- turned the house of God into a marketplace
- cheated worshippers coming to exchange their money for offerings or a lamb for sacrifice
- hindered "all nations" from coming to the Temple to worship and pray to God

• disobeyed God's commandment

Jesus exemplified the essence of prayer during His ministry, withdrawing Himself to a solitary place after a busy day's work in order to pray to His Father in heaven. Mark wrote, "Very early in the morning, while it was still dark, Jesus got up, left the house and went off to a solitary place, where he prayed" (1:35). Having observed prayer as an integral part of His ministry, the Disciples also came to Him with their request: "…'Lord, teach us to pray…' " (Luke 11:1). Accordingly, He taught His followers what is commonly known as "The Lord's Prayer" (Luke 11:2; Matt. 6:6–9).

It's important to be reminded at this critical point in the book that we *aren't* told to pray to any ancestor, god or goddess—the dead have no power to help the living here on earth; only the Lord, the Living God alone. He declares, "…'I am the LORD, and there is no other' " (Isa. 45:18).

Let's now begin by understanding what prayer's all about, for the sake of those who aren't familiar with the subject. They may ask the question:

What is Prayer?

Prayer is the audible or inaudible expression of our heart's concerns to God. Here's what hymn writer James Montgomery says about prayer:

> Prayer is the soul's sincere desire,
> Uttered or unexpressed,
> The motion of a hidden fire
> That trembles in the breast.
>
> Prayer is the burden of a sigh,
> The falling of a tear,
> The upward glancing of an eye
> When none but God is near.
>
> Prayer is the simplest form of speech
> That infant lips can try;
> Prayer the sublimest strains that reach
> The majesty on high.

> Prayer is the contrite sinner's voice
> Returning from his ways,
> While angels in their songs rejoice,
> And cry: Behold he prays!
>
> Prayer is the Christian's vital breath,
> The Christian's native air,
> His watchword at the gates of death;
> He enters heaven with prayer.
> (*MHB*, 533, verses 1–5 by James Montgomery, 1771-1854).

Knowing that God is Spirit, that no one else apart from Him can meet our spiritual, physical or emotional needs, and that *prayer* is the only means by which humans can communicate with Him, we must readily respond to His gracious invitation and come to Him with our problems. "And call upon me in the day of trouble; I will deliver you, and you will honor me."(Ps. 50:15). Again, in the gospel of Matthew, Jesus gently invites all people to come, irrespective of rank, race, color or sex: " 'Come to me, all you who are weary and burdened, and I will give you rest' " (Matt. 11:28).

Prayer is thus both the privilege and responsibility of every true child of God. It's a privilege because we're communicating with a God Who is "the King, the Lord Almighty," holy and too pure to look upon sin. Even the angels in heaven can't directly see Him; they have to cover their faces to praise His holiness and majesty, "...'Holy, holy, holy is the LORD Almighty; the whole earth is full of his glory' " (Isa. 6:3). In spite of His holiness, He bids us sinful humans to come to Him with all our concerns. Prayer is like coming to a loving parent willing to receive and listen to us unconditionally, regardless of the size of our need.

Prayer is the responsibility of every believer in obedient response to God's call to duty.

Additionally, prayer is the responsibility of every believer in obedient response to God's call to duty. Listen to this, for example: "if my people, who are called by my name, will humble themselves and pray and seek my face and turn from their wicked ways, then will I hear from heaven and will forgive their sin and will heal their land" (2 Chron.

7:14). We must simply obey His call to duty, because He has told us to pray.

It's thus evident that the purpose of prayer is to determine His will in our wishes and to pray for their fulfillment. As Christians, we ought to welcome the act of prayer as both a privilege and a responsibility to cooperate with the Triune God in the creative work of our fellow human beings. The following are several examples of the call on believers to pray.

"As for me, far be it from me that I should sin against the LORD by failing to pray for you. And I will teach you the way that is good and right" (1 Sam. 12:23).

"I urge, then, first of all, that requests, prayers, intercession and thanksgiving be made for everyone—for kings and all those in authority, that we may live peaceful and quiet lives in all godliness and holiness," (1 Tim. 2:1–2).

"And pray in the Spirit on all occasions with all kinds of prayers and requests. With this in mind, be alert and always keep on praying for all the saints. Pray also for me, that whenever I open my mouth, words may be given me so that I will fearlessly make known the mystery of the gospel" (Eph. 6:18-19).

" 'Watch and pray so that you will not fall into temptation. The spirit is willing, but the body is weak' " (Matt. 26:41).

All these references emphasize the point that the faithful saints' victories recorded in the Holy Scriptures came about "…'Not by might nor by power, but by my Spirit,' says the LORD Almighty" (Zech. 4:6), through the constant act of prayer, in which they invested much of their precious time, lives and ministries. As they waited patiently upon the Lord in prayer, He never disappointed them.

For the Scripture declares: "Call to me and I will answer you and tell you great and unsearchable things you do not know" (Jer. 33:3). The assurance we have from Paul is this: "The one who calls you is faithful and he will do it" (1 Thess. 5:24). Counting on God's faithfulness to His promises and knowing how much prayer can accomplish, he thus urges all believers to "pray continually" (5:17).

Prayer is a Priority and Discipline

As indicated in the above passage, a careful study of Jesus' ministry and life will show that prayer had the highest priority for Him, not only over physical rest but also social life and even food. Indeed, prayer was the primary communication link between Him and His Father. The same must be true for us, if we're truly His disciples. "After he had dismissed them, he went up on a mountainside by himself to pray. When evening came, he was there alone" (Matt. 14:23). "One of those days Jesus went out to a mountainside to pray, and spent the night praying to God" (Luke 6:12).

Can you imagine God's Son holding all-night prayer all by Himself on a mountain? Yet, He did it in order to be in tune with His Father—to receive the wisdom, power and direction necessary to accomplish His divine mission. And He got what He needed. That's the way our Master went, and we servants should follow the trail that alone can lead us to victory and glory in His name. Churches ought to occasionally organize prayer vigils to meet the needs of their members.

Prayer Is a Ministry unto God

The biblical concept of all believers' priesthood qualifies every Christian to be called "a priest unto the Lord." Hence, we always aim at ministering to Him before ministering to people. As His children, we mustn't fail to minister to Him through the acts of praise, worship and communion with Him through prayer and meditation in His name.

This duty is bestowed upon us not by virtue of our own righteousness, but by that of Jesus' blood. His sacrifice justifies our boldly entering the Holy of Holies with both humility and confidence in the very presence of God. Peter wrote, "But you are a chosen people, a royal priesthood, a holy nation, a people belonging to God, that you may declare the praises of him who called you out of darkness into his wonderful light" (1 Pet. 2:9).

In earlier verses he wrote, "As you come to him, the living Stone—rejected by men but chosen by God and precious to him— you also, like living stones, are being built into a spiritual house to be a holy priesthood, offering spiritual sacrifices acceptable to God through Jesus Christ" (2:5). Elsewhere in the Bible, "The LORD detests the sacrifice of the wicked, but the prayer of the upright pleases him" (Prov. 15:8).

Hence, as the people of God, we must always see it as a necessary duty and a privilege to minister to Him, thus receiving power, wisdom and direction before going out to minister to the world's problems and temptations.

Prayer Is a Unique Communication with God

This is our time spent with the Lord, because we love Him. During this time, our conversation reaches down to our deepest recesses, and our prayers turn into heart-to-heart dialogue with our heavenly Father. Just as "He made known his ways to Moses, his deeds to the people of Israel" (Ps. 103:7), so does He desire to do for those committed to His service in our time, through the Holy Spirit.

> *The LORD would speak to Moses face to face, as a man speaks with his friend. Then Moses would return to the camp, but his young aide Joshua son of Nun did not leave the tent. Moses said to the LORD, "You have been telling me, 'Lead these people,' but you have not let me know whom you will send with me. You have said, 'I know you by name and you have found favor with me.' If you are pleased with me, teach me your ways so I may know you and continue to find favor with you. Remember that this nation is your people." The LORD replied, "My Presence will go with you, and I will give you rest"* (Exod. 33:11–14).

Thanks to God that in these and many other ways, Moses, Israel's great intercessor, pleaded on their behalf in His presence and helped to deliver his people from the many afflictions that otherwise would have befallen them in the wilderness.

Whether you are somebody in authority or not, black or white, rich or poor, man or woman, it's important to know that as a Christian, your prayer can bring deliverance through faith in Christ. All the forces of evil that have crippled many Africans and non-Africans alike will lose their grip through the effectual prayer of believers in His matchless name. "…The reason the Son of God appeared was to destroy the devil's work" (1 John 3:8).

Prayer Opens Our Spiritually Blind Eyes

It's encouraging to know that through the act of prayer, the Lord graciously makes it possible for believers to see things in the spiritual realm that they can't see or know in any other way. Here are a few examples to stimulate your thirst for prayer:

- " 'Sacrifice thank offerings to God, fulfill your vows to the Most High, and call upon me in the day of trouble; I will deliver you, and you will honor me' " (Ps. 50:14–15).
- " 'Don't be afraid,' the prophet answered. 'Those who are with us are more than those who are with them.' And Elisha prayed, 'O

LORD, open his eyes so he may see.' Then the LORD opened the servant's eyes, and he looked and saw the hills full of horses and chariots of fire all around Elisha" (2 Kings 6:16–17).

The Bible describes demonic forces as "...the powers of this dark world..." (Eph. 6:12), and it's by prayer that the Lord generously enables believers to see what's hidden from natural sight. After revealing what our enemies have planned against us in the darkness, He empowers us in response to our prayer to overcome them. Thus Joseph Scriven exclaimed:

> O what a privilege we have in Jesus
> All our sins and grief to bear!
> What a privilege to carry
> everything to God in prayer!
> O what peace we often forfeit
> O what needless pain we bear,
> all because we do not carry
> everything to God in prayer!
> (*MHB*, 538, verse 1, Joseph M. Scriven, 1820-86).

Prayer Makes a Way for God's Will on Earth

What enduring knowledge it is that the power of heaven awaits church militants—all believers on earth, namely the universal Church—to pray for wonders.

Teaching His disciples how to pray, Jesus said, among other things, "your kingdom come, your will be done on earth as it is in heaven" (Matt. 6:10). He further assured them " 'I tell you the truth, whatever you bind on earth will bebound in heaven, and whatever you loose on earth will be loosed in heaven. Again, I tell you that if two of you on earth agree about anything you ask for, it will be done for you by my Father in heaven. For where two or three come together in my name, there am I with them' " (18:18–20).

What Christ clearly means is that His Father's divine purpose limits in some ways His activities on earth, but He nonetheless graciously awaits the prayers of His children before responding. I remember with a thrill John's vision of the 24 elders falling prostrate before the Lamb, holding "...golden bowls full of incense, which are the prayers of the saints" (Rev. 5:8).

Concerning believers' prayers, E. Stanley Jones said, "We align ourselves with the purpose and power of God, and He is able to do things through us that He could not do otherwise." He has delegated to believers a measure of His divine authority to be exercised through prayer, and so by calling on Him, we move, as it were, His "victorious right hand" to work mightily on behalf of His people. From time immemorial, He has sought an intercessor who would passionately plead for the people so that His perfect will and purpose might be done on earth as in heaven. The following is a fitting example in the history of Israel during the days of the prophet Ezekiel:

> *"I looked for a man among them who would build up the wall and stand before me in the gap on behalf of the land so I would not have to destroy it, but I found none. So I will pour out my wrath on them and consume them with my fiery anger, bringing down on their own heads all they have done, declares the Sovereign LORD"* (Ezek. 22:30–31).

Elsewhere in Scripture,

> *I have posted watchmen on your walls, O Jerusalem; they will never be silent day or night. You who call on the LORD, give yourselves no rest, and give him no rest till he establishes Jerusalem and makes her the praise of the earth* (Isa. 62:6–7).

In the two passages quoted above, we observe in the first instance that the lack of an intercessor would result in the destruction of Israel; whereas in the second case, prayer-warriors would keep watch and pray without ceasing until God's purpose was fulfilled in Jerusalem, which would cause everyone to praise Him. May I remind you, dear friend, that the intercessors aren't told to call on other gods or pour libation to Israel's ancestors; that wouldn't bring victory and honor to Jerusalem, but instead, defeat and disgrace.

Regrettably, that's exactly what's happening in most parts of the world today, especially in Africa. Therefore, if we really want to experience spiritual freedom and economic prosperity, we ought to have intercessors calling on God day and night, giving themselves no rest until He establishes Africa "…and makes her a praise on the earth."

> **If we really want to experience spiritual freedom and economic prosperity, we need intercessors**

Prayer Brings Deliverance

In 1 Samuel 7:7, we read about a vivid example of God's deliverance of Israel from the Philistines' hands when they had risen against her. Sensing defeat, the Israelites appealed to Samuel, in his double role as priest and prophet, to intercede on their behalf.

In compliance with their request, he stood before God and offered a sucking lamb in prayer to Him. "While Samuel was sacrificing the burnt offering, the Philistines drew near to engage Israel in battle. But that day the LORD thundered with loud thunder against the Philistines and threw them into such a panic that they were routed before the Israelites" (7:10)

An exciting New Testament example of deliverance that makes very interesting reading is the story of Peter recorded in Acts 12:6–17.

Additionally, there have been several instances of individuals' deliverance encountered in my ministry that space doesn't allow me to narrate here, but I can testify to this in my own life. My conversion and subsequent call to the ministry were the result of great deliverance that the Lord mercifully granted me while I suffered a near-fatal illness in the early 1960s. Close to death, I cried to Him in faith, confessed my sins and earnestly prayed for deliverance, promising to surrender my life to Him were I to be saved from oblivion. In the words of David, I may put it this way:

> *The cords of death entangled me, the anguish of the grave came upon me; I was overcome by trouble and sorrow. Then I called on the name of the LORD: "O LORD, save me!" The LORD is gracious and righteous; our God is full of compassion…For you, O LORD, have delivered my soul from death, my eyes from tears, my feet from stumbling, that I may walk before the LORD in the land of the living* (Ps. 116:3–5, 8–9).

Prayer Enables Believers to Receive Revelation

As we continue to walk closely with God in prayer and obedience to Him, He will reveal to us through the indwelling Holy Spirit for what He wants us to pray, pointing to a specific family problem or life situation. In His permissive will, He allows us to see what He sees, in order that we may move, through His will or action, to bring about a change for the better. As intercessors, we must be cautioned, however, to carefully guard against divulging secrets made known to us through prayer. We must seek God's clear guidance in obeying the timing and means for sharing the revelation with the people concerned.

While praying about 15 years ago, the Lord revealed to me that an acquaintance of mine was doomed, a grave being dug for him. *How would I break such news to him or even his wife?* What made it more difficult was that the man in question was fit and well, going about his business as usual. After praying for wisdom and guidance, I was told to go and share the Gospel with him and lead him to come into saving faith in Jesus Christ, using specifically John 5:24: " 'I tell you the truth, whoever hears my word and believes him who sent me has eternal life and will not be condemned; he has crossed over from death to life.' "

Without delay, I visited this man in the evening of the same day. I did exactly as I was told without mentioning the vision. A few days after my visit, I went back to follow up. His wife told me he had had to leave suddenly for his village near Kumasi, because some soldiers had been sent by Ghana's AFRC regime to arrest him. Why? Only God knows the answer, but whatever the reason might have been, he got the hint and left the city before the soldiers arrived. Those were the days when almost every well-to-do person in the country was suspected of ill-gotten money and charged with corruption by the previous AFRC regime. One could be arrested, taken to army barracks to be interrogated, beaten, imprisoned or killed, depending on the probe's findings.

It wasn't until I heard his story that I really understood the revelation granted me; surely the Lord knew what was to befall him and graciously delivered him from imminent death. He had indeed "crossed from death to life" because he believed in Jesus Christ as his Savior. I thank God for making me a vehicle through whom His message of salvation could arrive at the right time, or the man would have died, according to the revelation.

Here are some passages to confirm this truth about revelation through prayer:

> *Then Joshua tore his clothes and fell facedown to the ground before the ark of the LORD, remaining there till evening. The elders of Israel did the same, and sprinkled dust on their heads. And Joshua said, "Ah, Sovereign LORD, why did you ever bring this people across the Jordan to deliver us into the hands of the Amorites to destroy us? If only we had been content to stay on the other side of the Jordan!...The Canaanites and the other people of the country will hear about this and they will surround us and wipe out our name from the earth. What then will you do for your own great name?" The LORD said to Joshua, "Stand up! What are you doing down on your face? Israel has sinned; they have violated my covenant, which I commanded them to keep. They have taken*

some of the devoted things; they have stolen, they have lied, they have put them with their own possessions. That is why the Israelites cannot stand against their enemies; they turn their backs and run because they have been made liable to destruction. I will not be with you anymore unless you destroy whatever among you is devoted to destruction" (Josh. 7:6–7, 9–12).

In this passage, we find Moses's successor perplexed and sorrow-stricken, prostrating before the Lord in prayer from morning until evening hour. Then He revealed to Joshua the cause of Israel's defeat by her enemies: Achan had stolen some of the devoted things—a piece of silver, a robe and a bar of gold—and hidden them in his tent.

To purge Israel of this sin and set her aright, holy, and consecrated before the presence of God, Achan was brought out from his tribe and, together with his household, stoned to death and burned in fire. Thus cleansed, they were fully empowered by God to defeat their enemies.

The following passage describes Jesus praising His Father for the revelation to His disciples:

At that time Jesus, full of joy through the Holy Spirit, said, "I praise you, Father, Lord of heaven and earth, because you have hidden these things from the wise and learned, and revealed them to little children. Yes, Father, for this was your good pleasure. All things have been committed to me by my Father. No one knows who the Son is except the Father, and no one knows who the Father is except the Son and those to whom the Son chooses to reveal him" (Luke 10:21–22).

Paul, too, shares his experience of revelation:

To keep me from becoming conceited because of these surpassingly great revelations, there was given me a thorn in my flesh, a messenger of Satan, to torment me. Three times I pleaded with the Lord to take it away from me. But he said to me, "My grace is sufficient for you, for my power is made perfect in weakness." Therefore I will boast all the more gladly about my weaknesses, so that Christ's power may rest on me (2 Cor. 12:7–9).

We note here that, like the Apostle Paul, whenever we find ourselves struggling, we shouldn't hesitate to pray in order to know God's mind or revelation about it. With His revelation, we'll be able to bear our burden, knowing that His grace is sufficient to see us through.

It's very important to remind ourselves here again that no earthly being, ancestor or god has the power to deliver us from pain or suffering—only the Lord. "When our hearts are filled with pain," says David C.

McCasland, "it is good to call on God in prayer—morning, noon, and night."

Prayer Must Be in Accordance with God's Word

In order for our prayers to bear fruit, we should learn to pray in accordance with what God has said in the Holy Scriptures. This consists in speaking His Word in faith, not in special formulas or vain repetition, "…like pagans, for they think they will be heard because of their many words" (Matt. 6:7).

"The Spirit gives life; the flesh counts for nothing. The words I have spoken to you are spirit and they are life" (John 6:63); " 'Is not my word like fire,' declares the LORD, 'and like a hammer that breaks a rock in pieces?' " (Jer. 23:29). Therefore, if it's spoken in faith through the power of the Holy Spirit, it goes forth with anointing to perform what's intended. The following examples may be helpful.

> *As the rain and the snow come down from heaven, and do not return to it without watering the earth and making it bud and flourish, so that it yields seed for the sower and bread for the eater, so is my word that goes out from my mouth: It will not return to me empty, but will accomplish what I desire and achieve the purpose for which I sent it* (Isa. 55:10–11).

Peter observed the result of Jesus's words and said to Him,

> *…"Rabbi, look! The fig tree you cursed has withered!" "Have faith in God," Jesus answered. "I tell you the truth, if anyone says to this mountain, 'Go, throw yourself into the sea,' and does not doubt in his heart but believes that what he says will happen, it will be done for him. Therefore I tell you, whatever you ask for in prayer, believe that you have received it, and it will be yours"* (Mark 11:21–24).

The important key to the greatest resistance leading to victory over the Devil is prayer and fasting

The Bible reminds us further: "And without faith it is impossible to please God, because anyone who comes to him must believe that he exists and that he rewards those who earnestly seek him."

As you might have already noted earlier through the examples of Christ and the Apostles, the important key to the greatest resistance leading to victory over the Devil is *prayer* and *fasting*. Normal prayer *won't do it* unless it's ignited with fasting, as the Lord advised His followers.

Now, let's read on to see the key role that prayer and fasting play in the lives of Christian warriors.

CHAPTER 24

Let's begin by reminding ourselves once again of what Jesus said to His disciples, " 'This kind can come forth by nothing, but by prayer and fasting' " (*KJV*, Mark 9:28–29).

What is Fasting?

Fasting is the discipline of abstaining from food in order to "draw near to God" through prayer, referred to biblically as *afflicting the soul*: "Is it such a fast that I have chosen? a day for a man to afflict his soul?…" (*KJV*, Isa. 58:5) Fasting denies us our fleshly cravings, allows us to focus on matters of the Spirit that affect our relationship with God and our fellow human beings, and demonstrates the sincerity of our prayers.

How Must We Fast?

When we fast, we usually begin with brief abstention: from sundown to noon. Under more common circumstances, fasting lasts from sundown to sundown, say 6:00P.M. to 6:00P.M. the following day. During this period, we should spend time alone with God, reading and meditating on His Word, and listening for His counsel through the Holy Spirit (1 Kings 119:11–16, 33–37; John 10:27–30, 16:13–14).

When Must We Fast?

There are several biblical reasons for fasting:

- When facing a national crisis (Judg. 20:26; 1 Sam. 7:6; 2 Chron. 20:3; Ezra 8:21);
- For meeting individual needs (Matt. 17:21);
- During periods of distress (2 Sam. 3:35; Ps. 35:13);
- When facing spiritual decisions (Matt. 4:2; Acts 13:2);
- In anticipation of Christ's return (Luke 5:35).

Benefits/Blessings of Fasting

Heavy burdens are relieved through fasting (Isaiah 58:6ff):

- Wisdom is obtained (Dan. 10);
- Revival comes (Isa. 6);
- Recovery of a sick loved one may come (Ps. 35:13);
- God's protection from danger is secured (1 Kings 21:27-29);
- Inauguration of a great ministry may follow (Luke 4:1–13, 14–19);
- Deliverance from demonic possession or attack is secured (Mark 9:14–29).

The Scriptures are replete with evidence of the positive effects that prayer and fasting have on every human situation, even to the extent of dismantling strongholds and completely eradicating Satan's work. No military force or atomic bomb can do this except the Spirit of the Living God: "…'Not by might nor by power, but by my Spirit,' says the LORD Almighty" (Zech. 4:6). The example of Moses as a leader of the people of Israel may set the pace here.

When the Israelites rebelled against God in the wilderness, they came under His judgment. " 'I have seen these people,' the LORD said to Moses, 'and they are a stiff-necked people. Now leave me alone so that my anger may burn against them and that I may destroy them. Then I will make you into a great nation.' " (Exod. 32:9–10).

Moved with sympathy and compassion for his people, Moses prayed and fasted for 40 days and nights, pleading the Israelites' case before God at Mount Sinai (34:28). He asked for three things: first, that Israel might receive divine forgiveness; second, that he might have a vision of His glory; and third, that His presence might accompany them on their journey to the Promised Land.

In the end, God granted Moses' prayer and made a covenant with him. When he came down from the mountain, his face shone so brightly with His glow that the people of Israel couldn't look at him — he had to cover his face with a veil (34:35).

More than a month's worth of Moses' prayer and fasting resulted in the breaking of the powers of darkness and the moving of God's compassion for the restoration of Israel. Let me assure you that He Who gave Moses the light of righteousness has not changed. He "…is the same yesterday and today and forever" (Heb. 13:8). Therefore, if you're the head of a nation, community, church, family or business facing seemingly insurmountable problems, follow Moses' example. "…God is love," and "…cares for you" (1 John 4:8; 1 Pet. 5:7). He will surely answer your prayers for the blessing of your people, a testimony to His faithfulness and the glory of His Holy name.

Jesus Is Our Best Example

Now, let's move on further to the New Testament, where the Son of God exemplified the significance of prayer and fasting toward a successful ministry. He allowed his soul to be afflicted for 40 days and nights in the wilderness, resulting in His victory over Satan (Luke 4:1–12; Matt. 4:1–11).

We may think of prayer as *preparation* for battle, but Christ showed us that it is the battle *itself*—prayer and fasting were the heart of His ministry. Where was it that His sweat was like great drops of blood? It wasn't in Pilate's hall or on His way to Golgotha. It was right in the center of Gethsemane where He cried to His Father, offering up "…prayers and petitions with loud cries and tears to the one who could save him from death…" (Heb. 5:7).

When the test finally came, He walked up to the cross at Calvary with courage, "And having disarmed the powers and authorities, he made a public spectacle of them, triumphing over them by the cross" (Col. 2:15). Such a victory could only be the result of His soul's affliction.

Gordon Lindsay, on the first page of his book *Prayer and Fasting: The Master Key to the Impossible*, summed up the essence of Christ's prayer and fasting in the wilderness as follows:

> As Adam and Eve's disobedience by eating the forbidden fruit was the original cause of man's losing his God-given dominion in the Garden of Eden, so Christ's fasting forty days and nights in the wilderness, there overcoming the fiercest onslaughts of the enemy, made possible the restoration of man's dominion.

It's indeed my ardent, constant prayer that the religious and political leaders of Africa, and those of Ghana in particular, do their best to follow the examples of Jesus and the holy men and women of God. We have to team up together to fast and pray in order to experience His power, ushering in the spiritual, political and economic freedom He has promised to the obedient (Deut. 28:1–14).

King David prayed this way: "You are the God who performs miracles; you display your power among the peoples. With your mighty arm you redeemed your people…" (Ps. 77:14–15). Conversely, praying to ancestors and other gods amounts to nothing, because they have no power to help or save anybody. "My help," says the Psalmist, "comes from the LORD, the Maker of heaven and earth" (Ps. 121:2).

Following Christ's example, the early Church took prayer and fasting very seriously. Hence, the elders of the church at Antioch prayed and fasted before commissioning Paul and Barnabas for the missionary work in the Gentile world (Acts 13:1–3). Was theirs a failure or success? Under the guidance and anointing power of the Holy Spirit, they most definitely carried out a successful mission to His glory. Though they encountered problems and opposition from Jews and Gentiles alike, they were able to overcome every obstacle through the supernatural power of the Holy Spirit at work in them. What happened in Cyprus is a typical example of His prevailing power in their mission, as Luke reports:

> *They traveled through the whole island until they came to Paphos. There they met a Jewish sorcerer and false prophet named Bar-Jesus, who was an attendant of the proconsul, Sergius Paulus. The proconsul, an intelligent man, sent for Barnabas and Saul because he wanted to hear the word of God. But Elymas the sorcerer (for that is what his name means) opposed them and tried to turn the proconsul from the faith (13:6–8).*

Luke added the following :

> *Then Saul, who was also called Paul, filled with the Holy Spirit, looked straight at Elymas and said, "You are a child of the devil and an enemy of everything that is right! You are full of all kinds of deceit and trickery. Will you never stop perverting the right ways of the Lord? Now the hand of the Lord is against you. You are going to be blind, and for a time you will be unable to see the light of the sun." Immediately mist and darkness came over him, and he groped about, seeking someone to lead him by the hand. When the proconsul saw what had happened, he believed, for he was amazed at the teaching about the Lord (13:9–12).*

It's important for us to remember that Paul and Barnabas had been fasting and praying before they set off for their missionary work. Being filled with the Holy Spirit, they were able to overcome the Devil, who opposed them through Elymas. As Jesus warned us: " 'This kind can come forth by nothing, but by prayer and fasting' " (*KJV*, Mark 9:28–29).

Prayer and Fasting by the Household and Local Church

Besides individual efforts in prayer and fasting, a whole household led by a parent can engage in them for a worthy cause. Or it can be undertaken by the entire congregation of a church under the leadership of the pastor. In either case, there should be a particular purpose, a blessing to the participants and a glory to God. For instance, if a member of the family or church has contracted a serious illness, the entire group can enter into prayer and fasting on behalf of the afflicted. Intercessory prayers are necessary for victory over the enemy, as noted in the previous passages. Here, James encourages believers to pray in times of trouble or sickness:

Besides individuals, a whole household led by a parent can engage in prayer and fasting for a worthy cause

Is any one of you in trouble? He should pray. Is anyone happy? Let him sing songs of praise. Is any one of you sick? He should call the elders of the church to pray over him and anoint him with oil in the name of the Lord. And the prayer offered in faith will make the sick person well; the Lord will raise him up. If he has sinned, he will be forgiven. Therefore confess your sins to each other and pray for each other so that you may be healed. The prayer of a righteous man is powerful and effective (James 5:13–16).

Members of Calvary Redeeming Methodist Church, for instance, occasionally engage in a week of prayer and fasting as a necessary prelude to the annual revival—as well as other times, such as the Passion Week preceding Easter Sunday or Church Anniversary, as the occasion may demand. We also set aside a week to pray and fast in preparation for our outreach program in 2010.

Sincere prayer and fasting, as we saw in the examples of Christ and the Apostles, yield great power toward a successful ministry. In addition, I engage in personal prayer and fasting when I have a preaching appointment or counseling-and-deliverance session with someone demonically possessed. For example, I asked a female member of the church to join me in prayer and fasting for three days before facing the task of the Devil's exorcism from her seven-year-old stepson. When I went into prayer together with the mother, by the grace of God, the young boy was set free in the mighty name of Jesus Christ.

If a member of the family or congregation has a medical or physical condition making it unhealthy or impossible to fast, the patient should not be discouraged from praying; the Bible entreats Christians to "pray continually" (1 Thess. 5:17). That's the duty of all true believers.

I strenuously encourage you to start today: fast and pray earnestly to God in the name of His Son. Remember to confess your sin and forgive anyone who might have offended you. Then ask the Lord to forgive and cleanse you from every covert sin, because before Him no secret can be hidden. If you do this with a sincere heart, I guarantee your prayer will bear fruitful blessings for yourself and entire family.

Fasting Acceptable to God

Though there's no gainsaying the fact that prayer and fasting can achieve salutary results, their practice mustn't be mistaken for a magic wand performing wonders at any given time for one's own self-glorification—God frowns upon such prayers, even if we fast for many days. A situation very relevant to our discussion here occurred in the days of the prophet Isaiah, through whom God's Word came to the Jews in the land of Judah. Despite their elevated religious devotion, fasting and praying constantly to God seemed to have fallen on deaf ears. Listen to how He describes their fasting, their complaint and His final answer in the following passage:

> *"For day after day they seek me out; they seem eager to know my ways, as if they were a nation that does what is right and has not forsaken the commands of its God. They ask me for just decisions…'Why have we fasted,' they say, 'and you have not seen it? Why have we humbled ourselves, and you have not noticed?' Yet on the day of your fasting, you do as you please and exploit all your workers. Your fasting ends in quarreling and strife, and in striking each other with wicked fists. You cannot fast as you do today and expect your voice to be heard on high. Is this the kind of fast I have chosen…? Is not this the kind of fasting I have chosen: to loose the chains of injustice and untie the cords of the yoke, to set the oppressed free and break every yoke? Is it not to share your*

*food with the hungry and to provide the poor wanderer with shelter—when you
see the naked, to clothe him, and not to turn away from your own flesh and
blood?…Then you will call, and the LORD will answer; you will cry for help,
and he will say: Here am I…"* (Isa. 58:2–7, 9).

This passage teaches us the biblical principle that God is holy, and
we must be holy (1 Pet. 1:16). For that reason, we can't live in disobedience to His Word and still expect Him to have any regard for our fasting and prayers. For instance, praying and fasting for answers to particular problems, meanwhile betraying your spouse or cheating an employee in business circles, is an abomination. As His people, we need to
be reminded that He is a God of truth, and that nothing's hidden before
Him. "Made in God's image," we stand naked before His all-seeing
eyes, because He is omnipresent and omniscient, as declared in the
Scriptures (Ps. 139:1–5, 7–12; Prov. 15:3). It's only when we deal truthfully and honestly with one another and worship God in Spirit and truth
that we have access to His throne through His Son; our prayers will be
answered accordingly.

Let's do a little self-examination as we pore over these soul-search-
ing questions: *Where do we stand in our relationship with God? How are our relationships with household and friends?* If we're truly reconciled with Him
and our neighbors, our prayers won't be hindered (Ps. 66:18; Matt.
5:23). This being said, I sound another caution here: prayer isn't necessarily a means by which believers persuade God to grant their requests,
but rather a way to receive His grace in fulfilling His will in our lives.

Vernon Grounds reminds us: "Prayer isn't the way to get God to do
what we want. It's an expression of our trust in His power, wisdom, and
grace. No matter what we ask God to do for us, we are to have the attitude of Jesus, who said, 'Nevertheless, not as I will, but as You will' "
(Matt. 26:39). The key to a prayer's answer is found in the words of Jesus to His disciples in John 15:7: "If you remain in me and my words
remain in you, ask whatever you wish, and it will be given you."

In other words, if we keep His Word, His Spirit in us will guide
prayers aright and they'll be answered. It does assure all believers that
He answers prayers. Paul put it this way, "He who did not spare his
own Son, but gave him up for us all—how will he not also, along with
him, graciously give us all things?" (Rom. 8:32).

Therefore, we always need to remember that our Father in heaven
loves us so much that He will not deny His children anything that's best

for our lives. For we are His, and He is ours, and so whether we live or die, we belong to Him (14:8).

That thought should engender our dependence on God through our Savior, and not on ancestors or gods, spirits or angels. For " '…apart from me,' " says Jesus, " 'you can do nothing' " (John 15:5).

Now we turn to the following section for the subject of devotion's obstacles.

Hindrances to Prayer, with or without Fasting

Now, having spent a lot of time talking about prayer and fasting, it's important at this juncture to examine the ways our prayers could be hindered. One of the essential elements of prayer is our spiritual condition when in God's presence, because it could be a stumbling block in our path to prayer—regardless of our fasting. The Psalmist wrote, "If I had cherished sin in my heart, the Lord would not have listened; but God has surely listened and heard my voice in prayer. Praise be to God, who has not rejected my prayer or withheld his love from me!" (Ps. 66:18–20).

Since I've already dealt with the subject of *sin*, I won't write any further about it right now; however, I must add that it's always necessary to examine ourselves in the light of the Scriptures, becoming sensitive to the voice of the Holy Spirit. This will help us ensure that we have "…clean hands and a pure heart…" (24:4).

The following are common hindrances, whose presence should be noted and confessed before embarking on the holy path of prayer and fasting:

- Bitterness of heart or disharmonious relationship (1 Pet. 3:7; Matt. 5:23)
- Unforgiving spirit (Mark 11:25)
- Hidden or secret sin (Ps. 66:18; 1 John 1:8)
- Doubt (James 1:6–7)
- Inconsistency (Luke 18:1–8)
- Lack of determination (18:1–8)
- Self-righteousness or pride (18:10–14)

King David's classic prayer of confession after his sin against Bathsheba and the murder of her husband, Uriah—recorded in Psalm 51—may serve as a good example of a truly penitent heart. In his confession, he acknowledged his sin and prayed to forsake it completely, to be totally cleansed of it. He justified God for judging him on account of his sin and pleaded for renewal. He trusted in His everlasting love and asked for restoration, so that he might once again rejoice in salvation. He promised to tell others about His righteousness and to teach sinners about His ways. Finally, he declares his willingness to "offer a sacrifice of thanksgiving and a whole burnt-offering" acceptable to Him.

Commenting on this passage, Rev. Dr. John MacArthur pointed out that any true prayer of confession before the Lord must follow David's example. The next chapter will discuss how to offer prayer as a substitute for libation.

CHAPTER 25

Prayer as a Substitute for Libation

*H*aving studied how to pray and fast, we're now in a better position to replace the usual libation with a prayer—both biblically acceptable and effectual in the sight of the Lord. We're to pray to Him, our Creator and Father in heaven, Whose eyes and ears are always open to the prayers of those sincerely calling on Him "…Who richly provides us with everything for our enjoyment" (1 Tim. 6:17; *also* 2 Chron. 7:14). Our prayer must be offered or directed to Him in the name of His Son (John 14:13–14, 15:7) and by the power of the Holy Spirit (Rom. 8:26; Eph. 6:18). Thus, instead of libation, we ought to pray on any occasion such as a naming ceremony, funeral obsequies or annual festivals. The following is a suggested pattern for the celebration of an annual festival.

Celebrating an Annual Festival

As is customary for Ghanaian festivals, the function may be preceded by drumming, singing and dancing. Initially there may be drumming alone, calling people's attention to the great day, inviting everyone to celebrate the festival through the beating of the talking drum (*fontomfrom* in Akan): *Come one, come all to the festival and let us rejoice.* "This is the day the LORD has made; let us rejoice and be glad in it" (Ps. 118:24).

This could be followed with the singing of Akan lyrics that exhalt the name of God, offering Him praises, honor and adoration for His greatness and majesty. We must thank Him for His love, goodness and care in providing us with food, shelter, health, family, community and every other need. These festivities last about an hour, after which the rest of the program may continue as follows:

- An ordained minister, deacon or elder of any recognized church in the community or city may be invited by the paramount chief or king to offer prayers to God in the name of Jesus, on behalf of the chief, clan and entire community.
- In his prayer, he must mention the names of the founding fathers and ancestors of the community, thanking Him for their great achievements, wisdom and virtuous lives, all of which are challenging and worthy of emulation by posterity.
- He must also give thanks to Him for their families and the gift of children, for they "…are a heritage from the LORD, children a reward from him" (127:3).
- He must pray for His forgiveness of sins, both of commission and omission, and ask for the cleansing power of the blood of the Lamb of God to purify the people, making everyone spotlessly pure in His presence.
- He must pray for protection, brotherly love and the wisdom for sound judgment, good governance and prosperity for the chief, his elders and for all the families and people of the land, both at home and abroad.
- He must pray for any strangers among them so that all may dwell in safety and fear of God, living in loving relationship with one another for the well-being of all inhabitants.
- Finally, he must commit the future of the community and the nation to Him, thanking Him for all that is past and trusting Him for all that's to come.
- The king or paramount chief takes his oath of allegiance and addresses the audience.
- The function may come to a conclusion with drumming and dancing. This is the time for *nana*—the king or chief—and the queen to have the honor of taking the floor, dancing to the applause of the audience, during which the elders could join them on the floor.
- After *nananom* (the chief and his elders) have retired from the floor, the rest may continue until the end of the function.

Dismissal with Prayer

Since the function was started with prayer, it's equally important that it ends with the same devotion. The leader must thank God for a successful festival and commit the days ahead into His fatherly care.

In some places, the closing session of the festival may be marked with drumming and dancing as in the beginning, after which the celebrants disperse to their various homes with joy and new ideas, to consider all the important issues raised by the chief in his address. Since the chief, his elders and the entire community have been entrusted to God in prayer, all must put their faith to work by living in accordance with His Word, trusting that He is with them always to the end of the world (Matt. 28:20).

Thanksgiving Service to God

It's very important that *nana* and his elders cap all the activities with a special thanksgiving church service jointly organized and attended by all the churches of the town. Alternatively, *nananom* may decide to attend church service at a particular denomination of their choice, where the minister leads them to pray for divine wisdom, guidance, prosperity and protection for the chief, his elders and the people as a whole. For without the Lord, we humans can do nothing.

King David, as a newly installed monarch in place of Saul, realized he couldn't successfully govern Israel without the presence and power of God with him. So he summoned 30,000 people out of Judah and brought to the city "the ark of the LORD with shouts and the sound of trumpets" (2 Sam. 6:15). After the Ark's emplacement—representing God's presence among His people—we read the following about the king and his reign: "David reigned over all Israel, doing what was just and right for all his people" (8:15).

I trust that as pastors, kings, elders, and all people in authority begin to seek the face of God to do His will, He will surely begin to fulfill for us His rich promises, as set down in the following passage:

> **As people in authority begin to seek God to do His will, He will surely begin to fulfill for us His promises**

If you fully obey the LORD your God and carefully follow all his commands I give you today, the LORD your God will set you high above all the nations on earth. All these blessings will come upon you and accompany you if you obey the LORD your God: You will be blessed in the city and blessed in the country. The fruit of your womb will be blessed, and the crops of your land and the young of your livestock — the calves of your herds and the lambs of your flocks. Your basket and your kneading trough will be blessed. You will be blessed when you come in and blessed when you go out (Deut. 28:1–6).

Just as we humans won't entrust our treasure to a disobedient, careless son or daughter, neither will God, Who is holy and righteous. " 'Do not give dogs what is sacred; do not throw your pearls to pigs...' " (Matt. 7:6). But we're quite willing to entrust our precious goods or hard-earned wealth to our sons and daughters when we're secure in their maturity and trustworthiness. The following story may illustrate my point.

The Story of the Canaanite Woman

There's a story in Matthew's Gospel that brings home the point I'm trying to make here. He tells us that on one occasion in His ministry, Jesus and the Disciples withdrew to the region belonging to Tyre and Sidon, apparently to seek temporary relief from their busy schedule.

A Canaanite woman from that vicinity came to him, crying out, "Lord, Son of David, have mercy on me! My daughter is suffering terribly from demon-possession." Jesus did not answer a word. So his disciples came to him and urged him, "Send her away, for she keeps crying out after us." He answered, "I was sent only to the lost sheep of Israel." The woman came and knelt before him. "Lord, help me!" she said. He replied, "It is not right to take the children's bread and toss it to their dogs." "Yes, Lord," she said, "but even the dogs eat the crumbs that fall from their masters' table." Then Jesus answered, "Woman, you have great faith! Your request is granted." And her daughter was healed from that very hour (15:22–28).

The story of Jesus' encounter with the woman of Canaan illustrates the inclusive nature of His ministry. It expands beyond racial and cultural boundaries with grace and compassion, meeting the needs of all who truly seek Him; "...whoever comes to me I will never drive away" (John 6:37). For He has also said, " 'Ask and it will be given to you; seek and you will find; knock and the door will be opened to you' " (Matt. 7:7).

Therefore, with His promises, we must look to the future with high hopes, trusting in His providential care, He Whose "goodness and mercy" endure forever. Hence, I'm quite optimistic about the future, that God has something better for the world, particularly Africa — if we set our hearts to do His will through the power of the Holy Spirit given freely to believers. Let's now turn to the next chapter for a detailed discussion on the future of Africa.

CHAPTER 26

Africans Shall Rise and Shine

*T*his chapter focuses on the imminent and glorious future of Africa. In Isaiah 60:1–3, we're encouraged to

> *"Arise, shine, for your light has come, and the glory of the LORD rises upon you. See, darkness covers the earth and thick darkness is over the peoples, but the LORD rises upon you and his glory appears over you. Nations will come to your light, and kings to the brightness of your dawn."*

Isaiah's prophecy originally pointed forward to the coming of Christ, ushering in Israel's Messianic Age. He would establish the New Covenant through His ministry, death, resurrection, ascension and the outpouring of the Holy Spirit "upon all flesh:" believers in Christ, whether Jews or Gentiles, black or white, Asian or brown.

In hearing the same message for ourselves in the present situation, I'm fully convinced that the Lord has already bestowed upon Africa what Ezekiel calls "…showers of blessing" (Ezek. 34:26), so we might rise out of every shadow into His marvelous light, aglow with a new life of righteousness through faith in Jesus (Eph. 4:22–24). Surely this isn't our own doing, but the Lord's: "…and it is marvelous in our eyes" (Ps. 118:23).

Yes! I believe strongly that He expects us to be revitalized by the power of the Holy Spirit and to occupy our rightful place in every sphere of human endeavor—in the marketplace of economics, politics, science and technology, education, commerce and industry. Gone are

the days when we allowed ourselves and our fertile land to be exploit-
ed. In the words of the great Apostle Paul, we must exhort ourselves:

> *It is for freedom that Christ has set us free. Stand firm, then, and do not let
> yourselves be burdened again by a yoke of slavery* (Gal. 5:1).

Hence, he says to each of us:

> *"Wake up, O sleeper, rise from the dead, and Christ will shine on you." Be very
> careful, then, how you live—not as unwise but as wise, making the most of
> every opportunity, because the days are evil. Therefore do not be foolish, but un-
> derstand what the Lord's will is. Do not get drunk on wine, which leads to de-
> bauchery. Instead, be filled with the Spirit"* (Eph. 5:14–18).

This passage reminds me of the wonderful work of art cast in bronze
by an experienced sculptor depicting a map of Africa, with an African
male arising from slumber. It points to the fact that Africans will not remain on the bottom rung of the ladder forever; they've already begun to
rise by God's power with a new destiny. Although we can't change our
past, we shouldn't let it control what's to come; we must all look to a better life in Africa's future.

I'm personally convinced that that bronze refers to all peoples of
African descent who, for whatever reason, have migrated from their native countries in pursuit of fortune in other parts of the world. As aliens
sometimes far from home, we may be looked down upon by our employ-
ers, but sooner or later the Lord will make a way for us in rising up to
take our God-given positions wherever we may find ourselves.

President Obama Is Sure Proof

Barack Hussein Obama is the son of an African immigrant from a re-
mote village in Kenya, East Africa. His election and subsequent inauguration into office in January 2009 as the first African-American
president of the United States were historic and unprecedented. If it's
true that America is our generation's strongest nation, then with Obama's election to her highest position, I dare say without mincing words
that Africa has already risen and stands solidly on her feet. Indeed,
God's prophetic message is being fulfilled in this great son of Africa.

As most of us are aware, President Obama didn't suddenly rise to the
top as a national leader; he had as humble a beginning as any African
child. His father, a foreign student, married Ann, a white classmate, and

they gave birth in 1961 to a future leader. While still very young, his father went to Boston to pursue further studies at Harvard University's Law School. Due to lack of money, he couldn't bring his family with him and the marriage later fell apart.

Upon graduation, Obama Senior returned to Kenya to better his country's standing in Africa, where he passed away after some time. Though a heavy blow to young Barack, he managed to cope with his pain and sorrow all the same. Raised single-handedly by his mother—living occasionally with his white grandparents—he struggled through life in seeking his true identity as a young African-American man in the community. He even fell into the evil habit of following his black peers as they abused drugs. Nevertheless, he faced his challenges with courage and determination, using them as stepping-stones to higher ground.

He kicked cocaine, studied hard, did well in high school, played basketball, graduated college and finally excelled in law studies at Harvard, graduating with honors, *magna cum laude*. In his second year, his academic achievements were so outstanding that he won the presidency of *Harvard Law Review*. According to school records, Obama was the first African-American law student to have held that eminent position, by no means a small achievement. Even after graduation, he didn't seek high laurels in business circles, but chose first to serve his community, to identify with fellow black people in their struggles against racism and poverty, and to find the best means of giving service.

For instance, he worked hard to help them find employment and register to vote. While serving his community, his intelligence, social skills and good works shone forth so brightly in the public eye that he was elected to represent the State of Illinois in the U.S. Senate. Then, having contributed effectively to the Democratic cause and fueled by his rousing 2004 Democratic National Convention keynote address—which electrified and mobilized much of America behind him—Obama became the presumptive 2008 Democratic presidential nominee for the elections in November.

After his address, "the media instantly dubbed Obama 'Rising Star,'" says, Shel Leanne. All America witnessed Obama's convincing presidential win in 2008, with the greatest majority in American political history. Now, what is the secret of his success? From what source does he draw his wisdom and strength? As former members of pastor Jeremiah Wright's Baptist Church, I'm certain that both he and his

wife, Michelle, together with their two daughters (Malia Ann and Natasha), are Christians. Therefore, coupled with all his abilities, charisma and communication skills, Obama's trust in Christ, from whom all blessings flow, and without whom "…you can do nothing" (John 15:5), has lifted him to prominence as the President of the United States of America.

That's why it's very necessary for all of us to trust in God, feed fat on His Word and yield ourselves completely to His Son, so that the Holy Spirit might fill us, direct our paths and use us to fulfill His purpose for our lives on earth. As we might recall, Obama didn't allow the initial problems in his life to impede his education and progress. Like Paul, "…Forgetting what is behind and straining toward what is ahead, [he pressed] on toward the goal to win the prize for which God has called [him] heavenward in Christ Jesus" (Phil. 3:13). Truly, we can't change our past; but with trust in the Lord as our Shepherd, we'll never be found wanting. We're bound to succeed and enjoy better days ahead, because we "…can do everything through him who gives [us] strength" (4:13).

The vision of a future better life is a reminder of a similar message Jeremiah received from Jehovah concerning the Jews enslaved in ancient Babylon. He revealed to His servant that his fellow Jews would return to Jerusalem to rebuild their nation after 70 years of bondage. Here's part of the encouraging message the prophet Jeremiah delivered in Babylon:

> *This is what the LORD Almighty, the God of Israel, says to all those I carried into exile from Jerusalem to Babylon. "Build houses and settle down; plant gardens and eat what they produce. Marry and have sons and daughters; find wives for your sons and give your daughters in marriage…Also, seek the peace and prosperity of the city to which I have carried you into exile. Pray to the LORD for it, because if it prospers, you too will prosper"…This is what the LORD says: "When seventy years are completed for Babylon, I will come to you and fulfill my gracious promise to bring you back to this place. For I know the plans I have for you," declares the LORD, "plans to prosper you and not to harm you, plans to give you hope and a future"* (Jer. 29:4–7, 10–11).

In reading this vision, I had the conviction that just as the Lord graciously freed the Jews from bondage—leading them by Ezra's hand in their return to Jerusalem to revive their religion and rebuild their country—so will the people from Africa return someday for the reconstruction of their native lands. One may ask a legitimate twofold question: *When and how is God going to cause Africans to rise and shine?*

When Will This Happen?

My answer is that God's light has already begun to shine upon the continent. A good number of Africans have responded to God's call and are fulfilling their divinely appointed roles in various ways or ministries throughout the world. Let's begin with a few examples from the Bible.

From the records of the Bible, Africans have been utilized in accordance with God's plan of salvation for humankind from the beginning. When He called Abraham, the future patriarch left his country and came to Bethel, pitching his tent with the city to the west: "…There he built an altar to the LORD and called on the name of the LORD" (Gen. 12:8). But it's recorded that as he continued his journey southward, he encountered severe famine. Guess where God directed him to go for sustenance: Egypt in North Africa.

While there, Abraham and his nephew, Lot, became so wealthy in oxen, sheep, silver and gold that when they returned to Bethel, "…the land could not support them while they stayed together, for their possessions were so great that they were not able to stay together" (13:6). Consequently, they had to part company, with Lot choosing to settle in Jordan toward the east—close to the land of Sodom and Gomorrah—while Abraham lived in the land of Canaan (13:11–12).

Several years later, a similarly serious famine struck Jacob and his family, so they also took refuge in Egypt, where son Joseph by divine providence had been prepared to supply them all their needs in abundance. It was in North Africa that Jacob and his household of 70 people grew into the nation of Israel. This is how Mosy U. Madugba of Nigeria puts it:

> It is right to say that Africa played a significant role in the formation of Israel in the sense that the Israel that you see today was incubated in Africa. This shows that God has a covenant of preservation, a covenant of supply with that continent… Africans have always been used by divine election to run the last leg of the relay race in God's

> plan. When you come to the New Testament and consider the life of Jesus, as soon as He was born, the enemy came after Him. Satan wanted to snuff life out of Him, and God said to the earthly father, "take Him away. I have a place where I keep and nurture my people, take him to Africa." Thus Jesus was taken to Africa (*Africa's Time of Recovery*, pp. 43–45).

It's interesting to see how God in His sovereign will uses various people from generation to generation to fulfill His divine purpose. Thus, beginning with Abraham, the father of our faith, right up to Jesus Christ, the promised Messiah, Africa has been a safe haven for "all the agents of redemption whom God used."

Right now there are several African scholars being utilized to fulfill God's plan for freedom, peace and justice in the world. A good example to cite here is Ghanaian Kofi Annan, former Secretary General of the United Nations. He's served as efficiently and honorably as any of his predecessors. We also have Prof. Albert Wright, co-coordinator of the Task Force on Water and Sanitation for the United Nations' Millenium Development Project established by Annan. He's also the chairman of the Africa Water Task Force, a member of the Technical Committee of the Global Water Partnership, and a consultant in several developing countries on urban-sanitation policies. The importance of his work to Africa's development can't be over-emphasized.

Another Christian brother worthy of mention here is Dr. George Bonney of Rockville, Md. Professor in statistics and genetics at the National Human Genome Center of Howard University's College of Medicine in Washington, D.C., Bonney is also a conference speaker and has performed extensive community service. Teaming up with other medical specialists, he's advised people on certain hereditary or infectious diseases, such as HIV/AIDS and high blood pressure. Those needing treatment but lacking medical insurance receive necessary guidance in securing manageable insurance to meet their needs.

It'll excite you further to know what God is doing for Ghana through Horace Dei, who feels commissioned by God to undertake development projects called "Science Saves Lives" at Akwapem Mampong in the Eastern Region. Dei and his team of generous, devoted Christians have the vision to supply young people with both academic and biblical knowledge. They've learned from the Scriptures that academic achievement and material prosperity without spiritual insight or divine wisdom lead to pride, and pride leads to destruction (Prov. 11:2, 16:18). Hence, the team has established a computer-science school, Hershey Carpentry Center, a Cafeteria, Home Science Center and a Science Resource Center, where Bible knowledge is basic education.

Academic achievement and material prosperity without spiritual insight or wisdom lead to destruction

They also believe that if people are poor and hungry, they find it difficult, if not impossible, to heed the Gospel, so they offer "soft loans" to those who want to start farming and other businesses, guiding them toward self-sufficiency. As a staunch member of the Emory United Methodist Church in Washington, D.C., Dei solicits financial donations from generous individuals and private companies, such as Hershey, for the funding of these wonderful projects, hoping to extend his program to other regions in due course.

Among Ghanaian pastors working in several ways toward the development of the country are Revs. Kwabena and Christiana Darko, co-pastors of Oasis of Love Ministries in Ahodwo, a suburb of Kumasi in the Ashanti Region. Besides their vibrant church teeming with members, they've also established a beautiful school—from kindergarten to Junior Secondary School (JSS)—to serve rural youth. Their school helps to reduce the migration of students from the hinterland seeking admission to schools in the cities.

In addition to his pastoral and other responsibilities, Darko makes time for his thriving poultry business, which has become so successful that entrepreneurs from across Africa consult him concerning his business acumen. He's also one of the national executives of the Full Gospel Men's Fellowship, Ghana Chapter, and among a selected few religious leaders advising President Kufuor on religious policies. Whenever needed, he accompanies the leader on his international tours.

My friends, good news is evidenced in the previous passages: the Omnipresent God, in His mysterious way, is using His people not only from within, but also outside Ghana and Africa to fulfill His divine purpose for the nation in particular, Africa in general and the world at large.

At this juncture, I want to add to the list of God's Kingdom-builders another one of His servants, Rev. Seth Asare, senior pastor of the Newton United Methodist Church in Boston, Mass. Every year, he leads a Mission Team to undertake various much-needed development projects in underserved areas of the country. Last year's Mission Team—which included pastors Ruth, Dick, Julie Merriam, Dr. John Ogren, Donna Fish and others—was warmly welcomed at the Kotoka International Airport in Accra by Rt. Rev. Kow Egyir, then-bishop of the Sekondi Diocese of the Methodist Church, Ghana.

Viable projects carried out by the team were evangelistic activities in churches and a Vacation Bible School; the completion of a chapel at Azani Village near Busua, located a few miles from the Atlantic Coast; and the completion of a school wing for the chapel begun by Mission 2002.

The following is part of their Church Mission Report:

> Dr. John treated many hundreds of patients over a one-day period! Each patient got a free examination and was then given a prescription for medicine or else diagnosis to see a specialist. Money for the purchase of medicine was provided by the team ahead of time. Many had eye problems, including one boy with a large tumor.

The team has received land from the chief of Azani to start a palm-oil processing plant there. As a sign of commitment to the project, the bishop held a ground-breaking ceremony at the site. In March of 2004, Asare teamed up with the Most Rev. Dr. Robert Aboagye-Mensah, then-presiding bishop of the Methodist Conference, Ghana, for a massive Evangelistic Campaign that won hundreds of souls for Christ.

It's also very encouraging to know that equal progress is being made in the medical field. Among the great helping hands in this area is Thomas Oduro Kwarteng, who's busily engaged in a multi-medical industry and fitted with all kinds of computerized machinery for development projects in Ghana.

Negotiations are going on presently between Ghana's Ministry of Health and Healthcare Products International, Inc. for installing the HPI System, which according to their brochure "offers a patented system for the secure, comprehensive, and cost-effective transport of blood products, biologicals and organs and others that need consistent undisturbed temperature control." It's understood that financing the project in "qualifying countries"—of which Ghana is one—can be achieved through "grant in aid" or "soft loan" lending sponsored by international healthcare institutions such as WHO, the UN and USAID. Plans are in place for this to start soon and will be extended to other parts of Africa. Ghana's representative on the team is Papa Arko Arkhurst, the choir master of Calvary Redeeming Methodist Church in Rockville.

Keeping in mind these examples of the human instruments God has prepared for His development program in Ghana, Africa and other places, let's move on to the second part of the question.

How Is God Going to Do This?

In answering this question, I'm reminded of what Jehovah did for Israel. For instance, before He sent Moses to Egypt to deliver the Jews from bondage, He had prepared him for 40 years in the wilderness (Exod. 3–4). Before calling him to rest from his responsibility as a leader of His people, He had prepared young Joshua to take up the leadership role from his master, Moses (Josh. 1:1–9).

Before they reached the border of Jericho, God had sent ahead His captain to deliver plans to Joshua for capturing the city (5:13–6:20); and before the spies set foot in the city, He had already arranged for a harlot named Rahab to receive the spies into her home (2:1–24), thus enabling her to provide them the information needed for Jericho's overthrow.

As we've seen in the Bible, God truly does not work in a vacuum. Though He is all-powerful—and with Him everything is possible—in His divine wisdom and economy, He often uses human beings, regardless of rank, gender, or weakness, to achieve His purpose in the world. This demonstrates that He has never sent anyone to do anything in His name without the grace and power for fulfillment of His glory and the blessing of the people involved.

What He requires us to do is to "Trust in the LORD with all [our] heart and lean not on [our] own understanding; in all [our] ways acknowledge him, and he will make [our] paths straight" (Prov. 3:5–6). It's when we have nothing but Him alone to lean on that He is willing to lead us to victory in proving Himself mighty in our behalf—to perform His miracles in our lives. Then, the world will know assuredly that we serve a mighty, Living God, whose eyes " '…range throughout the earth to strengthen those whose hearts are fully committed to him…' " (2 Chron. 16:9).

When I read the following powerful statement made by Bishop T.D. Jakes, I was strengthened in my faith in the Lord and given confidence in what He can do with a believer. He said: "Never be intimidated by your dreams. It does not need to look like it will come true in order for it to come true. Because we believe, worship and pray to God Almighty, who 'is able to do exceeding abundantly above all that we can ask or think, according to His power that is at work in us' (Eph. 3:20), through His Son, Jesus Christ, our Lord." One of the dynamic African-American preachers of our time, Jakes was speaking to a large audience at a telecast church service in January 2003. I paraphrase below another of his statements:

> The gold, diamonds, bauxite, manganese and timber aren't in the United States, Europe or Asia, but in Africa. Yet many African countries live in poverty due to the corruption that's eaten into the very fabric of the continent. Nevertheless, if Africans would turn their hearts toward God, He would bring about a changed life, leading to righteousness, peace and prosperity, according to His power at work within them.

Indeed, this is a confirmation of my faith in what Jehovah can do with a people who put their trust in Him. It gladdens my heart and propels me to persevere in the ministry He has graciously entrusted to me by the inspiration of His Holy Spirit in the name of His Son. I strongly believe that He is at work in many individuals, fulfilling His purpose in diverse ways throughout the world.

In his book *Africa's Time of Recovery* (pp. 41–42), Madugba has this to say about Africa:

> The African continent has the largest reserve of mineral resources. It is the richest continent in the whole world, and God intentionally made it so for a purpose, so that at the appropriate time, Africa can help to preserve the world in times of need. If it is physically the richest continent in the world, the physical is a reflection of the manifestation of the spiritual. That means it also has the potential to be the continent with the richest spiritual content in the world.

With profound spiritual insight, Madugba reminds his readers of the famine in Abraham's time and how "he was led by divine providence to go nowhere else but Africa," where "he was blessed with wealth in the form of oxen, sheep, servants, both male and female, all manner of treasure in gold and silver." Thus, "God had made a preparation for Africa to be His treasure house," out of which God might extract both the physical and spiritual needs of the world's people. This may sound like a fairy tale to the skeptics, yet it's true, "For with God all things are possible" (Mark 10:27).

Africa as a Place of Refuge for God's People

Critical study of the Bible from Genesis to the New Testament elucidates God's divine providence and wisdom in making Africa a safe haven for His chosen people. Again, Madugba writes:

> It was in Africa that all agents of redemption whom God used were preserved from Abraham right up to Jesus Christ. As a newborn infant He was preserved from untimely death in Africa. Abraham was preserved physically on earth in Africa from untimely death through famine. Jacob too was preserved there; and Jesus Himself was preserved in Africa. It is evident by these that God has a covenant and of course a partnership with Africa. God does not forget covenants. Oh! He is a great covenant keeper and He has chosen in this season to remember Africa (p. 46).

I'm very much encouraged by what Jakes and Madugba have said about Africa, because I share a similar vision and hope for my fellow Africans. Moreover, the part of Jakes' message that lifts my aspirations to indescribable heights is what he said about Joseph, the dreamer, who was hated by his senior siblings.

Though sold into slavery by his jealous brothers and later imprisoned, he was released by divine intervention to become prime minister—next in authority to Pharaoh, king of Egypt. By implication, the same God who elevated Joseph from jail to a powerful position in a foreign land—delivering the Egyptians and his father's house from famine and death—will likewise rescue His precious sons and daughters in Africa from Satan's hands and the consequent evil life of selfishness, corruption and poverty.

My question is: *Is anything too hard for God?* No! With God, nothing is impossible (Jer. 32:27; Luke 18:27). Just as He inspired Nehemiah and Ezra in motivating their fellow Jews to rise up for spiritual renewal and the reconstruction of the walls and city of Jerusalem, so will Almighty God—"...the King eternal, immortal, invisible, the only God..." (1 Tim. 1:17)—raise converted, committed and anointed African leaders to rally their people toward spiritual, political, economic and social reformation on behalf of the entire continent. Although some of these leaders may still dwell abroad, they'll come home in God's time with divine zeal. I believe this spiritual reconstruction will begin with Ghana, where the light is already shining brightly in leading the way.

When this time arrives, Africa will have Spirit-filled men and women from all walks of life—attorneys, academicians, teachers, university and college graduates, middle-class workers. The continent will bear God-fearing, traditional kings and political leaders strong in the Lord, who'll seek to live and govern by the Book. They'll spread the seed of the Spirit through word and action, wherever they may be, in order to reap the harvest of love, peace, justice and unity in the land.

According to the records of the missionary agency run by Madugba and his colleagues in Nigeria, there are more missionaries in Africa than anywhere else on the surface of the earth, and they're seriously engaged in the spreading of the Gospel. This truth is reaffirmed by another African writer, Jean-Marc Ela from Cameroon:

> Nowadays, when the majority of Christians are no longer in the West but in the Third World, is it time for us Africans to reclaim the gospel, and bring our disinherited peoples face to face with it? For in the words of Paul VI, we face critical situations where "bold transformations" and "urgent reforms should be undertaken without delay" (*My Faith as an African*, p. 115).

Indeed, pastors and committed lay leaders must not only be more prayerful, but also move beyond their local congregations to bring the Bible to homes, villages and byways so that people in Africa and abroad might hear the Good News. "Bold transformations" and "urgent reforms should be undertaken without delay," said Pope Paul VI.

Ela made further observations on the shift in Christianity's center of gravity:

> Christianity has endured for a long time, maintaining its Greco-Latin heritage within the context of a society fashioned by Western models. Today the Church must examine that entire experience, recognizing that it has lost its cultural monopoly as well as the theological systems that seemed to guarantee it. A new age is beginning that gives great importance to non-Western Churches, and Africa plays a decisive role in this migration of the Church to the Southern hemisphere. While the loss of China has been felt as a heavy blow to the history of missions, Paul VI did not hesitate to declare that Africa is "the new homeland of Christ" (p. 116).

Thus, it's evident that my fellow believers Ela, Madugba and Pope VI see eye-to-eye with me in the present concentration of the Gospel on Africa. God is surely preparing the continent's men and women to conscript His army in its war against the Devil and every form of false religion that seems to deflect the people from following the true way of salvation in Christ. Ela concluded his observations as follows:

> The center of gravity of Christianity continues to shift. It is possible that the black continent will become a real prize for the church. The one hundred and fifty million Christians in Africa today are a significant resource on the religious map of the world and for the vitality of the Christian faith (pp. 115–116).

It follows that God will call believers to be rulers and others in authority, who'll use the natural resources of the land not for their own ends—as some selfish politicians and kings had done in the past—but for the progress and betterment of the people as a whole. This new brand of leadership will produce people who know for certain that sooner or later, they'll stand before the Judgment Seat of the Supreme Judge, Jesus Christ, "...the King of kings, and Lord of lords" (1 Tim. 6:15), to render to Him the account of their stewardship.

The African Enterprise Outreach

It's encouraging to know that since 1961, the African Enterprise—an interdenominational ministry consisting of seasoned evangelists and pastors—has been preaching the Gospel in the cities in partnership with local churches. Under the directorship of American Malcolm Graham and Canadian David Richardson, trained African evangelists are presently engaged in various Christian activities in 10 African cities.

I was greatly touched by the following report from Michael Cassidy of the African Enterprise:

> I want to encourage you as you pray about your response this month to our ministry, to seriously consider the incredible Training Programs undertaken by my colleagues around Africa. The measurement of their efforts undoubtedly comes in the feedback we receive from participants. For instance, Ms. Margaret Shomolo, Director of Research in the Provincial Government, South Africa, said: "It has been one of the most enriching courses I have attended. I am going back home a new person with a much better understanding of myself, my strengths and weaknesses" (*African Enterprise Newsletter*, Au-

gust, 2003).

In a recent report published in the *African Enterprise News Letter* under the title "Leadership Training," it was mentioned that Cassidy's African Enterprise Leadership Training Center (AELTC) in Pietermaritzburg, South Africa, is having a major impact on the continent's future leaders. With the average age of students between 25 and 35, it's poised to undergird the transformation of the continent by educating godly and biblically grounded church, business and civic leaders. Nearly 500 people have taken AELTC courses this year: 230 church leaders and 204 students and other youths.

One of the highlights was a course led by Ugandan archbishop Henry Orombi, who spoke on "Revival, Renewal and Moral Regeneration in National Transformation." With corruption and rampant sexual promiscuity as two of Africa's major problems, this course was highly relevant. After the training, Ayanda Mabaso, a student and youth leader said, "AE gave me the skills and training which I need to pass on to others, thus making disciples of all nations."

The following is another report, this time on Community Development:

> The AE Ghana Team exemplifies AE's aim not just to bring people to Christ, but to equip them to provide for themselves and become productive, contributing members of society. Thus they not only reach out with the Gospel but also spearhead practical training to prostitutes and other downtrodden women in the capital city of Accra. AE Ghana enrolls 20 women in the project twice per year, where they hear the Gospel, experience daily devotions and learn skills in batik, tie-die and baking, enabling them to start their own business or secure a job. The day after the last group graduated, one of them, Beatrice, was offered a job designing uniforms for the staff of a Ghanaian company. Beatrice called our Ghana Team and, through tears of joy, thanked the AE staff for the unconditional grace and love the team had shown her by spending so much time and effort to help both improve her life and introduce her to Jesus so that she can provide for her family and contribute products to her community (Stephen Lungu, International Team Leader, African Enterprise, December 2009).

This is very encouraging and much appreciated by those who attend and discover for themselves what leadership in Africa is all about.

Some of the topics tackled previously by the AE trainers, and reported in a previous article, included "Calling and Preparation into Leadership," "Dealing with Temptation and Failure in Leadership" and "Abandoning Power—Grace and Humility in Leadership." These training programs are wonderful opportunities for African leaders to grow in integrity and ability. Cassidy concludes this report with a plea: "Won't you stand with us in these worthy endeavors?" Having read about the good work being done by him and his colleagues, all lovers of Christ must endeavor to contribute generously in money and kind to support such a worthy ministry in Africa through these dedicated people of God.

As the Lord has graciously revealed in this vision, the greatest problem facing Africa isn't poverty, but the misappropriation of the land's resources by selfish individuals in high positions of authority. Why do they behave this way? The reason is that their hearts are corrupt; they have no fear of God and don't revere His son as their Savior. Hence, the Devil has lured them into believing the fallacy that they can make it without God, just as he did to Adam and Eve in Eden (Gen. 3:1–7).

Therefore, the good work being done by various missionary agents sponsored by other denominations around the world—including such religious bodies as the World Methodist Council of Churches, the All Africa Conference of Churches, World Vision, Africa House of Prayer, the Scripture Union and the African Enterprise Missionaries of Africa—in collaboration with local churches can't be overemphasized. There are yet other missions and individual evangelists engaged in spreading the Good News toward the total liberation of Africa and other parts of the world.

Space doesn't permit me to list all of the various groups and individuals here, but be assured that their work will never go unrewarded by the Lord, Who has called them into His ministry. Therefore, we must all contribute our quota financially, as well as by word and deed, to effect Africa's complete freedom from the dominion of demonic forces toward serving the Living God. Thus, we'll be His co-workers in ushering the entire continent and the rest of the world into the status of peace, righteousness, success and prosperity destined for humanity by the goodness and mercy of God through Christ.

Whatever our station in life as individuals, we need to order our lives daily in the fear of and obedience to the Almighty, looking to no other Master but "...the author and perfecter of our faith, who for the joy set before him endured the cross, scorning its shame, and sat down at the right hand of the throne of God" (Heb. 12:2), "…and is also interceding for us" (Rom. 8:34). Hence, King David speaks concerning Him: "…He guides me in paths of righteousness for his name's sake" (Ps. 23:3).

At this juncture, one may ask the question, *Where in Africa is God's light moving in a special way to achieve the divine goal for Africa and the world at large?* Madugba mentioned three countries—South Africa, Nigeria and Ghana—as unique places where spiritual revival has begun, where His mighty work is manifested in effecting visible changes in the religious, social, political and economic life of the people. Let's now turn to the next chapter to discuss the case of Ghana in more detail.

CHAPTER 27

*I*n 1983, while serving as a pastor of the Bethel Methodist Church at Samreboi, in the interior of the Western Region, Ghana, I had a dream in which I saw a bright star descending from heaven and settling on Ghana. Its brightness and beauty attracted many people, not only from Africa, but also from other parts of the world. Not long after that dream, I was visited by Daniel K. Fei, then national organizer for the Boys Brigade of the Presbyterian Church of Ghana, who was on a trip to Enchi, near the border of Côte d'Ivoire.

In our conversation, I shared the dream with Brother Fei. To my surprise, he told me that he had had a similar dream a few weeks prior to embarking on his regional tour. We both rejoiced, believing strongly that God was about to do something great in Ghana and that He would pour His Spirit over the nation in a special way to bring about a great revival in Ghanaians' lives. We believed further that through such a revival, He would draw into His Kingdom many people both from within and outside the continent. *Hallelujah!*

The dream reminded us of Isaiah's prophecy, as follows:

> *...The people walking in darkness have seen a great light; on those living in the land of the shadow of death a light has dawned. You have enlarged the nation and increased their joy; they rejoice before you as people rejoice at the harvest, as men rejoice when dividing the plunder...For to us a child is born, to us a son is given, and the government will be on his shoulders...* (Isa. 9:2–3, 6).

Fei and I were excited about this prophecy, believing that just as

God graciously brought His Son in the fulfillment of His Word for the salvation of "…the lost sheep of Israel" (Matt. 15:24), so will He do for Ghana and Africa as a whole. We surely stand in need of the great deliverance that can come from no one else but God.

In 1997, Ghanaian-American evangelist Edith Luray also had a vision that Ghana would lead in the spiritual awakening of Africa. Upon receiving this vision, she flew to Ghana and shared the vision's message with a number of ministers, who joined her in prayer and fasting for the nation. She said there was a drought in Ghana at that time. It hadn't rained for months, but while they fasted and prayed, God opened the waters of heaven and blessed the nation with a heavy downpour. "I believed," she said, "the rain was a sign of God's answer to our prayer," in fulfilling the vision of the country's revival and impacting the rest of Africa.

The testimony of this evangelist brings to three the number of people to whom God had revealed His plan for Ghana in particular and Africa in general. This third vision—coming from another servant of God in a foreign country—further strengthens my conviction in what He has said in this book. The Scriptures state that "One witness is not enough to convict a man accused of any crime or offense he may have committed. A matter must be established by the testimony of two or three witnesses" (Deut. 19:15; *also* Matt. 18:16). Therefore, I'm convinced that this vision, revealed to three of God's servants, will indeed be fulfilled in His appointed time. No matter how long it may tary, it'll surely come to pass (Hab. 2:3).

Ghana: God Has a New Africa

In light of the above testimony, I can see relevance in the profound, prophetic statement of hope for Africa declared in a sermon by Felton May, the then-presiding bishop of the Baltimore–Washington Conference of the United Methodist Church (U.S.A.) He said, among other things: "**God Has A New Africa**," whose acronym becomes GHANA, simultaneously symbolizing a new meaning for Ghana by virtue of the fire of revival set by God in the nation. It's making a positive impact on the rest of Africa in particular, and the world in general.

I suggest this as a new way to greet our fellow Ghanaians and Africans wherever we meet: "God has a new Africa." I believe that as we repeatedly use this salutation, we'll be charged consciously or unconsciously in becoming instrumental to the fulfillment of God's plan—not only for Ghana, but also for Africa as a whole.

His gracious work shouldn't be seen as a surprise to people, because He had done it before in Israel. After delivering the Israelites from exile in Babylon, God said "…you will be called Hephzibah and your land Beulah…" (Isa. 62:4), meaning *the Lord will take delight in you (Hephzibah), and you will be married (Beulah)*. These words reflected the new relationship God intended to establish with His people. This would eventually produce, by means of the indwelling Holy Spirit, the new life of righteousness He had purposed to begin with the remnant of Israel through the new covenant (Jer. 31:31–34). This messianic prophecy pointed forward to what Christ would do in believers, namely, give rise to His Church.

Now, we may ask the question: *Did God choose the nation of Israel because she consisted of the best people in the world?* No! He chose her by His grace and not by her works of righteousness or any virtue of her own (Deut. 7:7–8; John 15:16; Eph. 2:8–9; Titus 3:3–7).

Likewise, Ghana has been chosen to be a beacon of light, illuminating the way to real liberty in Christ and inspiring others to follow suit—solely by His Father's loving kindness showered on Ghana and its people. What a profound insight from May's lips! In his sermon, the bishop referred to the mighty work of God being done in Africa, which is now the focal point of evangelization, and wherein many souls are turning to the saving faith in Jesus Christ in our generation.

> **Ghana has been chosen to be a beacon of light, illuminating the way to real liberty in Christ**

Indeed, Ghana's founding fathers caught a glimpse of this truth from the very beginning of our independence and realized that the nation's progress depended not on human strength and wisdom, but on God alone—*Gye Nyame*. Hence, the words of our national anthem begin and end with God, as follows:

> God bless our homeland Ghana
> And make our nation great and strong,
> Bold to defend forever
> The cause of freedom and Right;

Fill our hearts with true humility,
Make us cherish fearless honesty,
And help us to resist oppressor's rule
With all our will and might evermore.

Raise high the flag of Ghana
And one with Africa advance;
Black star of hope and honor
To all who thirst for liberty;
Where the banner of Ghana free flies,
May the way to freedom truly lie;
Arise, arise, O sons of Ghanaland,
And under God march on for evermore.

The last line of the last stanza indicates our founding fathers' belief that Ghana can move forward successfully only under the power and guidance of God. Behold, He has graciously led the country through thick and thin these 53 years of sovereignty through His omnipotence, omnipresence and omniscience.

Ghana's Golden Jubilee in 2007

With Ghanaians' successful celebration, both at home and abroad, of their 50 years of independence on March 6, 2007, I have no doubt that Ghana is truly being led by God to become the Shining Star of Africa, as He Himself has revealed.

Do you recall that it was in 1983 that He showed me in a dream the great light that spotlit Ghana? And that due to its brightness, people from all over the world were drawn to her to see the light? I believe that the celebration of the golden jubilee—bringing in many visitors white and black to join Ghanaians to mark the occasion, seeing for themselves the wonderful developments in the spiritual, economic and social realms unfolding within—is a partial fulfillment of this dream. All the hotels in the city of Accra were full of visitors. Church services were held throughout the nation to give thanks to the Almighty God for the manifold blessings He had bestowed upon the country and its leaders since independence.

Wherever such services were held outside Ghana, prayers were offered for the well-being of the president, his cabinet, ambassadors and all others placed in authority under him, so that they might continue to submit to God's guidance for good governance, unity, peace, success and prosperity in the years ahead.

In the Washington Metropolitan Area, for instance, a unity service was held in the auditorium of Howard University Law School to commemorate the occasion. The celebration was attended by Ghana's former ambassador in Washington, Dr. Kwame Bawuah Edusei, his wife, and members of his staff. Pastors of various denominations, together with their choirs and congregations (more than 700 members) filled the sanctuary to its full capacity. Addressing his audience with a lesson read from Leviticus 25:10–19, Dr. Edusei exhorted Ghanaians to trust in Jesus Christ, to eschew selfishness, drugs and other forms of evil behavior that retard a country's progress.

He encouraged all Ghanaians to stay holy, because the Lord Who saved us from sin is holy. Aided by His Grace, we'll exhibit His love, a characteristic of the life of righteousness in exalting a nation. The celebration, which lasted for about two hours, began and ended successfully with the singing of Akan lyrics, songs of praise and worship, and dancing to the rhythms of the *fontomfrom*. We all rejoiced in the wonderful day the Lord had made, one that'll remain in memory forever.

Fulfillment of the Vision

As Ghanaians—especially those in authority, politicians, paramount chiefs, subchiefs, queen mothers, the elite, the citizenry—commit themselves daily to the Lord in His Word and prayer, and are strengthened by the mighty potential of the Holy Spirit, Ghana by the grace of God will become Africa's shining star. In continuing to champion the cause of freedom and the fire of great revival in the continent, the vision will have been fulfilled to His glory. The fire's illumination and energy will deliver multitudes out of the power of darkness into the marvelous light of the kingdom of God through faith in His Son.

You may ask, *How can you be certain of this?* My answer's based on the unchangeable, irrevocable truth of God's Word. I know to a certainty that what God has said He will surely perform (Luke 1:45), because "The one who calls you is faithful and he will do it" (1 Thess. 5:24). Moreover, we know that "God is not a man, that he should lie, nor a son of man, that he should change his mind..." (Num. 23:19). Therefore, I'm convinced that this vision will be fulfilled in due season.

Again, this conviction is based on previous prophecies the Lord had graciously fulfilled in the lives of many individuals—and in my ministry since 1968. Thus, we can place our faith in Him and, like Jeremiah, proclaim: "...for his compassions never fail. They are new every morning;

great is your faithfulness" toward all who trust in Christ for salvation (Lam. 3:22–3).

Examples of Fulfilled Prophecies

From 1978 through 1981, three American evangelists invited as keynote speakers to the Pastors' Conference at Kumasi Technical Institute—organized annually by the Ghana Evangelism Committee—had predicted that there would be religious revival in the country within the following five years. Rev. John Bassaw (of blessed memory) and I were among the many pastors, lay preachers and evangelists attending these annual conferences toward the edification of our personal lives and ministries. We took those prophetic messages very seriously, desiring to be a part of such an awakening in the country.

Today, as I speak, that prediction's come true. My five visits to Ghana—in 1992, 1999, 2002, 2004 and 2006—have offered me the privilege of seeing the mighty work of revival being done by the Lord through anointed ministers of the Gospel, evangelists, prophets and lay/local preachers. The fact that a number of venues previously used as movie theaters have been renovated into places of worship is clear evidence of the many souls He is drawing into the Church.

The reverse is taking place in Europe, where many churches have been converted to playhouses and restaurants due to lack of congregants. Ghana's seen a change in the lives of her people in turning from darkness to light, from the things of this world to the things of God and from the temporal to eternal issues of existence. We can say with David, " 'The LORD's right hand is lifted high; the LORD's right hand has done mighty things!' " (Ps. 118:16).

Let's take, for instance, the Odeon cinema hall in Ashanti Newtown, a populous suburb of Kumasi. It had been full of moviegoers, especially on weekends, but is now a temple of God, where believers meet together to worship the Lord and hear the Gospel. I'm speaking from personal experience here, because this was the place where my senior brothers and I used to watch movies on weekends in the 1960s before we became Christians. You can imagine my surprise when I saw for the first time, in July 1992, the most popular movie theater in Kumasi turned into a place of worship. Can you believe this? We can surely exclaim with the Psalmist and say, "the LORD has done this, and it is marvelous in our eyes...Give thanks to the LORD, for he is good; his love endures forever" (118:23, 29).

Today, my most senior brother, Joseph, and I are ministers of the Anglican and Methodist Churches, respectively. My elder sibling, Daniel (after whom I come), is an accountant with a Kumasi firm and a lay/local preacher and a chorister at the Bantama Methodist Church in the same city. Our only sister, Agnes (who comes after me), is married to the Rt. Rev. John Harvey Ewusi, former bishop of the Sekondi Diocese of the Methodist Church, Ghana. Indeed, the Lord is faithful, and has confirmed His Word:

> *For the Son of man is come to seek and to save that which was lost…But as many as received him, to them gave he power to become the sons of God, even to them that believe on his name* (KJV, Luke 19:10; John 1:12).

As I write this book, the Spirit of the Living God is moving mightily upon the souls of Ghana, the continent of Africa and the world at large, converting as many people as may hear and respond to His "…still small voice," (1 Kings 19:12), gently whispering into their ears the message of the Gospel. Just read, for example, the following brief testimony of Chip Ingram after his visit to Africa:

> Not long ago I traveled to Africa, and it was one of the most thrilling, challenging, and eye-opening experiences I have ever had. On my trip I encountered firsthand a "secret" that many people aren't aware of the fact that Christianity is growing at an amazing rate across Africa. It is incredible, but researchers estimate that approximately 18,000 people convert to Christianity every single day in Africa!

This testimony, together with others, certainly affirms the vision that Africa will rise and shine, because the Lord is still speaking to the hearts of thousands of individuals, calling them out of darkness into His marvelous light through the various anointed preachers of His Son's Gospel. He also may be calling you, whoever you are, in seeking to come into your life, save you from sin and bless you with the gift of a fruitful life. At this point, perhaps, you may be asking, *How do I become a child of God, a Christian?*

How to Pray to Become a Christian

At this point — if you sincerely desire birth into the family of God — I want to encourage you to boldly emerge, because it's not too late for you to be part of His universal Church. Just take a moment to pray sincerely to Him for salvation in the privacy of your room, hotel or wherever you may be at this hour. But do it now! Let nothing stop you from voicing the following prayer to receive Jesus into your life today. You'll be glad you did.

> O God, I acknowledge the truth that I am a sinner, and I repent of all my sins. I believe that You love me, and that You sent Your only Son, Jesus Christ, to die on the cross to save me from the penalty of all my sins. I believe that Jesus rose again from the dead and lives for evermore. O triumphant Jesus, I humbly invite You now to come into my heart to be my Lord and Savior for the rest of my life. Thank you, my Lord, for accepting me right now as Your child into Your kingdom, for Your name's sake. Amen.

If you've sincerely offered this prayer to the Lord, then believe that your sins are forgiven and that you're now His child (Isa. 1:18–19, 53:4–6; Mark 1:14–15; John 1:12; Acts 16:31; Rev. 3:19–20).

Many of the Youth Flock to Church

Nowadays, a considerable number of our young people, as well as many adults, no longer spend their money and time at the movies or dance halls like they used to. Where do we find them? We see them in churches, retreats, camp meetings, crusades, revivals and conferences, listening attentively to the Good News of Jesus Christ and various teachings on Christian life. They no longer have any time to fool around. Why? The logical answer is that Jesus has certainly done something new in their lives—they've found a new home in the House of the Lord. As lost sheep now found by their Shepherd, they love to hear His voice and follow Him wherever He leads them.

Like David, they're glad to hear: "…'Let us go to the house of the LORD.' Our feet are standing in your gates, O Jerusalem" (Ps. 122:1–2). Often, you'll find many youngsters gifted on the organ, guitar or trumpet in the church choir, choral group or praise-and-worship team, serving the Lord. Whatever part they feel called to play, they do so with joy and enthusiasm, leading the congregation to "Worship the LORD in the splendor of his holiness…" (96:9).

During my visit to Ghana in August 2002, I had the privilege of organizing a seven-day crusade from 7:00–9:30P.M. at the Good Shepherd Methodist Church in Tanokrom, near Takoradi. The place was packed to its fullest capacity every evening. The choral group that sang us into praise and worship consisted of youth dedicated to the service of God. I could feel the healing touch of their songs, because they're sung with heart and soul. These were the same young people—the cream of Ghanaian society—who until recently could be found loitering about in restaurants, parks, beer bars and dance halls. Thanks to "…the good shepherd…" (John 10:11), Who has graciously gathered the wanderers among his flock, gently leading them in various ways into the fold of His Church—His body. They now hear His voice and follow Him.

I can hear almost every African Christian saying with Isaiah, " 'Surely God is my salvation; I will trust and not be afraid. The LORD, the LORD, is my strength and my song; he has become my salvation" (Isa. 12:2). Our salvation as individuals and as a people of this world assuredly lies not in the hands of our politicians, but in Jehovah, the immutable God, Who is ever faithful to His covenant.

Obviously, I believe that experience has taught all of us—Africans in general, Ghanaians in particular, and other political leaders, chiefs, queens and athority figures—that without God, we humans can't make it. As I speak, neither a half-a-century of independence nor the myopic reliance on human ability, wisdom, political ideology and power have brought Ghana the political and economic freedom and material prosperity we had expected. I think we've sunk into this low economic position so that we might learn never to trust in ourselves or lean on human flesh again, but rather on the victorious, everlasting arm of God.

Traditionalists Preach "Sankofa"

In this time of religious awakening, it's sickening to witness traditionalists' efforts to convince society's ignorant members to return to the ancestral pagan practices we thought had been discarded 600 years ago. That was when our forebears worshipped idols made of wood, clay or stone, to which were offered sacrifices of sheep, goats and roosters in the hopes of obtaining their favor and protection against enemies, illness or untimely death. But could any of these material things rise to the challenges of our ancestors in time of need? No, not in the least.

Whenever a Ghanaian chief died in the past, for example, innocent servants, slaves, and strangers were beheaded and buried with him in the false belief that they would serve the dead ruler in the underworld. However, we certainly know that none of these beliefs is true and that no god, idol, fetish priest, priestess or diviner has the power to save anybody. If they did, they would have saved our fathers and the whole of

Africa from sin, poverty, slavery, demonic influences, illness and death. They would have ushered Africans into new life, peace, success, and prosperity here and now; but none of these things happened.

Such false prophets and entire households stand in dire need of deliverance from Satan's domination. Hence, the Scriptures declare,

> " '...Ignorant are those who carry about idols of wood, who pray to gods that cannot save. Declare what is to be, present it — let them take counsel together. Who foretold this long ago, who declared it from the distant past? Was it not I, the LORD? And there is no God apart from me, a righteous God and a Savior; there is none but me. Turn to me and be saved, all you ends of the earth; for I am God, and there is no other" (45:20b–21c, 22).

Kwame Gyekye, therefore, sounds the strong warning to all proponents of *sankofa* (return for it): "a return to the past must be guided by critical examination."

Caution: There Should Be No Looking Back

Having come this far, by the grace of God, and having discovered the Truth that's set us free from those vain idols formerly entangling and victimizing us, why should we return to damaging ourselves with traditions or cultural practices—libation, the belief in other gods, etc.? These religious practices didn't lead our ancestors to salvation, prosperity or success in life.

Why should we be made to return to the unprofitable idolatry we thought we had disgorged? A dog will return to its vomit, and a pig will return to wallow in the mud, regardless of the bath given by its owner. But, we're neither dogs revisiting what we have cast out, nor pigs rolling in filth after cleansing by Christ's precious blood through the baptism of the Holy Spirit. Like Paul, we must now "...[Forget] what is behind and [strain] toward what is ahead, [and] press on toward the goal to win the prize for which God has called [us] heavenward in Christ Jesus" (Phil. 3:13–14).

If as Africans we acted like pagans in the past, we no longer follow those beliefs and lifestyles or walk in darkness anymore. Paul put it this way: "And that is what some of you were. But you were washed, you were sanctified, you were justified in the name of the Lord Jesus Christ and by the Spirit of our God" (1 Cor. 6:11). "It is for freedom," he points out to the Galatians, "that Christ has set us free. Stand firm, then, and do not let yourselves be burdened again by a yoke of slavery" (Gal. 5:1).

We need to gather courage through faith in Christ, affirming that the God of our fathers Abraham, Isaac, and Jacob saved them and their descendants, and thus is more than capable in saving and sustaining us to the end of the age through His Son. Here's His promise: " 'If you are willing and obedient, you will eat the best from the land; but if you resist and rebel, you will be devoured by the sword.' For the mouth of the LORD has spoken" (Isa. 1:19–20).

Like the Galatians, we ought to closely guard our God-given salvation and freedom in Christ against traditionalists and false teachers of His Father's Word, who want to mislead believers—especially Ghanaian Christians—into darkness once again. Let's listen again to the words of Paul:

> *It is for freedom that Christ has set us free. Stand firm, then, and do not let yourselves be burdened again by a yoke of slavery. Mark my words! I, Paul, tell you that if you let yourselves be circumcised, Christ will be of no value to you at all. Again I declare to every man who lets himself be circumcised that he is obligated to obey the whole law. You who are trying to be justified by law have been alienated from Christ; you have fallen away from grace* (Gal. 5:1–4).

What he meant here is that believers are saved by grace (Eph. 2:8), and not by their good works, the law, or circumcision, because no one can be saved by his own good deeds. Therefore, anyone who turns away from grace through faith in Christ in following the Law makes void that grace and is under a curse (Gal. 3:10–11).

The curse signifies sinful bondage to Satan and eternal condemnation. Neither did the Apostle Paul want any of his converts to backslide into such a horrible situation nor do I want to find *any* human being, particularly believers, there. Therefore, *we should not look back*, lest we perish as Lot's wife did (Gen. 19:26).

Those Who Look Back Are Unworthy

Let's take the example of a new employee who keeps talking about and making references to his former job and all the benefits he used to enjoy. Such a worker can't be productive to the new employer in his business. The reason is that he can't focus on his present duties while still thinking about the former job and what he had left behind. Such reminiscing will sap his energy, dampen his interest in new responsibilities, and render him incapable of meeting the demands of the work for which he was hired. Guess what? His Master will say to him: "You're fired!"

The Effect of Looking Back

Talking about looking back reminds me of Jesus' words to a man desiring to follow Him, pleading: " '…but first let me go back and say good-by to my family.' Jesus replied, 'No one who puts his hand to the plow and looks back is fit for service in the kingdom of God.' " (Luke 9:61–62).

As Christians, looking back has the effect of diverting our attention or focus from Christ towards the material, eventually drawing us away from following the Lord. Hence, the admonition: *Don't look back*.

I would like to mention a practical example from my own life. While a student in middle school and later the Technical Institute, I was a member of the soccer and athletic teams, respectively, and participated in the 440×4, and 880×4 relays teams for my school. As a good long-distance runner, my nickname was Slow But Sure, because I had adopted a measured but steady style of competing in a race. Thus, even though starting slowly, I would increase my pace gradually during the race, finally speeding up toward the finish line to win the prize.

I still remember one of the stern warnings given by our coach to the runners: "Once you start the race, don't look back at the other athletes running closely behind you, trying to overtake you in the race." First, he explained that whenever you look back, your focus is shifted and, therefore, your speed's inevitably reduced within that critical time. Second, as you slow down, your opponent will overtake you. Third, as you look back, you may step into the next track, disqualifying you entirely. Fourth, looking back can be interpreted by your opponent as insecurity and the fear of losing. Looking back doesn't remove your fear, but compounds it, leading to certain defeat.

In short, a believer's "looking back" means spiritually backsliding into a former sinful lifestyle, a failure to stay on course. It means turning away from your trust in our Maker and Savior to other gods or any thing to which you had ignorantly given your utmost attention, love and loyalty. It follows that you're depending on the flesh, or what you or the world—with all its wisdom and technology—can enable you in your earthly accomplishments. James defines *looking back* as adultery or friendship with the world:

You adulterous people, don't you know that friendship with the world is hatred toward God? Anyone who chooses to be a friend of the world becomes an enemy of God. Or do you think Scripture says without reason that the spirit he caused to live in us envies intensely? (James 4:4–5)

"Sankofa" Can Lead to Idolatry

It follows clearly from James in the above passage that returning to traditional religious practice or ancestral worship (*sankofa*) amounts to the sin of idolatry, provoking the Lord to anger. For instance, in the days of Jeremiah, the idolatrous behavior of Israel so provoked Him that He refused to listen to prayers offered on their behalf:

> "So do not pray for this people nor offer any plea or petition for them; do not plead with me, for I will not listen to you. Do you not see what they are doing in the towns of Judah and in the streets of Jerusalem? The children gather wood, the fathers light the fire, and the women knead the dough and make cakes of bread for the Queen of Heaven. They pour out drink offerings to other gods to provoke me to anger. But am I the one they are provoking?" declares the LORD. "Are they not rather harming themselves, to their own shame?" (Jer. 7:16–19)

In avoiding the provocation of God toward anger, it behooves every true believer to prayerfully eschew the retrospective view: indulging in acts tantamount to idolatry. We must bear in mind that neither any human or earthly power nor wisdom or any other god can enable us to achieve our mission or purpose on earth. God alone, Who made us in His image and has graciously called us individually into His eternal Kingdom, has the ultimate, divine plan He wants each of us to fulfill. Besides, He alone and no one else has the power through which we can achieve our individual, divinely appointed goals. "Unless the LORD builds the house, its builders labor in vain. Unless the LORD watches over the city, the watchmen stand guard in vain" (Ps. 127:1).

Perhaps we need to be reminded that the Christian life is a relationship with God through His Son and with our fellow believers, meaning that you're not walking the path alone. Alternatively, it's like a relay race for which Christ has set the pace. Others have run the race before us and we're called upon, according to His Father's will, to snatch the baton as we move steadily toward our divine purpose's fulfillment in our generation.

As a believer, therefore, you must determinedly look straight ahead

> **Once you grasp the baton, you have to run with all your might, not looking back until you finish**

on your track, getting ready to move diligently forward as your teammate prepares to hand you the baton. Once you grasp it, you have to run with all your might, not looking back until you finish.

Looking forward versus backward has a lot of benefits. First, looking straight ahead has the advantage of inspiring you to exert your energy on the race set before you. Second, it requires you to stay focused on the race so that you don't step out of your track. Third, it enables you to sustain energy for increased speed in the final round to win the race. Similarly, as fellow believers, we're advised not to look behind in our walk with Christ, but always to look forward, our eyes fixed on "Jesus, the author and perfecter of our faith, who for the joy set before him endured the cross, scorning its shame, and sat down at the right hand of the throne of God" (Heb. 12:2).

Fixing our eyes on Him means remaining wholly focused on Him. It involves casting all our burdens on the Lord in every life circumstance. It means depending solely on Him to supply all our needs—physically, emotionally and spiritually—through the mighty labor of the Holy Spirit in us. Just as all the prophets and Apostles had to be filled with the Spirit of God in fulfilling their divinely appointed service, so those called by Him in these latter days ought to receive His anointing power in enabling the accomplishment of their own. It's "…'Not by might nor by power, but by my Spirit' says the LORD Almighty' " (Zech. 4:6). This isn't possible without total commitment, discussed in the final chapter.

CHAPTER 28

It Takes Total Commitment

*I*n order for any group of believers to be Spirit-filled vessels—to lift up the name of the Lord in their community—they have to be fully committed to God and to the task of increasing and extending His Kingdom in their part of the world. In one's full commitment to a job, one may ordinarily rely on one's own ability and plan to accomplish it; however, biblical commitment means surrender to God through faith in His Son. It means complete reliance on His plan and power for the achievement of that particular task or goal. There are several biblical models to encourage us.

For example, Zerubbabel and his team of Jewish leaders returning from exile realized at first the need to stay wholly committed to the Lord. That is, they set their hearts and minds to building God's altar in Jerusalem and worshipping Him according to the Scriptures (Ezra 3:1–6). Second, they were determined in accomplishing the divinely appointed task assigned to them in spite of obstacles encountered in the process. None of the leaders—neither Zerubbabel, Nehemiah nor Ezra—allowed himself to be drawn away from the labor expended rebuilding the walls and Temple of Jerusalem, and the renewal of their covenant relationship with God in accordance with the Holy Scriptures.

Most importantly, they depended on His power, wisdom and direction through daily prayer and adherence to His Word in every aspect of the project. Hence, notwithstanding the constant opposition encountered from Sanballat and Tobiah (Neh. 2:10) throughout, they were able to complete the rebuilding of both their protective barriers and house of worship. This is because they relied on Jehovah, not them-selves. The following is part of Nehemiah's report:

> *So the wall was completed on the twenty-fifth of Elul, in fifty-two days. When all our enemies heard about this, all the surrounding nations were afraid and lost their self-confidence, because they realized that this work had been done with the help of our God* (Neh. 6:15–16).

Another encouraging example is found in Acts 3, wherein the Apostles Peter and John healed the lame man at the Beautiful Gate of the Temple in Jerusalem, which miracle drew a large crowd to them. To direct attention to Christ instead of them, they began "…teaching the people and proclaiming in Jesus the resurrection of the dead" (Acts 4:2). But the religious leaders of the Jews had them arrested and thrown in jail. The following morning, they were made to appear before the Sanhedrin—the Supreme Court of the Jews—for questioning. One would have thought that facing such religiously authoritative judgment would frighten the Apostles into submission, but Peter's brave response to their questions stunned them:

> *…"By what power or what name did you do this?" Then Peter, filled with the Holy Spirit, said to them: "Rulers and elders of the people! If we are being called to account today for an act of kindness shown to a cripple and are asked how he was healed, then know this, you and all the people of Israel: It is by the name of Jesus Christ of Nazareth, whom you crucified but whom God raised from the dead, that this man stands before you healed. He is 'the stone you builders rejected, which has become the capstone.' Salvation is found in no one else, for there is no other name under heaven given to men by which we must be saved." (4:7–12).*

The Scripture says: "When [the high priest, religious leaders and the lawyers of the Supreme Court] saw the courage of Peter and John and realized that they were unschooled, ordinary men, they were astonished and they took note that these men had been with Jesus" (4:13).

It's further reported that on their release and after several threats, Peter and John neither relaxed on their oars, taking the matter for granted, nor did they claim any victory or glory for themselves in healing the cripple, but they "went back to their own people and reported all that the chief priests and elders had said to them. When they heard this, they raised their voices together in prayer to God" (4:23–24) as follows:

"Sovereign Lord," they said, "you made the heaven and the earth and the sea, and everything in them. You spoke by the Holy Spirit through the mouth of your servant, our father David: 'Why do the nations rage and the peoples plot in vain? The kings of the earth take their stand and the rulers gather together against the Lord and against his Anointed One.' Indeed Herod and Pontius Pilate met together with the Gentiles and the people of Israel in this city to conspire against your holy servant Jesus, whom you anointed. They did what your power and will had decided beforehand should happen. Now, Lord, consider their threats and enable your servants to speak your word with great boldness. Stretch out your hand to heal and perform miraculous signs and wonders through the name of your holy servant Jesus." (4:24–30).

The Apostles Experience Fresh Anointing

It's related in the Scriptures that, "After they prayed, the place where they were meeting was shaken. And they were all filled with the Holy Spirit and spoke the word of God boldly" (4:31). In their attempts to spread the Gospel, the Apostles were being threatened by the Jewish religious leaders, so they cried to the Lord. Their prayer was answered and they were empowered to boldly continue their ministry.

Today, He still answers prayers for all those truly committed to His Kingdom's agenda and glory. Those who sincerely call on Him will never be denied, but will receive help in due season in accordance with His promise (Ps. 50:15; Luke 11:9–13).

First, it's significant to note that the result of their prayer—"the shaking of the ground where they stood"—was primarily to break down the barriers of opposition erected by Jerusalem's religious leaders. Second, it was to imbue the Apostles with God's power in their continuous proclamation of the Gospel. Third, it ushered them into a strong bond of unity and love for each other. For up to this point in their Christian journey, there were still areas of weakness among them (as the body of Christ) that needed to be pruned, sanctified and strengthened to enable them to bear abundant fruit (John 15:1–5; Acts 5:1–11).

As we may recall, Jesus prayed to His Father for His followers "that all of them may be one..." (John 17:21) and also commanded them to " '...Love one another. As I have loved you, so you must love one another. By this all men will know that you are my disciples, if you love one another" (13:34–35).

Therefore, the answer to their prayer was the fulfillment of Jesus' high-priestly prayer for "love and unity." He knew that His disciples needed these supernatural qualities in order to root them deeply in the solid foundation built on unflinching faith in Him. He is "...the rock..." (1 Cor. 10:4) and the only foundation that can be laid (3:11), upon which stands the Church — the body of Christ.

Faith, love and unity emanating from the bond of the Spirit are inseparable virtues for the advancement of the Church. Following that answered prayer, we read that, "All the believers were one in heart and mind..." (Acts 4:32). For we know from the Scriptures and personal experience that a Church without solid faith, love and unity can't stand, let alone fight against any division or opposition that might come her way. Thus, fear, disloyalty, divisiveness and timidity among the Apostles — the leadership and its congregation — were eliminated and replaced with faith and boldness through the power of the Holy Spirit. We read, "With great power the apostles continued to testify to the resurrection of the Lord Jesus, and much grace was upon them all" (4:33).

Finally, the answer to their prayer provided them a financial breakthrough: the rich among them began to have compassion for the needy, giving generously to meet the needs of strangers and the poor, so that none was found wanting.

> *There were no needy persons among them. For from time to time those who owned lands or houses sold them, brought the money from the sales and put it at the apostles' feet, and it was distributed to anyone as he had need. Joseph, a Levite from Cyprus, whom the apostles called Barnabas (which means Son of Encouragement), sold a field he owned and brought the money and put it at the apostles' feet (4:34–37).*

The apostles prayed for power and guidance in the fulfillment of their great commission: to preach the Good News to all the nations, beginning in Jerusalem, and their prayer was answered because they aimed at seeking "...first his kingdom and his righteousness..." (Matt. 6:33), not their own welfare. Accordingly, the Lord empowered them with the Holy Spirit to enable them to satisfy both their spiritual and physical needs, as we read in the above passage. Now, those of us entrusted with the leadership of the Church in our time must follow the Apostles' good example.

Meeting the Needs of Believers Today

The needs of many church members today can't be met, because we don't pray enough. I believe we all have to yield to God in prayer in order to be renewed in faith, love and unity by the Holy Spirit. The regular routine of worship that we follow every Sunday has sometimes become so stale and empty of His Spirit that it doesn't inwardly touch or move the majority of worshippers to perform acts of kindness.

There are poor people in the Church today, especially in many parts of Africa. Nevertheless, the wealthy among us are so blind to their own spiritual needs that they ignore those of the poor, either because the wealthy aren't converted or are simply mere babes in Christ, not knowing how to use their resources to His glory.

When we pray, we don't see results, because as James says, "…you ask with wrong motives…" (James 4:3). It behooves us all—especially ministers and the leaders of the Church in Africa—to start now taking our own private devotional lives and that of the Church more seriously than we have in the past. There's an over-abundance of politics, jealousy, self-seeking and humanism in the Church these days. These attitudes defile us as the leaders in the body of Christ, causing divisions in churches, loss of focus and the failure to anoint the Spirit upon our lives.

This is particularly so with a number of Ghanaian Methodist churches in North America. We have to realize that wherever the Church is located—Europe or Africa, east or west, north or south—as pastors together with our lay leaders, we can't make headway toward growth unless we repent of our sins—including the lukewarm stance we take on God's work.

There's a need to pray for fresh anointing of the Holy Spirit upon our lives as pastors and leaders, the entire Church, and for the manifestation of our spiritual gifts in order to fulfill our individual ministries for the extension of the Kingdom of God in the world.

The ministry's awesome responsibility in furthering the work of God to which we're called is far beyond our human capabilities. As Paul pointed out, "Not that we are competent in ourselves to claim anything for ourselves, but our competence comes from God" (2 Cor. 3:5). To be blunt, we know that we can't do it unless we're empowered by Him Who called us to be His co-laborers.

It's certain that He will strengthen us if we ask Him, because He is aware of all our weaknesses. He has promised never to "fail or forsake" anyone sincerely trusting in Him. In fact, it was a similar awareness of the awesome responsibility of shepherding Christ's flock that led the Wesley brothers John and Charles to pour out their concerns in the following popular, solemn hymn of the Methodists:

A charge to keep I have,
A God to glorify,
A never-dying soul to save,
And fit it for the sky:

To serve the present age,
My calling to fulfill:
O may it all my powers engage
To do my Master's will!

Arm me with jealous care,
As in thy sight to live;
And O Thy servant, Lord, prepare
A strict account to give!

Help me to watch and pray,
And on Thyself rely,
Assured, if I my trust betray,
I shall forever die.
(*MHB*, 578 by Charles Wesley, 1707-88)

Like the Apostles, the Wesley brothers acknowledged their own in-adequacy in the task God entrusted to them. Hence, their complete reliance on Him through prayer for strength, wisdom, courage, dedication and guidance enabled the fulfillment of their calling. As a result, they were empowered by Him in the accomplishment of their ministries of church music and the preaching of the Gospel as faithful Methodist servants through faith, love and unity in Christ.

In his brief commentary on James 2:1–9, Dave Egner made the following observation concerning the ministry of Jesus: "He crossed traditional barriers to talk with tax collectors, sinners, non-Jews, people of mixed races, the poor, as well as the rich. He came to identify with each of us, and to pay the ultimate price on the cross for all our sins" (*Daily Bread*, Monday, October 27, 2003).

We need to follow the good examples of Christ and our predecessors by praying constantly for the fullness of the Holy Spirit. By so doing, we'll be strengthened in overcoming every obstacle that hinders the futherance of God's Kingdom, not only in Ghana, but also in Africa and the world at large.

It Calls for a Team of Prayer Warriors

In this connection, I'm afraid that our regular, routine prayers won't bring us the measure of divine strength required to achieve our goal. It's necessary to form a team of dedicated Christian adults as prayer-warriors who'll stand in the gap (Ezek. 22:30) day and night, interceding on behalf of the Church's progress. I believe there are seriously committed believers who love to pray, specially gifted in intercessory prayers in various churches in Africa and other parts of the world.

For instance, there is the Africa House of Prayer—consisting of the committed African church leaders of various denominations—led by Rev. Emeka Ngwampah of Nigeria. They meet at advantageous places interceding for the redemption of unbelievers from the powers of darkness. On the front page of the newspaper *Hope Africa*—published by I Go Ministries, Inc. and led by Rev. Dr. Nicku Mordi in Washington—it was reported that "for 13 years, intercessors have been [praying,] claiming Africa for Jesus" (Vol. 1 no. 2, July 2005).

Another powerful prayer house is Link Intercessors International, with Rev. Gifty Niboi as director. As their name implies, they link up with various prayer-warriors, particularly the women of various churches in Africa and Europe, who wail in prayer for God to send down His power for the release of all in sin's bondage throughout Africa and the rest of the world. The prayer-warriors of Calvary Redeeming Methodist Church in Rockville, Md., have teamed up with Link Intercessors International in their efforts to achieve this laudable goal for the glory of God.

Here in the U.S., He is doing mighty works through the Methodist Church of Ghana, North America Mission, consisting of more than 12 churches led by anointed preachers, bonding together to reach out to Africans, particularly Ghanaians, to seek the Lord while in a foreign country.

In addition, there are other great men and women of God, like Franklin Graham (son of Billy Graham), John Hagee, Kenneth Copeland, Anthony Hayford, John McArthur, Charles Stanley, T.D. Jakes, Paula Jones, Benny Hinn, Tony Evans, Seth Asare, Michael Youssef, Ravi Zacharias and Stephen Gyermeh—to mention only a few—as well as other pastors of the member churches of the Television Broadcasting Network (TBN), including other preachers of various Churches continually spreading the Gospel to win souls for Christ.

There are other preaching networks of white and black churches—

in Africa and across the globe—like those mentioned above, with prayer towers, whose unceasing intercessory prayers keep ministries on fire for the extension of God's Kingdom.

These are Prayer Giants, delighting in prayer for themselves, others and ongoing various ministries 24 hours a day. Their prayers yield fruitful results to the glory of God. As James stated, "…The prayer of a righteous man is powerful and effective" (James 5:16). Therefore, believers are obliged to join the prayer force to pray without ceasing (Luke 18:1; 1 Thess. 5:17). Jesus commands us to " 'Watch and pray so that you will not fall into temptation…' " Matt. 26:41).

In the book of the prophet Isaiah, God promised to establish a new Israel, a prototype for the Church of Christ, urging her to continue in prayer as follows:

> *I have posted watchmen on your walls, O Jerusalem; they will never be silent day or night. You who call on the LORD, give yourselves no rest, and give him no rest till he establishes Jerusalem and makes her the praise of the earth. The LORD has sworn by his right hand and by his mighty arm: "Never again will I give your grain as food for your enemies, and never again will foreigners drink the new wine for which you have toiled; but those who harvest it will eat it and praise the LORD, and those who gather the grapes will drink it in the courts of my sanctuary." (Isa. 62:6–9).*

This is Jehovah's clear message of promise to a reborn, penitent Israel under the new Covenant, initiated and made available to all believers by Jesus Christ for the past 2,000 years. Today, Israel stands as an independent sovereign nation, managing her own affairs despite the struggle with Palestine for occupation of certain portions of the land. Nevertheless, with the help of peace talks and negotiations mediated by the UN, and encouraged by the U.S. in particular, there's hope for lasting tranquility for both peoples in the end.

In much the same way, believers in Africa can be renewed by the Lord in order to fulfill the goals He has set before us, if only we deploy devoted Christians as prayer-warriors, interceding daily for the spiritual and physical well-being of the nations of this world, with a focus on Africa.

It uplifts our spirits to recall from the previous chapter that through the African Enterprise, the Lord has already instituted "a Christian interdenominational, cross-cultural ministry of evangelism, reconciliation, leadership training, relief and development." This missionary team works "with Church leaders to mobilize their congregations in outreach to Africa's cities." (African Enterprise, July/August, 2004).

The Prayer Request of African Enterprise

The bottom section of the paper has the following prayer request:

> Please, pray for an African city each day along with praying for an African Enterprise leader or event; and do remember all other missionary agents, as well, working in Africa and other parts of the world.
> 1. The Christians in the city, that they not be discouraged, that churches be united and minister with compassion.
> 2. The city government and business leaders, that they surrender their lives to God and lead with integrity.
> 3. The unsaved in the city, that they find salvation in Christ.
> 4. Resources, for the transformation of the cities.

Finally, there's a request to pray for John Reynolds, chairman of the African Enterprise, U.S.A. It's required of all believers to resolve as one people to commit themselves unreservedly, joining forces with the prayer-warriors of the world. We must aim at constant prayer to God for the redemption of the total continent of Africa, as well as the rest of the world. We need to pray for the fulfillment of His purpose in whatever area of service He has placed us.

Furthermore, we should be conscious of the truth that without Christ, all our efforts—as individuals or as the people of any nation—will continue to come to naught. But the Good News is that with Him, we can bring down "the walls of Jericho" and reduce every mountain to a plain, because we have the Almighty on our side; and "with God, all things are possible."

In this connection, I invite all readers of this book to join hands with me in intercessory prayer for every city on the continent of Africa, as well as the leaders, events and projects, as earnestly requested by the African Enterprise in previous pages. It was in the pursuit of such requests that Antoine Rutayisire, a representative of the African Enterprise, reports the following:

> AE seeks to mobilize prayer intercessors and others to pray in concert for important issues here in Rwanda. To this end, we organized a large Prayer Crusade at the Christian Life Assembly Church in Ki-

> gali. There were one thousand intercessors, pastors and lay people in attendance. We spent time in prayer for the country and also gave teachings on prayer and our vision for a national prayer network. Our hope is that the teaching will be put into action by those in attendance. These prayer crusades will continue on a monthly basis.

Nico Nteme of the Republic of Congo, also reports as follows:

> A Leadership Mission devoted to prayer for our Nation was held in partnership with a group of women from 8 different Christian women's organizations. About 250 women gathered and 54 committed their lives to Christ." (African Enterprise, July/August, 2003).

These encouraging words assure us of the great work that the Good Lord is doing in Africa. As believers, we should all unite to support the various groups of Christian workers and missionaries in these areas with both our constant prayers and financial support. Apart from praying regularly along with them, Calvary Redeeming Methodist Church will endeavor to offer them financial assistance as the Lord blesses us. It's hoped that other churches will follow suit, trusting that God will surely bring revival to the continent of Africa, because He has done it before in East Africa.

The East Africa Revival—A Living Example

In his book *Revolutionary Love*, Bishop Festo Kivengere, together with Dorothy Smoker, wrote about an inspiring revival that occurred in East Africa in the 1930s. It began with two devout Christian friends, Simeoni Nsibambi and Dr. Joe Church.

> They found each other by God's "accident" near Kampala, Uganda, when both were spiritually hungry to desperation. They dropped everything and sat together under a tree on Namirembe Hill, studying the New Testament for days to find more about the Holy Spirit. He found them, and led them to the cross of Christ and to a simple way of accepting its power daily for continuous personal reviving. (*Revolutionary Love*, 1983, p. 60).

According to the story, when they were ignited by the Spirit for Christ, the flame of revival gradually but intensely spread to schools, colleges and other parts of the country, converting teachers and students, the rich and the poor alike, and uniting them into one body in

Christ. For instance, "Teams were going out, invited or not, at their own expense, from Rwanda to Burundi and Tanganyika, from western and central Uganda to other provinces, and to Kenya and Sudan."

The revival of which Festo himself "became a part in 1940," when he was still a school teacher, was said to have lasted half a century. It's reported that the African Enterprise is one of the many fruitful results of the fire kindled by the Holy Spirit in the two friends' hearts.

If we band together, He will certainly tend the fire with us in our temples, as He did in the past

Undoubtedly, the same God that set ablaze these two "spiritually hungry" Africans in the 1930s will do it again in our day, if we would sincerely band together in small groups of friends in yielding to Him as vessels sanctified for His holy use. He will certainly tend the fire with us in our temples, as He did in the past. Will you, my friend, be part of this coming revival, even as Kivengere became a part when he was a teacher?

In your own capacity you can do nothing, but if you pray and cast yourself completely upon God through faith in His Son, He will accept you, fill you and use you in ways you had never imagined or thought possible. " 'What is impossible with men is possible with God.' " (Luke 18:27).

The South Africa Example: A Ray of Hope

I'm very much inclined to believe that the release of Nelson Mandela from a South African prison on February 11, 1990, didn't happen by chance but by divine intervention. It was certainly the result of the untiring efforts of thousands of Christians throughout the world, joining hands with Archbishop Desmond Tutu to lift up their voices in fervent prayers to God for the release of all those incarcerated in the country for political reasons. Speaking on behalf of his people to the UN Security Council, Tutu stated, among other things:

> I speak out of a full heart, for I am about to speak about... a land
> God had richly endowed with the good things of the earth, a land
> rich in mineral deposits of nearly every kind; a land capable of feed-

ing itself and other lands on the beleaguered continent of Africa, a veritable breadbasket; a land that could contribute wonderfully to the material and spiritual development and prosperity of all Africa, and indeed of the whole world.

And so we would expect that such a land, veritably flowing with milk and honey, should be the land where peace and harmony and contentment reigned supreme. Alas, the opposite is the case. For my beloved country is wracked by division, by alienation, by animosity, by separation, by injustice, avoidable pain and suffering. It is a deeply fragmented society, ridden by fear and anxiety.

Nevertheless, with constant prayers and hard work, Tutu—together with members of the Executive Committee of the South African Council of Churches—held emergency sessions with P.W. Botha to work out lasting solutions to the rapidly deteriorating situation. Tutu continued:

As a result of our peace initiative, we did get to meet two cabinet ministers, demonstrating thereby our concern to carry out our call to be ministers of reconciliation and ambassadors of Christ. We deplore all forms of violence, the violence of oppressive and unjust society and the violence of those seeking to overthrow that society; for we believe that violence is not the answer to the crisis of our land.

In saying so, he endorsed the view being stressed in this book that "Unless the LORD builds the house, its builders labor in vain..." (Ps. 127:1), because it's "...'Not by might nor by power, but by my Spirit,' says the LORD Almighty" (Zech. 4:6). He concluded as follows:

We dream of a new society that will be truly nonracial, truly democratic, in which people count because they are created in the image of God. We are committed to work for justice, for peace, and for reconciliation (*Modern History Sourcebook: The Question of South Africa*, pp. 1, 4).

Dream Fulfilled: "Free at Last!"

On Mandela's release from prison, after more than a quarter-century of confinement in the South African apartheid system, the freed leader of the African National Congress (ANC) walked through those prison gates to enter a car on the other side. "I felt, even at the age of 71, that my life was beginning anew...I was a free man for the first time in 27 years." Surely the dream of Tutu, Mandela and many others, both within and outside South Africa, had been fulfilled.

He continued: "I thank all those in the ANC and the democratic movement who had worked so hard for so long." Standing on the same podium with him was Coretta Scott King, wife of the great freedom fighter Martin Luther King, Jr., who had flown from the U.S. to be among his welcoming guests. Mandela added, making reference to King's "immortal words:"

> "This is one of the most important moments in the life of our country. I stand here before you with deep pride and joy—pride in the ordinary, humble people of this country. You have shown such a calm, patient determination to reclaim this country as your own, and now the joy that we can loudly proclaim from the rooftops—'Free at last, free at last!'

> "I stand before you humbled by your courage, with a heart full of love for all of you. I regard it as the highest honor to lead the ANC at this moment in our history. I am your servant... It is not the individuals that matter, but the collective... This is a time to heal the old wounds and build a new South Africa."

Indeed, after about 300 years of colonial rule, with bright skies the greatest of all days dawned on the land of South Africa—the day of Mandela's inauguration as the president of the Republic of South Africa on May 10, 1990. Frederik Willem de Klerk, second deputy president, was the first to be sworn in, followed by Thabo Mbeki as the first deputy president. When it was Mandela's turn, he said, "I pledge to obey and uphold the Constitution and to devote myself to the well-being of the Republic and its people." To the assembled guests and watchful world, he said:

> Today, all of us do, by our presence here... confer glory and hope to our newborn liberty. Out of the experience of an extraordinary human disaster that lasted too long, must be born a society of which all humanity will be proud. We, who were outlaws not long ago, have today been given the rare privilege to be host to the nations of the world on our own soil. We thank all of our international guests for having come to take possession with the people of our country of what is, after all, a common victory for justice, for peace, for human dignity. We have, at last, achieved our political emancipation. We pledge ourselves to liberate all our people from the continuing bondage of poverty, deprivation, suffering, gender, and other dis-

> crimination. Never, never, and never again shall it be that this beau-
> tiful land will again experience the oppression of one by another...
> The sun shall never set on so glorious a human achievement. Let
> freedom reign. God bless Africa! (*Long Walk To Freedom*, 1994, pp.
> 539–541).

I believe it's the dream of all Africans and anyone who yearns for world peace that what happened to our brothers and sisters in South Africa will also come true for us in the near future. The God Who opens and none can shut, shuts and none can open is still on the throne overseeing His creation to fulfill His purpose on earth.

It may interest you to know that Mandela was 44 when he became a political prisoner and 71 when he was released, having gradually but steadily and courageously rallied his people to ultimate freedom. Finally, when the mandate was given to the ANC to form a government, he said:

> I saw my mission as one, preaching reconciliation, of binding the
> wounds of the country, of engendering trust, and confidence. I knew
> that many people, particularly the minorities, whites, coloreds, and
> Indians, would be feeling anxious about the future and I wanted
> them to feel secure. I reminded people again and again that the lib-
> eration struggle was not a battle against any one group or color, but
> a fight against a system of repression. At every opportunity, I said all
> South Africans must now unite and join hands and say we are one
> country, one nation, one people, marching together into the future.
> (p. 115).

Warren W. Wiersbe wrote: "What people do with authority is a test of character. Do they use their authority to promote themselves or to help others? Do they glorify themselves or glorify God?" (*Be Committed: Doing God's Will Whatever the Cost*, p. 96).

Thus, in spite of the apartheid regime's atrocities committed against his fellow South Africans, Mandela didn't seek revenge, mindful of the written Word of God, "...'It is mine to avenge; I will repay'..." (Rom. 12:19). With that in mind, he sought for reconciliation and unity of the entire population—black or white, Indian or Asian—fully believing that "...'With man this is impossible, but not with God; all things are possible with God.'" (Mark 10:27).

In order to achieve his aim of reconciling and uniting the people of his country, Mandela appointed Tutu—who had retired as Anglican

Archbishop of Cape Town—chairman of the South African Truth and Reconciliation Committee. The Committee's good work resulted in a measure of peace and unity that played a large role in the economic and political stability of South Africa under Mandela's leadership.

"Good leaders," says Herb Vander Lugt, "don't rely on domineering self-assertion—neither at home, nor in church, nor in business. Rather, they balance self-assertiveness (which isn't wrong in itself) with the principle of submitting to one another (Eph. 5:21). They listen respectfully, admit when they are wrong, show a willingness to change, and mix gentleness with firmness. That's submissive leadership—and it works!"

Ghana on the Path of Reconciliation

When President John Agyekum Kufuor, leader of the New Patriotic Party (NPP), took office as the head of the Republic of Ghana in 2001, he was faced with a major decision: whether to toe the line of those arguing for retaliation against the members of J.J. Rawlings's military regime for the death of their family members, or to bury the past and follow the path of reconciliation. As a Christian, Kufuor, like Mandela, chose the latter. He quickly set up a special National Reconciliation Committee, whose objective was to seek reconciliation among all factions in the country in working towards the unity, peace and progress of people from all walks of life toward the common good.

That was the kind of leadership that Kufuor adopted during the eight years of his presidency. Bolstered by the prayerful support of Ghanaian Christians and other religious bodies both within and outside the country, he steered the course of peace, unity and economic development in Ghana.

Talking of the achievements of the Kufuor government, Ivor Agyeman-Duah, Minister-Counselor of Public Affairs of the Ghanaian embassy in Washington, D. C., stated, "There is freedom, unity and peace in the country as compared to the period before he took office. There is growth in the economy, inflation is down, and there are new initiatives by the government, adding value to raw materials." With these positive changes in Ghana, the minister was optimistic that Kufuor would win the forthcoming presidential elections in December 2004, to enable his government to continue with the good work already in progress.

That's the kind of leadership I believe will succeed in Africa in particular and the world at large. Like Mandela, We patiently wait in hope for revival of the people everywhere by the Spirit of the Living God, whose timing is always the best for His people.

As the majority of Ghanaians expected, President Kuffuor did win a second four-year term in office, and continued with his good governance as much as he could. But, he was eventually succeeded by the NDC (National Democratic Congress), led by Arthur Mills. Despite the change in government, Ghanaians still looked forward to the best in the years ahead.

Solomon wrote: "There is a time for everything, and a season for every activity under heaven: a time to be born and a time to die, a time to plant and a time to uproot, a time to kill and a time to heal, a time to tear down and a time to build… He has made everything beautiful in its time…" (Eccl. 3:1–3, 10).

The Lord our God, will graciously bring a great revival to the land in due season, even as He promised the following to Israel in the days of Ezekiel:

> " *For I will take you out of the nations; I will gather you from all the countries and bring you back into your own land. I will sprinkle clean water on you, and you will be clean; I will cleanse you from all your impurities and from all your idols. I will give you a new heart and put a new spirit in you; I will remove from you your heart of stone and give you a heart of flesh. And I will put my Spirit in you and move you to follow my decrees and be careful to keep my laws. You will live in the land I gave your forefathers; you will be my people, and I will be your God* (Ezek. 36:24–28).

In fact, signs of revival are evident in several places around the country. With the conversion of a number of kings and queen-mothers, who are making a positive impact on their subjects, and the opening of new churches in many cities and urban and rural areas of the land, we must acknowledge the moving of the Holy Spirit on the lives of Ghanaians, giving the praise and thanks due Him.

Furthermore, we anticipate with joy a much more extensive revival affecting everyone. We're trusting in God and His promises, always relying on His power through prayer to do His will, because we know that "He gives strength to the weary and increases the power of the weak" (Isa. 40:29). We ought to constantly remember the greatness of His faithfulness. He is never late, and in His own time, He brings deliverance, freedom and peace to all who wait for Him.

The Psalmist said, "I am still confident of this: I will see the goodness of the LORD in the land of the living. Wait for the LORD; be strong and take heart and wait for the LORD" (Ps. 27:13–14). "For the revelation awaits an appointed time; it speaks of the end and will not prove false. Though it linger, wait for it; it will certainly come and will not delay" (Hab. 2:3).

When the day dawns on this vision's fulfillment, Africa, as well as the rest of "the earth will be filled with the knowledge of the glory of the LORD, as the waters cover the sea" (2:14). Then, we'll all—black and white alike, together with our children—exclaim, "No one could have done this, except the Lord (*Gye Nyame*)." We'll rejoice with the Psalmist and the Apostle John, respectively, and shout, "the LORD has done this, and it is marvelous in our eyes…'To him who sits on the throne and to the Lamb be praise and honor and glory and power, for ever and ever!'" (Ps. 118:23; Rev. 5:13).

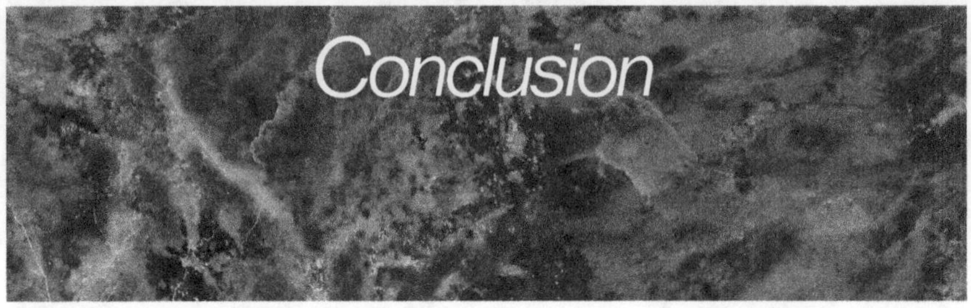

In bringing the recounting of this vision to its conclusion, I want to first give thanks to the Almighty God for using me as a vessel in which to receive His vital message to my fellow Ghanaians, to other Africans and all other people of this world—black or white, male or female, young or old, rich or poor. Second, I would like to remind my readers that God granted me this vision for the following reasons:

- To confirm the truth that He created all humans equal in His image, He loves all human beings and does not desire that anyone should die in sin due to the ignorance of His Will, as revealed in the Holy Scriptures.

- To teach us that we can't save ourselves from the consequences of our sins. This circumstance has been aggravated by the worship of idols and ancestors, with adverse consequences burdening families, communities, nations, and the world at large, particularly Africa, with Ghana as a prime example. This has allowed the Devil to gain a foothold in numerous people, black and white alike, whose habit has become to commit acts of wickedness, murder, terrorism, fear, mistrust and insecurity in the world.

    Nevertheless, through God's merciful kindness toward us, He revealed to me not only the cause of our woes, but also the way of deliverance from these evils and "…from the coming wrath" (Matt. 3:7). Deliverance consists in turning away from sin, idolatrous practices, occultism and Satanism toward saving faith in Jesus Christ, Who offered His life as sacrifice on the cross at Calvary for the penalty of our sins (John 3:16; 1 John 1:9, 2:1–2).

- That in spite of the woeful condition in which we find ourselves, the Scriptures assure us that if we sincerely repent of our sins and accept Jesus as our Lord and Savior, we'll receive His Father's forgiveness and new life in Christ. The Holy Spirit will set His eternal seal upon the soul of each of us as the guarantee of our new relationship with Him—as the sons and daughters of our Father in heaven (1 John 1:9, 5:11–12; John 1:12, 3:16; 2 Cor. 6:14–18).

- That God expects all in positions of authority to realize they're accountable to Him and should use the trust vested in them by their people for the common good. Hence, they're to rely on Him for power, wisdom and direction, and find peace and the fulfillment of their goals. Furthermore, as individual Christians, we're to conduct ourselves in such ways that our new life of righteousness positively impacts the lives of our entire household and communities at large (Matt. 5:13–16; Acts 16:31). For "Righteousness exalts a nation, but sin is a disgrace to any people" (Prov. 14:34).

- That God wants all who've come to know the Truth (Jesus Christ) to share the Good News with their neighbors, "for all have sinned and fall short of the glory of God" (Rom. 3:23); that sinners must repent and turn to Him for salvation while it's day. For "…Night is coming, when no one can work" (John 9:4).

- That human beings—whether black or white, from the East or West—aren't made to be independent of God, irrespective of our economic, scientific and technological advancement. Hence, it's only in maintaining our relationship with Him through faith in His Son that we're enabled by the power and guidance of the Holy Spirit to achieve our lifelong, divinely appointed goals.

- That there's no other God except our Creator; that there's no other Savior or Mediator between God and humans except our Lord Jesus Christ. Therefore, we must cling to the truth of His Word; otherwise, we'll discover the utter disappointment and misery that all our toils and earthly existence are altogether fruitless in the end. As Solomon regrettably came to know in his latter days, "…everything was meaningless…" (Eccl. 2:11).

- That by all means the Lord is coming again, at the hour of His own choosing, to judge the living and the dead, requiring that they give account of their lives before the holy and righteous God (Eccl. 12:14; Rev. 22:12; Rom. 14:12).

- That since " '…God does not show favoritism' " (Acts 10:34), every individual—black or white, male or female, young or old—has a share in the abundance of His grace, gifts and unlimited resources in meeting life's spiritual, physical and emotional demands (Phil. 4:19). For He is the One "…who richly provides us with everything for our enjoyment" (1 Tim. 6:17).

Come one, come all! Everyone is invited—particularly my fellow Africans—to get into Jesus Christ's heavenward wagon. Our Master declares that He is " '…the way and the truth and the life. No one comes to the Father except through me' " (John 14:6). I believe strongly that this is our time to rise and shine, because light has arrived (Isa. 60:1). No one should lag behind; the Lord graciously saves, heals and abundantly blesses all who sincerely call on Him. It's soul-refreshing to remember that God gave His Son " '…All authority in heaven and on earth…' " (Matt. 28:18) and has

> *…seated him at his right hand in the heavenly realms, far above all rule and authority, power and dominion, and every title that can be given, not only in the present age but also in the one to come. And God placed all things under his feet and appointed him to be head over everything for the church, which is his body…* (Eph. 1:20–23).

The Good News is that if we accept Jesus right now and are willing to follow Him the rest of our lives, He will surely lead us to the end, every step of the way, by means of the Holy Spirit, Who dwells in every believer. Thereafter we'll be with Him in heaven, where the righteous live in peace and glory in the presence of God and His holy angels forever.

Conversely, if we reject Him as our Savior and Lord, we'll certainly be condemned at His judgment seat and cast out together with Satan into hell, where there's " '…eternal fire prepared for the devil and his angels' "…and " '…where there will be weeping and gnashing of teeth' " (Matt. 25:41, 8:12).

The irrefutable and irrevocable truth of the matter is that no religion in this world except Christianity has the solution to the problem of sin facing humanity. Furthermore, of all the religious founders who ever lived, only Jesus Christ—as the Son of God and conceived by the Holy Spirit—lived a sinless life. Though tempted at all points during His earthly existence, He never succumbed to sin (Heb. 5: 7–10), because

He was God in human form, both fully God and fully human (John 1:1, 14).

Therefore, He was the only perfect man in solving the problem of sin, which had separated people from God since the fall of Adam and Eve. That's why Christ declared: " 'For the Son of Man came to seek and to save what was lost' " (Luke 19:10). Through His Father's providence, He offered His life on the cross for the forgiveness of the world's sins. Scripture says, "It was now about the sixth hour, and darkness came over the whole land until the ninth hour, for the sun stopped shining. And the curtain of the temple was torn in two" (23:44–45). Commenting further on this statement, Ray C. Stedman asked,

> Why was this curtain torn in two? Because the Holy of Holies was now to be opened up for the first time to human gaze! And because the Holy of Holies of the human spirit was now to be opened up for the first time to the gaze and habitation of God! When the Son of man died, God ripped the veil wide open. He passed through the Holy place, and penetrated into the Holy of Holies, into the secret of humanity—and the reality of humanity's spirit was unveiled. (*Adventuring Through Matthew, Mark, and Luke*, p. 44).

Since Jesus' sacrificial death on the cross had opened the gateway to eternal life for all believing in Him, the writer to the Hebrews penned the following message of comfort to all believers in Christ:

> *Therefore, brothers, since we have confidence to enter the Most Holy Place by the blood of Jesus, by a new and living way opened for us through the curtain, that is, his body, and since we have a great priest over the house of God, let us draw near to God with a sincere heart in full assurance of faith, having our hearts sprinkled to cleanse us from a guilty conscience and having our bodies washed with pure water* (Heb. 10:19–22).

"That is where we stand now", Stedman declared. It's such a blessing, my friends, to grasp the following insight shared with us on the benefits of the work of Christ for humanity:

> The secret of humanity is open to anyone who opens his or her own heart to the Son of Man, the perfect man. He alone has penetrated the depths of human spirit. He alone re-establishes the lost relationship with God that enables us to be what God intended us to be. He alone saves and restores what was lost in the fall of man, in the entrance of sin into the world. He alone can restore the marred, distort-

ed image of God in our lives.

> All the possibility of a fulfilled humanity is available to anyone in whom the spirit of Christ dwells. All that you deeply want to be in the innermost recesses of your heart, you can be. I'm not talking about your goals in life, such as becoming a millionaire or an Olympic gold medallist. No, I'm talking about the deepest, most inexpressible yearnings of your heart-your desire to be connected to God, to know Him, and be known by Him; your desire to have your life count for something in the eternal scheme of things; your desire to be clean and whole and forgiven. Jesus makes it possible for you to fulfill God's best for you, so that you will be mature and Christlike, filled with love, forgiveness, wholeness, and good works (p. 45).

Therefore, everyone who believes in Christ receives eternal life from His Father here and now, through the transforming power of the Holy Spirit in the name of Jesus. Why? Because "God made him who had no sin to be sin for us, so that in him we might become the righteousness of God" (2 Cor. 5:21).

For the first time in your life, you'll surely discover in Christ the amazing truth and assurance—through the work of the Holy Spirit in you—that you're accepted as a child of God. Besides, since He has no inferior children, you'll find out how much He loves and cares for all belonging to His family equally. Paul confirms this in the following passage:

> *Praise be to the God and Father of our Lord Jesus Christ, who has blessed us in the heavenly realms with every spiritual blessing in Christ. For he chose us in him before the creation of the world to be holy and blameless in his sight. In love he predestined us to be adopted as his sons through Jesus Christ, in accordance with his pleasure and will—to the praise of his glorious grace, which he has freely given us in the One he loves* (Eph. 1:3–6).

The Apostle added, "Consequently, you are no longer foreigners and aliens, but fellow citizens with God's people and members of God's household" (2:19).

Dear reader, armed with the Scripture quoted above, you might have now realized your need to receive Jesus into your heart as your Savior and Lord. If not, perhaps the following simple questions may help you to make up your mind before it's too late:

Who have you decided to follow the rest of your life?

Who is your chosen Leader or Master in this life?

To whom do you owe allegiance?

As a human being made in God's image—regardless of your position in society or family—to whom do you look for love, peace, strength, protection, courage, success, joy and comfort in your daily life?

David McCasland made this observation:

> Even when life seems overwhelming, we can cry out to the Lord and find His deliverance from distress. It is not health or wealth, but God's unfailing love that sets us free in every circumstance of life. (*Daily Bread*, Wednesday, November 28, 2002).

The unavoidable questions each of us needs to answer are: *Where will I spend eternity? Do I have hope in heaven with the Lord after my death or will I be condemned to hell through rejection of Christ?* As you prayerfully meditate on what answers to give yourself, I offer this brief but precious story by Vernon C. Grounds to guide your decision-making process:

> During World War II, B-17 bombers made long flights from the U.S. mainland to the Pacific island of Saipan. When they landed there, the planes were met by a jeep bearing the sign: "Follow Me!" That little vehicle guided the giant planes to their assigned places in the parking area.
>
> One pilot, who by his own admission was not a religious man, made an insightful comment: "That little jeep with its quaint sign always reminds me of Jesus. He was (a lowly) peasant, but the giant men and women of our time would be lost without His direction."
>
> Centuries after our Savior walked the streets and hills of Israel, the world with all its advances still needs His example and instruction. When His ways aren't followed, numerous problems and evils arise in our world—including immorality, crime, and greed. How do we follow Jesus's ways?

The writer answers the question by reiterating what I had said earlier in my conclusion:

> First of all, we turn from our sin and entrust our lives to Him as our Savior and Lord. Then we seek His will in His Word each day and put it into practice by the power of the Holy Spirit within us. We learn to deny our selfish desires and give ourselves completely to following Jesus (Mark 8:34–35) (*Daily Bread*, March 5, 2003).

As I conclude the documentation and explanation of this vision, my heart's thrilled to know that the Almighty has confirmed His message to me through the story told by Grounds, a dedicated man of God working with the RBC Ministries in Grand Rapids.

Indeed, God is faithful and will always honor His Word to those who sincerely trust and obey Him. Therefore, without any doubt or fear, I'm convinced that this vision's message will be fulfilled, as He has always done according to His Word. That's why He told me to put it in writing: so that everyone may read this book and turn from their sins to His Son, the friend of sinners (Luke 15:1–7). I want to encourage you to put your faith in Him. If you're willing and ready, I want to invite you right now to pray the following with all your heart:

> O God, my heavenly Father, thank you for creating me in your image. Thank you for all the spiritual and material provisions you have in store for me through your Son, Jesus Christ. I believe He died on the Cross for all my sins, and that He rose again from the dead. I beseech you, O God, to forgive me all my sins. I humbly invite your Son, Jesus Christ, into my heart, to be my Savior and Lord all the days of my life. Thank you, Father, for accepting me as one of your children, through Jesus Christ, my Lord. Amen.

If you've sincerely prayed as above, believing with all your heart, then you can be certain you're a changed person and that your name's recorded in "…the Lamb's book of life" (Rev. 21:27). It means that henceforth, Christ is in you, and you are in Him (John 15:3–4; Rev. 3:20). His abiding promise is that " '…I am with you always…' " (Matt. 28:20). Trust in Him with all your heart, because He is able to save to the utmost all who come to Him and wholeheartedly depend on His finished work on the cross (John 1:12, 10:27–30; Acts 16:31).

May I remind you that I'm a living witness—as is the entire universal Church, Christ's body—to what God's saving Grace, through faith in His Son, can do. All that He has done through this ministry—plus the writing of this important vision into a book—must enlighten all skeptics concerning what our Maker can do for anyone trusting in Him.

The message of this book is that without God, we can't make it. This is summed up in the two Akan words *Gye Nyame* (except for God), which is to say: unless God sustains us spiritually, emotionally, mentally and physically by His infinite power, no living thing, including the universe, can exist. It is He Who upholds His own creation by His omnipotence, and no other god. Again, only He alone and no one else can heal and fill the emptiness of our aching hearts. We live by His power.

The same breath of life that God breathed into the first man — "...man became a living being" (Gen. 2:7) — is the one sustaining every human being on earth. Hence, He has the power to retain or withdraw it from any of us at any time, and no one can stop Him (Job 42:2; Luke 12:20). Habakkuk put it this way: "Has not the LORD Almighty determined that the people's labor is only fuel for the fire, that the nations exhaust themselves for nothing?" (Hab. 2:13). Jesus confirmed this message when He declared: " '...apart from me you can do nothing.' " (John 15:5).

The truth emphasized repeatedly in this book is that God made us in His image, in order for us to have a personal relationship with Him and depend on Him in all our ways. We weren't intended to exclude Him in any aspect of our lives in the pursuit of our earthly goals, lest we perish. But being humans with free will, we went our own way instead of His and have been separated from Him since the fall of our first parents (Gen. 3).

Nevertheless, out of God's infinite love and compassion for lost humanity, He came to our rescue by sending His only Son, Jesus Christ — whose substitutionary death on the cross has paid for our sins — as the holy and righteous demands of the Law required (Rom. 6:23; Heb. 2:2). Through His sacrifice, God has made us who believe accepted in the beloved (Eph. 1:6).

It means, therefore, that all believers in Christ will be forgiven of sins, blessed with a new life in Him, and avoid condemnation to hellfire. All believers will be in heaven with the Lord and rewarded for their fruitful life in Christ through the work of the Holy Spirit (John 14:1–3; Matt. 25:40–43, 44–46; Gal. 5:22; 2 Cor. 5:17; Rev. 22:12–15).

It's the prayerful yearning of my heart that as you come to the conclusion of this urgent message from God, you'll join me and all others concerned in committing our lives afresh to His Son. Don't let the sun go down without making a decision about your destiny: to take hold of the unlimited, unconditional, and eternal love of God through faith in Jesus.

He is looking for people like you and me who are ready to offer themselves "as living sacrifice," as God's sanctified vessels, to reach out to the lost, and to bless their families, communities, nations and the world at large. Or we can instead be a tool for destruction in Satan's hands.

Let me give you an example here. An unseen arsonist rose up against the communities of the Washington Metropolitan Area several years ago, burning down people's houses—not because the victims had done him any wrong, but simply because he was full of anger and wickedness, an agent of the Devil who "…comes only to steal and kill and destroy…" (John 10:10). By November 20, 2003, the arsonist had burned down 32 houses in Washington, D.C., Maryland, and Virginia. There were many reported injuries in this violence and one death.

What did he gain by being so cruelly destructive to innocent people? We prayed that he would soon be arrested and convicted of his cowardly and dangerous acts under the cover of dark. God knows him and his every move. Last year, the man was caught and brought to justice.

Now, friend, having come thus far in this book, I'm confident that you're aware of the truth that our choices ultimately affect our destiny. We also know that we can't be neutral in matters of the spirit: we can either be on the right or wrong side of the journey through life. The choice is in our hands.

If we choose God by faith in His Son, He will be with us forever here on earth and hereafter in heaven. But if we decide to live on our own terms and be our own captains, then we leave ourselves open for Satan's domination and destruction in the end. You can make this day one of salvation for " '…you and your household' " (Acts 16:31). In this connection, I humbly but seriously challenge you—white or black, male or female, young or old—in the words of Joshua:

> **We can't be neutral in matters of the spirit: we can either be on the right or wrong side of the journey through life**

> *"…choose for yourselves this day whom you will serve, whether the gods your forefathers served beyond the River, or the gods of the Amorites, in whose land you are living. But as for me and my household, we will serve the LORD."* (Josh. 24:15).

I counsel you to choose Christ, Who is " '…the way and the truth and the life…' " (John 14:6). It's only by choosing Him through faith that we all, together with members of our families, can be saved, living eternally in "...righteousness, peace and joy in the Holy Spirit" (Rom. 14:17), with Him, all the Apostles and fellow believers in the Kingdom of God.

It's declared in the Holy Scriptures, " 'In the time of my favor I heard you, and in the day of salvation I helped you.' I tell you, now is the time of God's favor, now is the day of salvation" (2 Cor. 6:2). Since you're now fully aware of the situation we're in as human beings—particularly as Africans—may I invite you to participate in the following tasks?

- At this juncture, please join me in thanking God for His goodness in revealing to me this vision to share with all people.
- If you haven't done so already, pray to God to forgive you all your sins and accept His Son as your personal Lord and Savior. Here's the promise of the Lord to all who sincerely turn to Him with a penitent heart: "Here I am! I stand at the door and knock. If anyone hears my voice and opens the door, I will come in and eat with him, and he with me" (Rev. 3:20). That's His assurance of your salvation by grace through faith in Him (Eph. 2:8).
- Pray for the salvation and well-being of your family, both far and near.
- Let's join together to intercede for Africa in particular and the world in general, so that the leaders will submit to God of all power and wisdom, through faith in Jesus, and that they'll be guided and controlled *not* by any other power—political, economic, technological, or demonic—but solely by His, the Holy Spirit, our Comforter and Advocate (John 14:26; Rom. 8:26).
- Pray for Barak Obama, the first African-American president of the strongest nation in the world, so that he might be led to govern with true justice for all, in wisdom and fear of God, leading to peace and true freedom for America and the world at large. Through Obama, God has fulfilled His prophetic Word: "Africa shall rise from its slumber." Indeed, I believe this is happening.

Additionally, we should be praying for all the leaders of other countries, so that they might all seek God's counsel during their tenures, acknowledging the truth of the following Scriptures:

> *"Counsel and sound judgment are mine; I have understanding and power. By me kings reign and rulers make laws that are just; by me princes govern, and all nobles who rule on earth...The fear of the LORD is the beginning of wisdom, and knowledge of the Holy One is understanding. For through me your*

> *days will be many, and years will be added to your life"* (Prov. 8:14–16,
> 9:10–11).

I'm confident that if we team up together with heads of governments and make these our daily concerns in prayer, we'll certainly become partners with God and experience not only a miracle of New Life, but also success and prosperity in our families, communities of faith and nations, overcoming our own failures and the diabolical works of our archenemy, the Devil, who "…comes only to steal and kill and destroy…" (John 10:10).

Albert Einstein said, "There are two ways to live your life. One is as though nothing is a miracle. The other is as though everything is a miracle." Since miracles don't happen by chance—except by the power of God, Who made heaven and earth, including everything in it—it follows that He loves His creation and is actively engaged in it, miraculously accomplishing His purpose of redemption among humanity day by day through Jesus Christ. I believe Einstein might have made the above statement based on his own observation of the irrefutable truths revealed by the Holy Spirit in diverse ways through what is theologically known as general revelation or natural theology.

With God's power, we'll fulfill His loving and eternal purpose for humankind, both spiritually and physically in this life and in the world to come. As you know by now, His marvelous work of salvation in this world can be accomplished only through those who embody His Holy Spirit and act in faith and obedience to His Word. Furthermore, it's good to be reminded that our lives are but shadows that pass away (James 4:14). In order for us to be counted worthy of the Lord, we must live in Christ and He in us by means of the power of the Holy Spirit. With Him as our Lord and Savior, "The Spirit himself testifies with our spirit that we are God's children" (Rom. 8:16).

Let's pause here briefly to examine this: if the word *Christian* is broken into two syllables, we have *Christ* and *ian*. Thus, without the word *Christ*, the syllable *ian* has no meaning in itself. Therefore, the letters IAN can be interpreted as *I Am Nothing*. So the full statement reads *without Christ [in me], I am nothing*. But regardless of my race, color, sex, status or rank in society, *with* Him, I *am* a Christian, a precious *somebody*, a child of God: the object of His love, sealed by the Holy Spirit (Eph. 1:13) and bound for heaven by virtue of His grace through faith in Jesus (John 1:12, 14:3; Eph, 2:8).

Hence, Jesus declared: " '…He who believes in me will live, even though he dies; and whoever lives and believes in me will never die…' " (John 11:25–26). Knowing His victory over death, He assured His followers, "…Because I live, you also will live" (14:19). Therefore, with "…Christ in you, the hope of glory" (Col. 1:27), you are fully certain of eternal life together with Him in His Father's Kingdom. Hence, whether we live or die, we live eternally by His power.

Therefore, banish doubt from your mind and ensure that you are truly a child of God by committing your life completely to His Son, so that from this day forward "…the author and perfecter of our faith…" (Heb. 12:2) may begin to lead you on your Christian journey. Let's be reminded that without Him, we are nothing, for " '…dust you are and to dust you will return' " (Gen. 3:19). Besides, "…we brought nothing into the world, and we can take nothing out of it" (1 Tim. 6:7).

Think seriously about this: if God, Who "…formed the man from the dust of the ground and breathed into his nostrils the breath of life…" (Gen. 2:7) were to stop the air we breathe for just a minute, how terrible the consequences would be. I propose that otherwise, all human beings, including every living thing—birds of the air, fish in the sea, trees of the forest, grass of the field, flowers of the garden, the minutest creatures imaginable—would be dead.

Because of His infinite goodness, mercy toward humanity and the gift of the Holy Spirit—as revealed in the life, atoning death, resurrection, and ascension of Jesus Christ—God does not consume us in spite of who we are as human beings. That makes Jesus unique in human history, and believers must embolden themselves in convincing others that He is the only way to God.

Dave Branon spells it out specifically as he comments on the following theme: "Jesus: Unique in All the World."

> Jesus is unmatched in history—His very being cries out for us to entrust our lives to Him. Jesus Christ is:
> Unique in substance: He alone is both God and man (John 10:30).
> Unique in prophecy: No other leader's life was foretold so clearly and accurately (Mic. 5:2).
> Unique in mission: Jesus alone came to save us from our sins (Matt. 1:21).
> Unique in birth: Only Jesus was born of a virgin (1:23).
> Unique in ability: No one but Jesus has power to forgive sins (Mark 2:10).

Unique in existence: Jesus alone existed before the beginning of
time (John 1:1-2).
Unique in position: No one else is equal with God (Phil. 2:5–6).
Unique in reign: Only Jesus reigns forever (Heb. 1:8).

With such exceptional uniqueness embodied in Jesus, we must fully
agree and boldly declare with Branon: No one in history is like Him. He
alone deserves our trust, and He alone is the path to His Father. Finally, he concludes with a poem by Brandt:

No other name can save me.
No other name beside,
But Jesus Christ the risen Lord,
Who once was crucified.
(*Our Daily Bread*, July 7, 2006)

Therefore, since God, out of His unconditional love, graciously provided the world with all the means of grace for salvation in His unique
Son, I cordially invite all those who haven't yet become His children to
be part of His uncountable family in the Eternal Kingdom through faith
in Christ (Rev. 3:19–21, 7:9–17)—*right now*. This is an unspeakable
privilege, so we mustn't let it slip through our fingers. We must altogether seriously heed God's gracious call to all people—black or white,
rich or poor, male or female, old or young, including our little children
(Mark 10:13–15). As Isaiah declares:

*"Gather together and come; assemble, you fugitives from the nations. Ignorant
are those who carry about idols of wood, who pray to gods that cannot save. Declare what is to be, present it—let them take counsel together. Who foretold this
long ago, who declared it from the distant past? Was it not I, the LORD ? And
there is no God apart from me, a righteous God and a Savior; there is none but
me. Turn to me and be saved, all you ends of the earth; for I am God, and there
is no other* (Isa. 45:20–22).

At this juncture, having discussed all this, I consider it essential to
conclude the message with a prayer for all who read this book, so that
they may be richly blessed by its contents. St. Paul offered these words
daily to God on behalf of the Ephesian Christians:

*I keep asking that the God of our Lord Jesus Christ, the glorious Father, may
give you the Spirit of wisdom and revelation, so that you may know him better.
I pray also that the eyes of your heart may be enlightened in order that you*

> *may know the hope to which he has called you, the riches of his glorious inher-*
> *itance in the saints, and his incomparably great power for us who believe. That*
> *power is like the working of his mighty strength, which he exerted in Christ*
> *when he raised him from the dead and seated him at his right hand in the heav-*
> *enly realms, far above all rule and authority, power and dominion, and every*
> *title that can be given, not only in the present age but also in the one to come.*
> *And God placed all things under his feet and appointed him to be head over*
> *everything for the church, which is his body, the fullness of him who fills every-*
> *thing in every way* (Eph. 1:17–23).

I earnestly invite you to join me in this prayer every day for ourselves and for all others, believers and non-believers alike. Let's look to the Lord as He continues with His wonderful work of transformation in our lives, our families, communities, cities, countries in Africa in particular, and the world at large. We should never forget to rely on Him daily in all we do, keeping in mind His Word, and sharing the same with people: "Unless the LORD builds the house, its builders labor in vain. Unless the LORD watches over the city, the watchmen stand guard in vain;" for, " '…apart from me,' " He says, " 'you can do nothing;' " "…'What is impossible with men is possible with God' " (Ps. 127:1; John 15:5; Luke 18:27); and that "…'Everything is possible for him who believes' " (Mark 9:23).

It's "…'Not by might nor by power, but by my Spirit,' says the LORD Almighty" (Zech. 4:6) that we're able to fulfill our purpose to His glory. That means it's only His Spirit in us that reveals His purpose for our lives and gives us the power to live and fulfill the same (John 16:12–14; Acts 1:8).

With these words of the Holy Scriptures reminding us of our need of the Lord and His power and for His glory, let's eschew every form of tradition that hinders our faith in Christ. As a close reader of this book, you may exonerate me from the charge of being against tradition *per se*, as could be wrongly assumed. Rather, what I've set forth here offers a better way of living our lives—not by the traditions of our ancestors or by any other means—but according to the will of God by His power, knowing that *without Him, we can't make it.*

A life with God honors Him and us as His children. It uplifts our community and is a blessing to posterity, because it leads to success and prosperity (Josh. 1:8–9). It's such holy living that'll lead us as a people and our nation as a whole to possess and enjoy all the spiritual and material blessings of God (Deut. 28:1–14) without conflicting with the

Holy Scriptures or His will.

Therefore, we must trust and obey the Lord, continuing to love and serve Him and our neighbors as we do ourselves. We must keep His Word alive and pray without ceasing until the return of His Son, Who will take us into the mansion God has prepared for us in heaven (John 14:3). As it's written: "…you were slain, and with your blood you purchased men for God from every tribe and language and people and nation. You have made them to be a kingdom and priests to serve our God…" (Rev. 5:9–10). Moreover, we "…know that [our] labor in the Lord is not in vain," "…for at the proper time we will reap a harvest if we do not give up" in living by His power (1 Cor. 15:58; Gal. 6:9).

In the end, we'll each receive "…a crown of life" as a reward for our faithful service (Rev. 2:10) and join "the loud voices in heaven" to proclaim:

> *"Worthy is the Lamb, who was slain, to receive power and wealth and wisdom and strength and honor and glory and praise!"…The kingdom of the world has become the kingdom of our Lord and of his Christ, and he will reign for ever and ever" (5:12, 11:15).*

APPENDIX 1

Abbreviations of the Books of the Bible

Acts	Acts	Lev.	Leviticus
Amos	Amos	Luke	Luke
Col.	Colossians	Mark	Mark
Dan.	Daniel	Matt.	Matthew
Deut.	Deuteronomy	Mic.	Micah
Eccl.	Ecclesiastes	Neh.	Nehemiah
Eph.	Ephesians	Num.	Numbers
Esther	Esther	Phil.	Philippians
Exod.	Exodus	Prov.	Proverbs
Ezek.	Ezekiel	Ps.	Psalms
Ezra	Ezra	Rev.	Revelations
Gal.	Galatians	Rom.	Romans
Gen.	Genesis	Titus	Titus
Hab.	Habakkuk	Zech.	Zechariah
Hag.	Haggai	1 Chron.	1 Chronicles
Heb.	Hebrews	1 Cor.	1 Corinthians
Hosea	Hosea	1 John	1 John (Epistle)
Isa.	Isaiah	1 Kings	1 Kings
James	James	1 Pet.	1 Peter
Jer.	Jeremiah	1 Sam.	1 Samuel
Job	Job	1 Thess.	1 Thessalonians
Joel	Joel	1 Tim.	1 Timothy
John	John (Gospel)	2 Chron.	2 Chronicles
Jon.	Jonah	2 Cor.	2 Corinthians
Josh.	Joshua	2 Kings	2 Kings
Judg.	Judges	2 Sam.	2 Samuel
Lam.	Lamentations	2 Tim.	2 Timothy

www.ingramcontent.com/pod-product-compliance
Lightning Source LLC
Chambersburg PA
CBHW051458030726
47592CB00006B/1990